Approaches to the Fiction of
Ursula K. Le Guin

Studies in Speculative Fiction, No. 4

Robert Scholes, Series Editor

Alumni/Alumnae Professor of English and
Chairman, Department of English
Brown University

Other Titles in This Series

Approaches to the Fiction of
Ursula K. Le Guin

by
James W. Bittner
Adjunct Assistant Professor
Department of English
Iowa State University
Ames, Iowa

UMI RESEARCH PRESS
Ann Arbor, Michigan

Produced and distributed by
UMI Research Press
an imprint of
University Microfilms International
A Xerox Information Resources Company
Ann Arbor, Michigan 48106

Library of Congress Cataloging in Publication Data

Bittner, James W. (James Warren)
    Approaches to the fiction of Ursula K. Le Guin.

    (Studies in speculative fiction ; no. 4)
    Revision of thesis (doctoral)–University of Wisconsin,
1979.
    Bibliography: p.
    Includes index.
    1. Le Guin, Ursala K., 1929-   –Criticism and
interpretation. 2. Fantastic fiction, American–History
and criticism. I. Title. II. Series.
PS3562.E42Z56 1984   813'.54   84-8507
ISBN 0-8357-1573-6

ἡμεῖς δέ, τίνες δὲ ἡμεῖ
And we, who are we, anyhow?
—Plotinus, *Enneads*

"Hard and cruel as it may seem," said the Cardinal, "yet we, who hold our high office as keepers and watchmen to the story, may tell you, verily, that to its human characters there is salvation in nothing else in the universe. . . . For within our whole universe the story only has authority to answer that cry of heart of its characters, that one cry of heart of each of them: *'Who am I?'*"

—Isak Dinesen, *Last Tales*

In memoriam L.B., who, having traveled
the way over eight other mountains,
had reached, finally, the ninth.

Contents

Preface

Critical evaluations of Ursula K. Le Guin's individual novels and stories and formulations about the direction of her development and about the shape of the whole body of her fiction must, at this time, be exploratory and provisional. If she is productive into her seventies and eighties as both her father (anthropologist A.L. Kroeber) and her mother (author Theodora Kroeber) have been, then she is still in the middle of her literary career. She is, after all, still "pushing out toward the limits—my own and those of the medium," as she once said.[1] Each new work she creates will affect the meanings of those that preceded it; each new publication will alter, subtly or dramatically, the configuration of her literary achievement.

The appearance of *Orsinian Tales* in 1976 is a case in point. Before Le Guin published this collection of tales, she was known, on the one hand, as the author of a superb fantasy trilogy for adolescents, and, on the other, as one of the best science fiction writers at work today. Until 1976, almost all of her fiction seemed to fall into one of two imaginary realms, either the Earthsea Archipelago (her "Inner Lands," as she calls them), or the Ekumenical Scope of the Hainish worlds (her "Outer Space"). Critical comment usually focused on one of these Secondary Worlds to the exclusion of the other, perhaps because of the critics' taste, or perhaps because of what Le Guin calls "adult chauvinist piggery": readers of fiction written for adults rarely consider stories written for juveniles, relegating them to the children's librarians or to teachers of the elementary grades.[2] Thus, when an entire issue of *Science-Fiction Studies* was devoted to Le Guin's work in 1975, all the essays dealt exclusively with her science fiction, referring to her fantasy in brief asides, if at all. Moreover, some of the essays proposed schemes or patterns to explain her development, taking *Rocannon's World* (1966) as a starting point and passing over the Earthsea trilogy. But after the publication of *Orsinian Tales,* a collection of short fiction set in an imaginary Central European country that Le Guin invented more than a decade before she wrote *Rocannon's World,* it is obvious that criticism concentrating on her science fiction alone can give only a partial account of her development. It is clear, in fact, that Le Guin's major fiction through the mid-seventies divides itself not into two, but three different imaginary worlds, and that her growth as a writer begins not with *Rocannon's World* and the science fiction she published in the sixties, but with the Orsinian tales and novels she started writing in the early fifties.

The following chapters do not propose a single picture of the whole range of Le Guin's work. This is not an introduction to the fiction of Le Guin, nor is it a collection of detailed readings of her major novels. Rather than emphasizing the separateness of her individual works by concentrating attention on them one by one, and instead of drawing boundaries around her fantasy and science fiction (as much of the criticism had done), I will be making exploratory approaches towards an understanding of the relationships within and among her novels and short stories. My goal is to see some of the connections between part and part and between part and whole, not to identify those qualities that divide and separate.

Making connections, or, better yet, understanding and appreciating the relationships and connections that already exist, is the abiding theme of all of Le Guin's work, a theme she identifies as marriage:

> the "person" I tend to write about is often not exactly or not totally, either a man or a woman. On the superficial level, this means that there is little sexual stereotyping . . . and the sex itself is seen as a *relationship rather than an act.* . . . Once, as I began to be awakened, I closed the relationship into one person, an androgyne. But more often it appears conventionally and overtly, as a couple. Both in one: or two making a whole. Yin does not occur without yang, nor yang without yin. Once I was asked what I thought the central, consistent theme of my work was, and I said spontaneously, "Marriage."[3]

Le Guin is here discussing only one aspect of her fiction, characterization, and concentrating on but one aspect of that, relations between male and female. Her reference to yin and yang, however, gives the word "marriage" the widest possible range of meanings, for yin and yang symbolize much more than just male and female. They play a major role in Chinese theories of cosmogony and cosmology. They are the

> two complementary forces, or principles, that make up all aspects and phenomena of life. . . . [They] proceed from a Supreme Ultimate (T'ai Chi), their interplay on one another (as one increases the other decreases) being a description of the actual process of the universe and all that is in it. . . . [They] lend substance to the characteristically Chinese belief in a cyclical theory of becoming and dissolution and an interdependence between the world of nature and the events of man.[4]

On another occasion, Le Guin said that the *t'ai chi,* symbolized by the yin-yang circle ☯, is not only "a central theme in my work. It's a central theme, period."[5] So when she says that marriage is "the central, consistent theme" of her work, we can understand her to be referring to any complementary, correlative, or interdependent relationship between what we may perceive as opposites or dualisms, but which are in reality aspects of a whole, or moments in a continuous process. Because the idea of complementarity, represented by the yin-yang circle, encompasses Le Guin's theme of marriage, being both more general and abstract than the idea of marriage, yet also more specific and concrete, I use it to define not only Le Guin's central theme, but also her fictional techniques, her modes of thought, and ultimately, her world view.

The idea of complementarity has been, in one form or another, an element of Western and Eastern thought for twenty-five centuries, from Anaximander and Heraclitus in Ionia (sixth century B.C.) and Lao Tzu and Chuang Tzu in China (sixth and fourth centuries B.C.), down to Niels Bohr, C.G. Jung, and Robert Ornstein in our own century. As J. Robert Oppenheimer said in his 1953 Reith Lectures on the BBC,

> complementary modes of thought and complementary descriptions of reality are an old, long-enduring part of our tradition. . . . the experience of atomic physics gives us a reminder, and a certain reassurance, that these ways of thinking and talking can be factual, appropriate, precise, and free of obscurantism.[6]

Thus in the twentieth century, an essentially mythical or mystical idea—even an occult idea—has found a place in fields as different as quantum mechanics and analytical psychology, and has touched virtually every problem in philosophy. Bohr argued that a complete description of the wave-particle duality in quantum phenomena must be complementary, and then, in lectures to various audiences from 1930 to 1960, extended the idea of complementarity into biology, psychology, ethics, and anthropology, hoping to establish it as a major philosophical concept.[7] As Jung explored the structures and operations of the psyche, he developed concepts and models which turned out to be remarkably similar to those developed by Bohr, Heisenberg, and other physicists. After Jung discovered the correspondences between psychology and physics, he often pointed to the analogies between what he was discovering about the psyche and what the physicists were discovering about the fundamental units of matter-energy.[8] Robert Ornstein has made the idea of complementarity a guiding concept in his studies of the psychology of consciousness and the physiology of the brain.[9]

For Erwin Schrödinger, atomic physics is "part of our endeavor to answer the great philosophical question which embraces all others, the one Plotinus expresses by his brief τίνες δὲ ἡμεῖς;—*who are we?*"[10] Another part of that endeavor is Jung's analytical psychology. It is significant that physics, which has penetrated far into the external world of matter, and psychology, which has penetrated far into the internal world of spirit, should have arrived at the same concept: complementarity (thereby calling into question the very divisions between matter and spirit, external and internal, object and subject). Still another part of the endeavor is the art of storytelling. Le Guin knows as well as Cardinal Salviati, the narrator of Isak Dinesen's "The Cardinal's First Table," that the story is a tool for answering the question "Who am I?" Like the Cardinal, who has been "schooled in the art of equipoise," and who generates a "reconciling synthesis" not only in his family but also in his complementary roles as priest and artist,[11] Le Guin has learned that the artist's aesthetic modes and the scientist's rational modes are complementary means to the same end. By themselves, art and science are of limited value; together, they offer answers. As Schrödinger says in *Science and Humanism,*

> the isolated knowledge obtained by a group of scientists in a narrow field has in itself no value whatsoever, but only in its synthesis with all the rest of knowledge and only inasmuch as it really contributes in this synthesis something toward the demand τίνες δὲ ἡμεῖς; who are we?[12]

It is with the intent of contributing something toward answering that demand that Le Guin writes *science* fiction. In the same ways that physicists use mathematics, psychologists use dreams and myths and anthropologists use a culture's artifacts, Le Guin uses the story: as a tool for discovery and exploration, for describing reality and for synthesizing answers to "the great philosophical question which embraces all others." Along with Bohr, Jung, and Dinesen's Cardinal, Le Guin has found that the question must be formulated and answered in complementary ways. Because Le Guin also has been "schooled in the art of equipoise," her fiction offers a reconciling synthesis: science, dreams, myth, and religion (in the form of Taoist philosophy and mysticism) are integral parts of her stories and novels.

Each of the following chapters offers one way toward understanding complementarity in Le Guin's fiction. Chapter one approaches the idea through a theoretical discussion of the poetics and rhetoric of the romance genre, the characteristic fictional form of most of Le Guin's work. The romance, a literary form whose purpose or final cause is a moment of vision from enchanted ground, a moment of synthesis in which contradictions are *aufgehoben* (annulled by each other, absorbed into each other, and transcended), is Le Guin's principal narrative tool for marrying opposites and thus for creating an image of the world and of ourselves that transcends by synthesizing the opposition and conflict immanent in all reality. The romance answers the question "who are we?" by transforming dualisms into complements and contradictions into correlates.

The complementarity of realistic and fantastic literary modes is the primary focus of chapter two, an analysis of *Ornsinian Tales* and its relation to Le Guin's other works. As Le Guin weaves together historical fact and romantic vision in *Orsinian Tales,* she marries history and art to create an imaginative reality that is, and at the same time is not, like our familiar world.

Just as the complementarity of yin and yang entails a cyclical theory of becoming and dissolution, the complementarity of realism and fantasy in *Orsinian Tales* entails circularity. I show how this circularity operates in the last tale in *Orsinian Tales,* "Imaginary Countries." The chapter concludes with a look at *"An die Musik,"* a tale in which Le Guin suggests that the function of art is celebration, the spontaneous burst of joy that comes when opposites and tensions are resolved and transcended.

After opening with a brief discussion of the interrelationships between Le Guin's fantasy and science fiction, chapter three explores the complementarity of myth and science in Le Guin's fiction, approaching her work through a study of sources. Myth and science are generally taken to be mutually exclusive modes of understanding, but Le Guin marries them in both her juvenile fantasy and in her adult science fiction. Norse myth and relativity physics are complementary in "Semley's Necklace," and Celtic-Teutonic myth and modern anthropology are married in the Earthsea trilogy to produce the institution of magic, itself a metaphor for Le Guin's art, which connects complements.

Chapter four is an account of the development of Le Guin's science fictional future history from its origins in "Dowry of the Angyar" (1964) through "The Day Before the Revolution" (1974). My approach will be to study the internal dynamic that has generated the major portion of Le Guin's work so far, her science fiction. Le Guin's Hainish future history, a metaromance and metahistory spanning over a million years, springs from a dialectical interplay between the conventions of pulp science fiction on the one hand, and myth and anthropology on the other. This interplay is the surface manifestation of a deeper dialectic: the dynamic marriage of myths of beginning and ending, a synthesis of the social contract and the utopia. The complementarity of etiology and teleology is the root of Le Guin's mode of experiencing time and historical vision. This vision, embodied in a narrative time that is a marriage of historical time *(chronos)* and mythic time *(mythos),* illuminates the present moment, actuality. The recovery of the past and the projection of a future ideal are complementary and interdependent acts that create the present. Utopian possibilities latent in the present emerge when we understand it as a marriage of the past and the future.

It is, finally, a pleasure to acknowledge the help and encouragement of many people. I am deeply grateful to my wife Carolyn and son Ross for graciously accommodating what became a guest that was with us long after it had worn out its welcome. Their support has been indispensable. Michael Bemis shared his experience, strength, and hope at crucial times. Professors John O. Lyons, Annis Pratt, and Barton R. Friedman read and commented on the manuscript at various stages. I thank them for their suggestions both on matters of detail and on the larger design of the whole project. Numerous people provided information, shared materials, answered queries, and offered suggestions: John Bangsund, Eddy C. Bertin, Martin Bickman, C.H. Blanchard, Jan Bogstad, Elizabeth Cummins Cogell, Herrlee G. Creel, Joe De Bolt, Richard D. Erlich, John P. Fleming, Lawrence Flescher, Jeffrey Frayne, Robert Galbreath, Chuck Garvin, Betsy Harfst, Denys Howard, Naomi Lewis, Lesleigh and Hank Luttrell, Ugo Malaguti, Robert H. March, J. Wesley Miller III, Joseph Needham, Henry-Luc Planchat, Eric S. Rabkin, B.R. Raina, Catherine Rasmussen, Thomas J. Remington, Joanna Russ, Roger C. Scholbin, Robert Scholes, Kathleen Spencer, Darko Suvin, Grant Stone, Pierre Versins, Ricardo Valla, and Susan Wood. I owe a special debt to Jeffrey H. Levin, Le Guin's first bibliographer, who shared graciously his incomparable resources and knowledge. And I am most grateful to Ursula K. Le Guin herself for her wit, candor and door-opening. Her answers to queries have made this not a dry and tedious scholarly exercise, but at many moments a pleasure, and, at rare and unexpected times, a joy.

Acknowledgments

The author gratefully acknowledges permission to quote extracts from the following works:

Rocannon's World. New York: Ace Books, 1966. Copyright © 1966 by Ace Books, Inc. Reprinted by permission of The Berkley Publishing Group.

Planet of Exile. New York: Ace Books, 1966. Copyright © 1966 by Ursula K. Le Guin. Reprinted by the permission of The Berkley Publishing Group.

City of Illusions. New York: Ace Books, 1967. Copyright © 1967 by Ursula K. Le Guin. Reprinted by the permission of The Berkley Publishing Group.

The Left Hand of Darkness. New York: Ace Books, 1969. Copyright © 1969 by Ursula K. Le Guin. Reprinted by the permission of The Berkley Publishing Group.

A Wizard of Earthsea. Berkley: Parnassus Press, 1968. Copyright © 1968 by Ursula K. Le Guin. Reprinted by permission of the author.

The Farthest Shore. New York: Atheneum, 1972. Copyright © 1972 by Ursula K. Le Guin. Reprinted by permission of the author.

The Dispossessed. New York: Harper & Row, 1974. Copyright © 1974 by Ursula K. Le Guin. Reprinted by permission of the author.

The Wind's Twelve Quarters. New York: Harper & Row, 1975. Copyright © 1975 by Ursula K. Le Guin. Reprinted by permission of the author.

Very Far Away From Anywhere Else. New York: Atheneum, 1976. Copyright © 1976 by Ursula K. Le Guin. Reprinted by permission of the author.

Orsinian Tales. New York: Harper & Row, 1976. Copyright © 1976 by Ursula K. Le Guin. Reprinted by permission of the author.

"An die Musik." *Western Humanities Review,* 15 (1961). Copyright © 1961 by Ursula K. Le Guin. Reprinted by permission of the author.

"The Word of Unbinding." *Fantastic* (January, 1964). Copyright © 1964, 1975 by Ursula K. Le Guin. Reprinted by permission of the author.

"The Dowry of the Angyar." *Amazing* (September, 1964). Copyright © 1964 by Ursula K. Le Guin. Reprinted by permission of the author.

"Winter's King." *Orbit 5,* ed. Damon Knight. New York: Putnam, 1969. Copyright © 1969 by Ursula K. Le Guin. Reprinted by permission of the author.

"The Word for World is Forest." *Again, Dangerous Visions,* ed. Harlan Ellison. New York: Doubleday, 1972. Copyright © 1972 by Ursula K. Le Guin. Reprinted by permission of the author.

"The Day Before the Revolution." *Galaxy* (August, 1974). Copyright © 1974 by Ursula K. Le Guin. Reprinted by permission of the author.

"Schrödinger's Cat." *Universe 5,* ed. Terry Carr. New York: Random House, 1974. Copyright © 1974 by Ursula K. Le Guin. Reprinted by permission of the author.

"Prophets and Mirrors." *The Living Light,* 7 (Fall, 1970). Copyright © 1970 by the National Center for Religious Education. Reprinted by permission of the publisher.

"A Citizen of Mondath." *Foundation,* no. 4 (July, 1973). Copyright © 1973 by Ursula K. Le Guin. Reprinted by permission of the author.

"Dreams Must Explain Themselves." *Algol* 21 (November, 1973). Copyright © 1973 by Ursula K. Le Guin. Reprinted by permission of the author.

"The Child and the Shadow." *Quarterly Journal of the Library of Congress,* 32 (1975). Copyright © 1975 by Ursula K. Le Guin. Reprinted by permission of the author.

"American SF and the Other." *Science-Fiction Studies,* 2 (1975). Copyright © 1975 by Ursula K. Le Guin. Reprinted by permission of the author.

"A Response to the Le Guin Issue." *Science-Fiction Studies,* 3 (1976). Copyright © 1976 by Ursula K. Le Guin. Reprinted by permission of the author.

"Is Gender Necessary?" Aurora: Beyond Equality, ed. Vonda McIntyre and Susan Anderson. Greenwich: Fawcett, 1976. Copyright © 1976 by Ursula K. Le Guin. Reprinted by permission of the author.

"The View In." *A Multitude of Visions,* ed. Cy Chauvin. Baltimore: T-K Graphics, 1975. Copyright © 1975 by T-K Graphics. Reprinted by permission of the author.

"The Cardinal's First Tale," by Isak Dinesen. *Last Tales.* New York: Random House, 1957. Copyright © 1957 by Random House. Reprinted by permission of the publisher.

"In Praise of Limestone" and "In Memory of W.B. Yeats," by W.H. Auden. *Collected Shorter Poems 1927-1957.* New York: Random House, 1966. Copyright © 1966 by W.H. Auden. *W.H. Auden: Collected Poems,* ed. Edward Mendelson. Copyright © 1976 by Edward Mendelson, William Meredith, and Monroe K. Spears, executors of the Estate of W.H. Auden. Reprinted by permission of Random House.

The Gayety of Vision: A Study of Isak Dinesen's Art, by Robert Langbaum. New York: Random House, 1965. Copyright © 1964 by Robert Langbaum. Reprinted as *Isak Dinesen's Art: The Gayety of Vision.* Chicago: University of Chicago Press, 1975. Reprinted by permission of the author.

1

Of Jewels, Stories, Patterns, Visions, and Worlds: The Dialectical Plots of Le Guin's Romances

The concept, which some would see as the sign-unit for whatever is comprised under it, has from the beginning been instead the product of dialectical thinking in which everything is always that which it is, only because it becomes that which it is not.
—Max Horkheimer and Theodor Adorno, *Dialectic of Enlightenment*

While European philosophy tended to find reality in *substance,* Chinese philosophy tended to find it in *relation.* . . . Behind the metaphysical idea of "substance" . . . lies the logical idea of "identity," and Western philosophers laid down as a basic principle of thought that a thing cannot both be and not be at the same time. Chinese philosophers, on the other hand, laid down that a thing is always "becoming" or "de-becoming," all the time on the way to something else.
—Joseph Needham, *Science and Civilisation in China*

The best entry into Le Guin's fiction is not her apprentice work, nor is it her first published story. It comes *in medias res,* in her third novel. Midway through *City of Illusions,* Falk reaches Es Toch, the goal of the quest he began at Zove's House, among the Forest People. Drawn by a faint hunch or hope, Falk has believed that Es Toch holds the key to his lost identity and past. He discovers that his hunch is true, but this discovery immediately uncovers a larger truth. While the Shing hold the key to his identity, he, in turn, is the key to their efforts to locate and subdue his home planet, which had until then escaped their domination. So he is not merely Falk, a strange looking alien who six years previously had wandered into a forest clearing, fully grown physically, yet mentally a *tabula rasa;* he is also Ramarren, the greatest mathematician-astronomer from his home country Kelshy on Werel, the navigator of the spaceship *Alterra.* He is a "two-minded man."[1] His quest, he discovers, began not 2,000 miles away at Zove's House, but 142 light years away on another planet, and of those who made the journey with him, only one, (the boy Orry), has survived the Shing attack on the *Alterra* as it neared Earth. But Falk does not have the faintest idea of any of this until after he hears the story told by Orry.

After Estrel had delivered Falk to the Shing, and after they have tried to get the information they want with mind-altering drugs, they introduce Orry to him. Falk is baffled and confused by Orry's recognition of him as Ramarren, but because Zove and All-Alonio have taught him the "Old Canon of Man" (Taoism), he remains open to the possibility that Orry can help him towards the truth about himself. In response to Falk's questions "Will you tell me who...who we are?" and "Why did we come here?" (pp. 306, 307), Orry answers with a long "childish narrative" (p. 310). As he listens, Falk begins to comprehend who he is: he recovers the 1,200 year-long history of the Terran colony on Werel, their home planet in the Gamma Draconis solar system, and he learns their reasons for traveling the 142 light years to Earth. After Orry has finished, "Falk kept gazing in his mind at the jewel that might be false, and might be priceless, the story, the pattern—true vision or not—of the world he had lost" (p. 307).

This scene from Le Guin's third novel may very well be the *locus classicus* of her central formal and thematic concerns. Just as Shakespeare often staged plays within his plays in self-conscious commentary on his own art, Le Guin includes here a story within a story, and provides us with some clear indications of what she is about. What is significant in this situation in Es Toch, not only in terms of the relationship between the characters in the text, but also in terms of the relationship between us as readers and the text is this: Falk recognizes who he is, and begins to reconstitute his identity, as he listens to a story, a "childish narrative," *the protagonist of which is none other than himself.* At the same time, our reading of *City of Illusions* is analogous to Falk's listening to Orry's story. In a sense *we* are the protagonist of Le Guin's narrative. "The message of all romance," says Northrop Frye, "is *de te fabula:* the story is about you."[2] And as Le Guin herself has written, "we read books to find out who we are...the story—from *Rumplestiltskin* to *War and Peace*—is one of the basic tools invented by the mind of man, for the purpose of gaining understanding." She goes on to say that no human society has lacked stories, while some great ones have lacked the wheel, hinting that we are not merely *homo faber,* or even *homo sapiens,* but we are, perhaps most importantly, *homo narrans.*[3] "Stories have been told as long as speech has existed," says Dinesen's Cardinal, "and *sans* stories the human race would have perished, as it would have perished *sans* water."[4]

What we experience as we read *City of Illusions* is the story of Falk's quest for his origins and identity. The story Falk hears Orry tell is the story of the quest—guided by Ramarren—of nineteen descendants of Terran colonists of Werel for their origins on Earth and for an understanding of their relationship with the rest of humanity. Both Le Guin's story and Orry's story are romances, the characteristic narrative form of most of Le Guin's fiction. The expanding pattern of relationships, historical, cultural, social, and personal, that is the shape of Falk's journey in *City of Illusion* is at once process and result. Le Guin's typical protagonist discovers his or her identity during a journey, most often in some sense a journey home. This journey is a process of discovering roots and recognizing a destiny prefigured in those roots. It is a process of recognizing one's relationship with his environment, material or imaginative, social or personal, and generally both. Whether mediated through the science fiction conventions of her Hainish stories *(Rocannon's World, Planet of Exile, City of Illusions, The Left Hand of Darkness, The Word for World is Forest,* and *The Dispossessed),* or through the conventions of juvenile fantasy in her Earthsea trilogy *(A Wizard of Earthsea, The Tombs of Atuan,* and *The Farthest Shore),* the pattern of this discovery process in Le Guin's fiction is the romance quest.

Not only the form itself of Le Guin's stories (the poetics of the romance) but also the relationship she creates between her stories and their readers (the rhetoric of the romance) is their content. What we experience as we read *City of Illusions*—imaginatively traveling into the far future to trek with Falk across North America—is analogous to Falk's traveling 142 light years from Werel to Earth, then 2,000 miles from the Applachians to the Rockies, in order to discover who he was, who he is, and who he might be. The rest of this chapter will be devoted to an examination of how the story, "one of the basic tools invented by the mind of man, for the purpose of gaining understanding," may be used to discover, to explore, and to constitute who we are.

I

The sentence Le Guin uses to describe Falk's reaction to Orry's "childish narrative" points to the major concerns of the romance. The jewel that Falk gazes at in his mind is at once a conventional symbol of the precious object of the quest and also a symbol of the Self (in the Jungian sense). It echoes other jewel images in *City of Illusions.* The patterning frame, used by the Prince of Kansas to give an enigmatic forecast of Falk's destiny, contains an opal which stands for Falk. This image is recalled at the end of the story as Falk-Ramarren and Orry are escaping in a comandeered Shing spaceship, as they watch sunlight creating dawn on the Earth's Eastern Ocean, "shining like a golden crescent for a moment against the dust of stars, like a jewel on a great patterning frame" (p. 370).

So the jewel Falk gazes at after hearing Orry's story turns out to be both a symbol for his self and an image of a planet seen from a spaceship, a "world." The merging of self and world in the image of the jewel is analogous to the syntax of the whole sentence, which collapses and synthesizes into apposition the words "jewel," "story," and "pattern," modified by "vision," all modifying "world": "the jewel that might be false and might be priceless, the story, the pattern—true vision or not—of the world he had lost." The "world" Falk has lost is in one sense the planet Werel, and in another, it is his identity as Ramarren. At the same time that it is a physical environment, a culture, a history, a home, it is also selfhood, "world" as *"Welt"* in *Weltanschauung,* a configuration of concepts, a pattern or mode of perceiving with which one individually responds to and orders his experience. Thus a "world" is the totality of the dialectical interplay of individual self and environment, a *Gestalt* which can be either a conglomeration of alienated fragments or an integrated unity, an identity. This "world" is no ahistorical, static entity, though, for it exists as a "story," and therefore unfolds in time, in an ordered and coherent fashion, structured according to a particular "pattern," a plot, which leads up to and expresses a "vision." It is here, in the apposition and interweaving of the words "jewel," "story," "pattern," "vision," and "world," that the meaning of Le Guin's fiction is embedded. A "world" is the way things happen, not a thing. It is the path (Tao) that all events take, and as such it includes the way (tao) an individual perceives and acts, whether in violation of it, or in harmony with it. This is the foundation of Le Guin's ethics. The plots of her romances carry the protagonist and the reader from a situation in which the protagonist's world is fragmented and alienated, quite often because of something he or she did, toward a momentary vision of harmony, balance, and identity of world as self and world as environment, an identity of Self and Other.

A story is the tool Falk uses to discover-recover and to understand his world, just as it is, according to Le Guin, the tool we use to do the same thing. What Falk needs in the Shing city of illusions is a way of seeing, a mode of vision that will enable him to make the proper choices. Orry's story helps him to achieve this. Similarly, for readers of stories, fantasy and science fiction can provide glimpses of reality more penetrating than those offered by realism, which Le Guin regards as "the least adequate means of understanding or portraying the incredible realities of our existence."[5] Who we are may be more readily understood with the romance than with realism; realism may merely reinforce and legitimate the obstacles that stand in the way of true vision. To the degree that we, like Falk, are imprisoned in cities of illusions, we need the vision that the romance offers. A view in may be the way out.

Le Guin's concern with the value of story telling for acquiring and forming perception and vision is central not only to *City of Illusions;* it animates most of her other fiction as well. The same cluster of imagery that carries the idea in *City of Illusions* is the vehicle for the theme in her other novels. The opening paragraphs of her first published novel, *Rocannon's World,* and the opening paragraphs of *The Left Hand of Darkness,* announce it. An anonymous storyteller prefaces his narrative about Rocannon with these words:

> In trying to tell the story of a man, an ordinary League scientist, ... one feels like an archeologist amid millennial ruins now struggling through choked tangles of leaf, flower, branch and vine to the sudden bright geometry of a wheel or a polished cornerstone, and now entering some commonplace, sunlit doorway to find inside it the darkness, the impossible flicker of a flame, the glitter of a jewel, the half-glimpsed movement of a woman's arm.[6]

And Genly Ai opens his "report," *The Left Hand of Darkness,* with these remarks:

> I'll make my report as if I told a story, for I was taught as a child on my homeworld that Truth is a matter of the imagination. The soundest fact may fail or prevail in the style of the telling: like the singular jewel of our seas, which grows brighter as one woman wears it, and, worn by another, dulls and goes to dust. Facts are no more solid, coherent, round, and real than pearls are. But both are sensitive.[7]

These two storytellers have similar purposes. One, in "trying to tell the story of a man," feels like an archeologist groping through the detritus of nature and history, searching for a *pattern* ("geometry of a wheel") which when discovered appears like a *vision* or a *jewel* ("sudden bright ... flicker ... glitter"). The storyteller's goal here is discovery through recovery. Genly Ai, on the other hand, certainly no positivist, proceeds toward his goal, Truth, by invention rather than discovery, for story telling is obviously inventive. He wants to offer facts set in a *story* so that they produce a *vision;* he knows that facts without aesthetic value are as dull and dusty as jewels without a beautiful setting. For both narrators, facts are perceived in flashes and glimpses and have meaning only when understood as elements in a pattern. Although one emphasizes discovery and the other emphasizes invention, the two processes are really one. The dialectic of invention-discovery is the story teller's art just as it is Falk's method of reconstituting his identity: he adds "guesses and extrapolation" to Orry's "childish narrative" (p. 310).

Story tellers have no monopoly on the method of invention-discovery— and here is a point where fiction and science fuse to form science-fiction—for the great experimental and theoretical physicists of the twentieth century have used it to understand the nature of reality when their standard paradigms or categories have failed them. *Gedankenexperiment* (thought experiment) is the name Ernst Mach coined late in the nineteenth century for the procedure of using entirely fictive or fantastic constructions or situations in order to discover or explain something about reality.[8] Many physicists after Mach, Einstein and Schrödinger most notably, used *Gedankenexperimenten* to explore problematic aspects of quantum theory, and they have been followed by science fiction writers, including Le Guin, who consciously and deliberately use *Gedankenexperimenten* to ask questions about who we are.[9]

II

But what, one might ask, is invented-discovered by the storyteller? An artist, of course, uses imagination and invention to make discoveries, reach understandings, and communicate truths about who we are. The specific nature of the discoveries, understandings, and truths crafted with a particular tool will depend on the capacities and qualities of the tool, as well as on the ways the tool is used. Before we can understand how Le Guin uses her tools, we have to understand the tool itself. If, as Bohr and Heisenberg have taught us, and as artists have repeatedly shown us, our instruments form a constitutive part of the reality they help us see, then the forms a writer chooses to communicate meaning will be a constitutive part of that meaning.

I believe, along with E.D. Hirsch, Jr., that generic conceptions are heuristic devices that a writer uses to constitute meanings. Fantasy and science fiction—Le Guin's major forms—are subgenres of the romance, so fantasy and science fiction should exhibit the same general configurations that the romance does. We must recognize, however, that generalizations about the romance carry us only part of the way toward an understanding of the specific forms Le Guin uses. The following discussion of the poetics and the rhetoric of the romance should not, therefore, be taken as an attempt to provide a final and inflexible pattern, but is intended only to identify the most central generic patterns and impulses and the most significant rhetorical strategies in Le Guin's fiction. We are for the moment concerned with *langue*, not *parole*, with what Todorov calls a theoretical genre rather than a historical genre.[10]

"The most important principle in any genre," says Darko Suvin, following Aristotle and more recent theorists like R.S. Crane, E.D. Hirsch, Jr., and Claudio Guillén, "is its *purpose*, which is to be inferred from the way the genre functions."[11] According to Hirsch, the notion of purpose, "the most important unifying and discriminating principle in genres," is similar to an Aristotelian final cause. It is "an entelechy, a goal-seeking force that animates a particular kind of utterance."[12] Literary forms, of course, are not organisms with a vital force that "animates" them, so the notion of entelechy is metaphorical. But if literary forms are not part of first nature, like acorns which become oaks, they may be thought of as operating according to second nature. Because definite meanings become associated with different literary forms, even to the point of becoming virtually identical with them, we "naturally" expect certain specific meanings when we encounter well established conventions and usages. When a story begins "once upon a time," we "naturally" form a whole system of expectations, which are in a sense the genre itself. Genre is, in Hirsch's words, "an anticipated sense of the whole."[13] We can, with Guillén, speak of a genre's "informing drive."[14]

What, then, is romance's informing drive; what is the purpose or final cause that can be inferred from the way romances operate; does the romance have an end like that inferred by Aristotle to be the end of tragedy, the arousing and purging pity and fear? A. Bartlett Giamatti supplies one: he argues that the "Romance, at its heart, constantly yearns" for moments of vision from enchanted ground.[15] Giamatti's formulation, resting on the personified yearning heart of the genre, embodies the notion of vital force or entelechy. "Impulse" is another word he uses to describe the cause of those moments of vision when "the reader, or protagonist of chivalric romance—or both—discovers an image of permanence and perfection through the reconcilation of opposites."[16] For Spenser and his contemporaries, this moment is symbolized with the gesture of raising a visor or a helmet. Although it may appear to be a violation of historical and cultural relativity to extend Giamatti's definition of the telos of the romance to apply to all romances, whether Greek, Continental, English, or American, Ancient, Medieval, Renaissance, Romantic, or Modern, this is not necessarily the case. The raising of the visor or helmet is native to the romances the yielded Giamatti's observation and cannot be replanted in different cultural soil without shock. But as Frye points out, "the conventions of prose romance show little change over the course of the centuries, and conservatism of this kind is the mark of a stable genre."[17] As a matter of fact, Giamatti's thesis is reaffirmed in other recent studies of the romance. Fredric Jameson, for example, writes that "the romance must seal the hero's mission by some form of revelation, of which the most celebrated is of course the appearance of the enigmatic grail itself,"[18] and Kathryn Hume speaks of an "epiphanic vision [that] is proper to the special world [of the nonprobable in romance]."[19]

The essential parts of Giamatti's formulation of the purpose or final cause of the romance are: (1) the enchanted ground (if not a world of the marvelous and the improbable, at least a strange and different world, what Tolkien calls a "Secondary World"); (2) the vision of permanence and perfection (or of unity, balance, wholeness, and harmony—the absence of, or the momentary synthesis of contradictions and conflicting opposites); and (3) the sharing of the vision by protagonist and reader alike. Thus there is, built into the very being of the romance genre, a drive, a yearning, or an impulse, analogous to the acorn's drive to become an oak tree, toward a visionary reconciliation and synthesis. That the genre is personified in this formulation is evidence that the poetics and the rhetoric of the romance are cognate: the anticipation and expectation aroused in the reader *are* the shape of the genre.

Having posited this much as the purpose of the romance, we can make some initial statements about the potential and the limits of the form. Unlike comedy, romance cannot resolve conflicts between social groups (like young and old) with a social ceremony (marriage); rather, it resolves psychological and metaphysical opposition and contradictions, including related ethical problems, with a visionary experience, or even a magical event. One should not expect from romances, then, at least not from the relatively conventional and traditional ones, very much in the way of realistic and direct social statement. On the contrary, one can expect the resolution of conflicts—even those which may appear on the surface to be social conflicts—to be effected by magic of some sort. As Auden says, perhaps too categorically, the traditional quest tale "provides no image of our objective experience of social life"; instead, it is a "symbolic description of our subjective personal experience of existence,... *the literary mimesis of the subjective experience of becoming.*"[20]

This definition of the romance need not exclude social meanings. Our subjective selves, our individual worlds, however private, do not exist in a vacuum, but are influenced by, and formed in response to, the world around us. Romance forms, because they have always contained a latent "identity between individual and social quests," are liable to "kidnapping," argues Frye, by absorption into "the ideology of an ascendant class."[21] Whoever the kidnapper, though, the resolution of class conflict or ideological contradiction is still magical. To the extent that political or social concerns are identified with the fundamental concerns of the romance, which are psychological and metaphysical, to the degree that the special enchanted world of the romance represents or corresponds to or directly contradicts the reader's world, the resolution of the conflict in the romance will have some social and political resonance.

This is not to say, however, that a visionary or magical resolution is not "true." The sense in which the resolution of a romance plot is "true" is rooted in its rhetorical power to create in its readers an intense absorption in the experiences of the protagonist. And this absorption, which may be more intense with the romance than with other genres like comedy or tragedy, arises from the congruence between the pattern or structure of the romance (its poetics) and the most fundamental psychological processes in every reader. The reader responds to a romance quest in much the same way that a tuning fork in one corner of a room begins to vibrate when an identical tuning fork is struck in another part of the room. This congruence accounts for the existence in the romance of the enchanted world, as well as for the fact that protagonist and reader alike share the vision (the rhetoric of the romance) that comes from experiences in that special secondary world.

Kathryn Hume's essay "Romance: A Perdurable Pattern" presents a useful outline of the basic structure of the romance. The article calls for close attention on two accounts. First it provides a fuller understanding of the rhetoric of the romance, the ways in which romance is *de te fabula,* and second, it elaborates a poetics of the romance, one paradigmatic or ideal-typical plot against which we can perceive and appreciate Le Guin's artistry in constructing her own romances.

Hume's essay is essentially an elaboration of Auden's incisive remark that the romance is the mimesis of "becoming." While Auden explains "becoming" in conscious and existential terms, Hume draws on the psychological understanding of ego development in order to explain the nature of the "becoming" that is re-presented and reiterated when a storyteller presents a romance quest. Ever since the early psychoanalysts noticed similarities between the pattern or logic of dreams and the structures of myth, hero legends, folk tales, and fairy tales, psychological explanations of the "meaning" of myth and folklore have been commonplace. Hume, however, makes a distinction between the archetypal infrastructure of the romance and its culturally conditioned literary reflexes or projections. Implicitly, she makes the same distinction that Frye, borrowing Schiller's terms, makes between "naive" and "sentimental" romances.[22]

Hume begins by establishing the congruence between the development of the ego (her model for that being the theory of Centroversion from Neumann's *The Origins and History of Consciousness*), and the core pattern of the hero myth (the tripartite process of Departure, Initiation, and Return outlined in Campbell's *The Hero With a Thousand Faces*). She then proceeds to set forth her own tripartite organization of the romance hero's experiences, choosing terminology which emphasizes the "state of the hero mentally and socially" (p. 135). Like the ego's development, the prototypical romance hero's experiences can be described in three stages: Equilibrium, Struggle, and Higher Harmony.

The first stage, Equilibrium, shows us a hero at home with himself and his world. In this relatively helpless and unthinking state, the hero feels secure, comfortable, and sheltered. That his needs are taken care of is often indicated by his high social status: he really does not have to do anything. But this idyllic situation is interrupted by what Campbell calls the Call to Adventure. The hero either responds to a summons (rumor of damsel in distress, someone's demand for help), or he is precipitated outright into the adventure by being kidnapped, dispossessed, drugged, or otherwise carried away against his will from the state of Equilibrium. Quite often the romance hero is merely a passive observer who finds himself caught up in a conflict larger than himself, but who nevertheless undertakes the quest and somehow emerges from it victorious. Many of Le Guin's protagonists unwittingly precipitate the action by some deed for which they alone are responsible: Ged releases his Shadow in Earthsea and Genly Ai's very presence on the planet Gethen creates the situation which forces him to trek across the Ice with Estraven. Because Le Guin's heroes are responsible for creating the need for the journey and for making the journey themselves, her romances have a strong ethical dimension.

The second stage, Struggle, takes place in a special world ridden by magic and irrational forces. This world, radically different from the one the hero has known, is closed. To enter it, the hero must cross a threshold, whether it be by going through a door or a gate, by entering a forest, by crossing a body of water by bridge or boat, or by crossing interstellar distances in a spaceship. Sometimes the hero must defeat or outwit the guardian of the passage to the special world. The hero's adventures in this world, which correspond to the ego's struggles in the unconscious during the process of Centroversion, are epitomized by a fight with a monster or a dragon. These fearsome opponents may be represented by wicked step-kin, satanic adversaries, witches, wolves, cannibals, or foreign invaders. In *A Wizard of Earthsea* it is Ged's own Shadow, and in *The Left Hand of Darkness,* Genly Ai's adversaries are the categories he uses to interpret reality, the most obvious being the dualism of male and female. But the hero does not face these enemies alone. At some point he receives help in the form of luck, wisdom, or magic. He may get advice from a wise old man or wizard, assistance from animals, or help from devices like magic swords, spears, purses, rings, or other identity tokens. Whatever forms these malignant and benign beings take, they are, says Hume, "identical with the symbols collected from the study of dreams, the dragon fight being both prime expression of the ego's struggle and the most basic of romance adventures" (p. 144). Like the ego which must venture into the unconscious and struggle there with "all manner of powers,... all extra-rational [and] not regulated by reason or logic (p. 132), the romance hero must enter upon enchanted ground and face ordeals more extreme and more terrible than anything he has experienced in his normal world. Because these powers inhabit a realm totally alien to the hero's normal world (and alien to the ego's rationalism and logic), they assume hyperbolic characteristics. Thus, there is little subtlety in the characterizations in romance; to ask for subtle delineations of character in a romance is to ask the unconscious to speak the language of consciousness. What Erich Fromm calls "the forgotten language," what Le Guin calls "the language of the night"—these are the native tongues in romance's enchanted world.[23]

Of paramount significance to the reader of romance is the equivalence between the nonprobable world depicted in romances and his own unconscious. Because of this, argues Hume, the special world of romance is "relevant to every member of the audience whether in its past or present development" (p. 144). It is this equivalence which makes possible Frye's statement that "the message of all romance is *de te fabula*," and also makes possible the likelihood that the reader will share the protagonist's vision from enchanted ground. Moreover, this equivalence accounts for the reader's sense that the fictional experiences depicted in romances, even the most hyperbolic ones, are "true," even while they are not, as is often charged, "true to life." As Auden says, these experiences "correspond to an aspect of our subjective experience." The struggle in the quest tale, he continues, "must be dualistic": it must be "a contest between two sides, friends and enemies."[24] In slightly different terms, Frye writes that "the central form of the romance is dialectical: everything is focused on a conflict between the hero and his enemy, and all the reader's values are bound up with the hero."[25]

Hume accounts for this polarization by referring to the related "nexus of concerns" that the world of romance and the unconscious share. Just as the forces in the romance are "sharply polarized into good and evil," the forces confronted by the ego in the unconscious may be "destructive at one stage [and] helpful at another, but at any given point in the conflict, evil is evil because it can harm the ego, and good is good because it has the potentiality to help" (p. 144). This of course applies more to "naive" than to "sentimental" romances. A writer like Le Guin, conscious of the potentialities of the genre, can exploit them for numerous effects by manipulating the reader's expectations. In *City of Illusions* the guide-helper Estrel turns out to be a betrayer, and in *The Left Hand of Darkness,* Estraven, who initially seems to be Ai's enemy, turns out to be his guide and double. At any moment in Le Guin's romances, friend and enemy may be sharply distinguished, but then again, their differences may, at another moment, be confused and ambiguous. Ultimately when we see them whole, we realize that friend and enemy are complementary parts of a unity. Like Estraven, Ged's Shadow initially appears as the hero's enemy, but ultimately we recognize it as a helpful though fearful guide and an integral part of Ged's Self.

The third and final stage of the romance, Higher Harmony, shows us a hero in a new equilibrium, the most common being the standard "they lived happily ever after" ending, which Hume regards as "axiomatically demanded by the romance construct" (p. 141). We see a hero who, having passed out of the strange world, is older, more mature, more experienced, and radically changed. The harmony and balance that characterized the first stage, Equilibrium, is regained, but it is qualitatively different in that it is more secure and lasting. Borrowing a phrase from Campbell, Hume describes the hero as a Master of Two Worlds: he has experienced both the baleful and helpful forces of the strange world, and has had a vision during which he has experienced a "sense of wholeness, peace, affirmed identity" (p. 143).

Although Hume mentions "affirmed identity" as a probable result of the hero's experiences in the enchanted world, she is not as concerned with this dimension of the romance as Frye is. Unlike Frye, whose exposition of the structure of the romance in *The Secular Scripture* centers on the hero's loss of identity, alienation, and subsequent recovery of identity and self-recognition, Hume is more interested in establishing the romance as "an objective correlative to the related unconscious troubles" (p. 134). While Frye's ultimate object is to demonstrate that secular romances form "a single integrated vision of the world, parallel to the Christian and biblical vision," and more than that, that they are a "revelation from God," he does discover along the way toward this goal valuable insights which can stand by themselves apart from the conclusions he pursues.[26]

I have used recent theories about the romance in order to show that the words that head this chapter—"jewel," "story," "pattern," "vision," and "world"—refer to essential aspects of the romance. Giamatti's essay on Spenser opened the discussion of vision, and Hume's essay on the "perdurable pattern" of the romance led into a treatment of pattern and story. What still needs separate treatment is the concept of world. Frye's emphasis on the romance hero's identity leads us directly to that. Frye proposes that in the romance

> heroes and villains exist primarily to symbolize a contrast between two worlds, one above the level of ordinary experience, the other below it. There is, first, a world associated with happiness, security, and peace: the emphasis is often thrown on childhood or an "innocent" or pregenital period of youth, and the images are those of spring and summer, flowers and sunshine. I shall call this world the idyllic world. The other is a world of exciting adventures, but adventures which involve separation, loneliness, humiliation, pain, and the threat of more pain. I shall call this world the demotic or night world. Because of the powerful polarizing tendency of romance, we are usually carried directly from one to the other (p. 53).

These landscapes are synonymous with the state of the protagonist's self: in the idyllic world he has a sense of identity, and in the demotic world, he is reified and alienated:

> Reality for romance is an order of existence most readily associated with the word identity.... It is existence before "once upon a time," and subsequent to "and they lived happily ever after." What happens in between are adventures, or collisions with external circumstances, and the return to identity is a release from the tyranny of these circumstances. Illusion for romance, then, is an order of existence that is best called alienation. Most romances end happily, with a return of the state of identity, and begin with a departure from it (p. 54).

In most romances, we follow the protagonist as he makes a cyclical movement through these two worlds: descent into the night world and return to the idyllic world.

Rather than organizing the structure of the romance in three parts, Frye concentrates his discussion on these two movements. Descent begins with the "motif of amnesia": the hero experiences "some kind of break in consciousness [involving] forgetfulness of the previous state" (p. 102). Just as the hero in Hume's scheme leaves the state of Equilibrium, Frye's prototypical romance hero experiences a sharp descent in social status which may take the form of dispossession, even slavery (e.g., Arren's capture by pirates in *The Farthest Shore*). Whatever form the descent takes, though, "the structural core is the individual loss or confusion or break in the continuity of identity" (p. 104). From that point on, there is further descent into the demotic world, and the hero progressively loses his sense of freedom. The central images during this descent into alienation are metamorphosis and doubling: "every aspect of fall or descent is linked to a change in form in some way, usually by associating or identifying a human or humanized figure with something animal or vegetable" (p. 105). During the earlier stages of descent, the doubling image appears in the "Narcissus theme" in which the hero exchanges his original self for his mirror image or shadow, while at later stages in the descent, this theme appears in the form of the Doppelgänger or shadow figure who threatens the hero with disaster and death. This is clearly what happens in both *A Wizard of Earthsea* as Ged confronts his Shadow and in *The Farthest Shore,* when Arren is nearly seduced by Sopli and when Ged confronts Cob. With increasing loneliness and alienation, the hero approaches the nadir of the descent, and just when he seems to be impossibly imprisoned or caught in enchantment and binding spells, or captured in the bowels of a monster, he escapes, the "standard escape device of romance [being] that of escape through a shift of identity, the normal basis of the recognition scene" (p. 136). This shift of identity usually comes at the moment of vision from enchanted ground. I will discuss the nature of the moment of vision in Le Guin's fiction later.

Ascent, argues Frye, is movement toward self-recognition and identity, and "all the Narcissus and twin and Doppelgänger themes that occur in the descent are reversed" (p. 152). When the demotic enchantment of the double or the shadow is broken, the severed current of memory is restored. Crucial to this process is that moment when by some paradox, the hero releases himself from bondage and enchantment, and achieves separation from the demotic by "consolidating and defining it" (p. 142). For Frye, the end of romance, the outcome of the upward journey which began at the moment of recognition or death/rebirth, is the creation of a model world, "not like a past state to return to, but an inner model or social vision to be recreated out of our 'lower' world of experience" (p. 184). Implicit in this statement is the suggestion that utopian vision is a direct result of the romance pattern. One could go beyond Frye at this point and argue that the utopia is the logical consequence of the romance. This seems to have been the case with Le Guin's career from 1966 to 1974. After she had written a few straightforward romance quests in the sixties, she produced a utopia, albeit an "ambiguous" one, *The Dispossessed*, in the seventies.

One thing that Frye does not make clear is the precise nature of the relationship between the idyllic and demotic worlds on the one hand, and identity and alienation on the other. His notion that the ascending movement in romance is "an upward journey toward man's recovery of what he projects as sacred myth" (p. 183) suggests that the downward journey, conversely, is similarly a consolidation of projected demotic qualities, but he does not say this in so many words. Le Guin would contend that the consolidation of projected demotic qualities is the *sine qua non* of the recovery of utopian vision (she might not search for sacred myth as Frye does).[27] Not only is the dystopia on Urras a necessary precondition for the utopian society on Anarres; they are complementary, for they both orbit around a common center of gravity.

In Fredric Jameson's essay on the romance, we find a discussion of two senses of the word "world," a discrimination which clarifies the relation between the protagonist's state of mind (and the reader's) and the worlds we see represented in the romance. In one sense, says Jameson, a "world" is an object of representation, and as such "never completely severs its connection with sense perception, even when it has become relatively figurative," as for example, when it is used to refer to detached realms of good and evil in romances.[28] This is "world" as it is used in Frye's definition of the idyllic and demotic worlds. In another sense, though, the word "world" reflects its origins in the phenomenological movment; Jameson writes that

> it originally designated something like the frame or the *Gestalt,* the overall organizational category within which the various empirical innerworldly phenomena are perceived and various innerworldly experiences take place. In this sense, then, a *world* cannot . . . be itself the object of experience or perception, for it is rather that supreme category which permits all experience or perception in the first place and must thus lie outside them as their own first condition.[29]

Given these two senses of "world," Jameson proposes the following definition of the romance:

> romance is that form in which the *world-ness* of *world* reveals itself. . . . romance as a literary form is that event in which *world* in the technical sense of the transcendental horizon of my experience becomes precisely visible as something like an innerworldly object in its own right, taking on the shape of *world* in the popular sense of nature, landscape, and so forth.[30]

This definition is compatible with Giamatti's and Hume's. When Jameson says that the romance as a literary form is an "event" in which "the *world-ness* of *world* reveals itself," he is speaking of the genre's tendency to culminate in a visionary moment on enchanted ground. And this visionary moment would involve, in the Jungian terms that are the substratum of Hume's account of the romance, the hero's confrontation with his shadow. The struggle between two "worlds" (the one unconscious and hence opaque to perception by the rational mind, and the other a projection), issues in the creation of a new "world" in the instant that the horizon separating the two worlds ceases to exist. This is the moment when the ego embraces the shadow, a pure example of which is Ged's naming of his Shadow. This is the moment Frye refers to as "consolidation and definition"; it is the moment of the hero's escape from alienation and tyranny "through a shift of identity, the normal basis of the recognition scene." The shift of identity is a shifting of the horizons of a "world" in the phenomenological sense; it is the radical transformation of the categories and configurations which had constituted the old *Gestalt*. This is, indeed, precisely what Falk experiences in *City of Illusions* as he listens to Orry's narrative; it is the "event" experienced by most of Le Guin's protagonists as they stand on enchanted ground.

The enchanted ground in *The Left Hand of Darkness* and the moment of vision experienced by Genly Ai are characteristic of the moments of vision in Le Guin's other romances. In the world of ice, snow, and extreme cold on the Gobrin Ice, in this world of total whiteness, nothing can be distinguished from anything else. Genly Ai sees "no sun, no sky, no horizon, no world. A whitish-gray void." In "the place inside the blizzard," there are no shadows; there is only "bland blind nothingness," what Estraven calls "the Unshadow."[31] The "world" as a *Gestalt* that makes perception possible floats free because there is no "world" as a landscape for it to perceive. Here, on the Gobrin Ice, the world-ness of Genly Ai's world reveals itself. The categories (e.g., male-female, and all other dualisms) he has used to see Estraven vanish, and he can, when he is otherwise blind, perceive Estraven as he-she really is. Genly Ai experiences the "shift of identity" Frye speaks of when the ways in which he sees, which *are* his identity, shift. As Estraven and Ai pull the sledge across the glacier, they create a new world, the nucleus of a community, through their interaction and mutual aid. The moment of vision when Ai sees Estraven truly is not to be dismissed as a private mystical experience; it is a social act. The void Ai experiences on the Ice is not something that creates angst and fear for Le Guin; resembling more the Oriental than Occidental void, it is the source of all creativity, including the creativity necessary for building a community. Le Guin's characters often enter this void with another person or with a guide, and there experience a moment of vision, transcend dualistic categories as they see things whole, and emerge with the seeds of a new social organization, a new understanding of the moral order underlying all existence, and a new realization of self based on a relationship with an other.

It is important to understand that the moment of vision in the romance is the culminating event in a story that unfolds in time. Rather than speaking of romance's dualistic images and polarizing forces, we should instead conceive of the romance as a dialectical process. Two boxers squaring off, one wearing white trunks and the other black, is not dialectical. A dialectical process begins when an initial element (thesis) creates out of its own contradictions an inverted image of itself (antithesis). The conflict and opposition between thesis and antithesis are resolved into a synthesis, a resolution which can be denoted best by the untranslatable German word *aufheben,* which means three things simultaneously: negate, absorb, and transcend.[32] Good and evil, friend and enemy, helper and harmer, idyllic and demotic—these are not eternally separate and conflicting opposites or dualities; rather, they are *complements,* by themselves incomplete moments in a unified process, but together internally related parts of a coherent whole. Each exists *only* by virtue of being the inverted or negated counterpart of the other. As Horkheimer and Adorno say, "everything is always that which it is, only because it becomes that which it is not". Things are, according to Chinese philosophers, "all the time on the way to something else." Becoming, not Being, is the way we are and who we are.

So it is with the concepts identity and alienation. An individual's or a social group's attempt to create and maintain an identity dialectically creates its antithesis and alienation, for in the ego's or group's conscious desire to keep its inner world constant and in the act of reaffirming its organizational categories merely by using them, it unconsciously ignores and excludes whatever does not conform to its *Gestalt.* Ged looses his Shadow from his inner into his outer world and Anarresti children watch propaganda films, relieving them from most all responsibility for their own feelings and shortcomings. The ego cannot see whatever is outside the horizons of its world. It has conceptual blind spots. Thus a "world" in the phenomenological sense cannot exist without its horizons; it cannot exist without alienating whatever contradicts or threatens its identity. In order for the ego to maintain its identity in the form that its organizational categories determine to be good and worthwhile, it must alienate whatever is evil and worthless, and avoid humiliation or annihilation by creating a shadow. The ego's fear of admitting to itself that it is evil or worthless is then directed outward as the shadow is projected onto others. Contradictions are expelled beyond the horizon of the ego's world; the Other assumes ownership of all that is alienated. Thus Self and Other may be bound together with fear and suspicion into a society in which individual and social alienation are the main cohesive forces.

A social group, like the individual, needs to alienate all that threatens its ideological consistency so that it can preserve its identity. If something happens within a society which the society cannot admit to its collective conscience, it can expel it, imprison it or blame it on outsiders, thus removing it from its collective consciousness. Since an individual cannot have an identity without membership in some social group, the opportunities for individual alienation and social alienation to reinforce each other are legion. As Frye says, "an identity between individual and social quests has always been latent in romance."[33] It is manifest in *The Dispossessed.*

To recall Frye is to return to the consideration of the romance genre as a tool for invention and discovery, for constituting meanings and stating truths about who we are, in all our manifold alienations and identities. The singular power of the romance consists in its ability to complete (in the course of the imaginative experience of reading) the dialectical synthesis of identity and alienation into a new identity characterized not by what it *excludes,* but rather by what it *includes.* The only way to resolve the contradictions between identity and alienation, in their interrelated individual and social forms, is to resolve them into a synthesis in which the old horizons that had separated one world from another are *transcended* as they are *negated* by means of an *absorption* of one into the other at the moment that what had been forgotten or repressed or alienated or excluded from consciousness is recognized as part of the whole self. This is the telos of the completed romance quest. When Ged and his Shadow say each other's names *at the same time* and embrace each other, the horizons between them are *aufgehoben.* "'I am whole, I am free,'" Ged says to Estarriol. And in his wholeness and freedom, he transcends whatever would have power over him: "naming the shadow of his death with his own name, [Ged] had made himself whole: a man: who, knowing his whole true self, cannot be used or possessed by any power other than himself, and whose life therefore is lived for life's sake and never in the service of ruin, or pain, or hatred, or the dark."[34] Ai's moment on the Gobrin Ice is similar, as is Shevek's moment on Urras when he sees the fundamental unity of Sequency and Simultaneity. All three of these moments take place away from "home," in an alien environment, on enchanted ground where the rules of habit and logic are suspended. As sailors in Earthsea say, *"Rules change in the Reaches."*

The completed romance quest, then, is pre-eminently a tool for dealienating alienation; it is the mediation by which, in dialectical terminology, we negate the negation. The "natural" and "appropriate" language for this, said Le Guin in a lecture presented at the Library of Congress, is fantasy. "The great fantasies, myths, and tales," she said, "are indeed like dreams":

> they speak *from* the unconscious *to* the unconscious, in the *language* of the unconscious— symbol and archetype. Though they use words, they work the way music does: they short-circuit verbal reasoning, and go straight to the thoughts that lie too deep to utter. They cannot be translated fully into the language of reason. . . . They are profoundly meaningful, and usable—practical—in terms of ethics; of insight, of growth.[35]

For Le Guin, the journey into the unconcious is not only a psychic journey; it is a moral journey as well. It is, she believes, "the individual's imperative need and duty."[36] The individual who projects his shadow "denies his own profound relationship with evil" and therefore "denies his own reality."[37] On another occasion, she said,

> If you deny affinity with another person or kind of person, if you declare it to be wholly different from yourself—as men have done to women, and class has done to class, and nation has done to nation—you may hate it, or deify it; but in either case you have denied its spiritual equality, and its human reality. You have made it into a thing, to which the only possible relationship is a power relationship. And thus you have fatally impoverished your own reality. You have, in fact, alienated yourself.[38]

So the denial of affinity and relationship, the ego's exclusion from its world of whatever threatens its limited and limiting identity, creates reification, alienation, and power relationships. What the romance genre can do is help the reader discover the real relationships and affinities, affirm rather than deny profound relationships with evil, and it does this through what Le Guin calls the "very strong, striking moral dialectic" that we find in the greatest fantasies. This dialectic, she says, is "often expressed as a struggle between the Darkness and the Light. But that makes it sound simple, and the ethics of the unconscious—of the dream, the fantasy, the fairytale—are not simple at all. They are, indeed, very strange."[39] What the "standards of conscious, daylight virtue" find when they enter this strange dialectic are not actions which are "good" and "bad"; rather, they will find that

> evil...appears in the fairytale not as something diametrically opposed to good, but as inextricably involved with it, as in the yin-yang symbol. Neither is greater than the other, nor can human reason and virtue separate one from the other and choose between them. The hero or heroine is the one who sees what is appropriate to be done, because he or she sees the *whole,* which is greater than either evil or good.[40]

What romances can do—and Le Guin believes they are "usable" and "practical" in terms of ethics and insight—is provide both the means and the end of the process of moral discovery, a discovery which comes in the form of a vision of the wholeness that transcends the ethical horizons of the conscious world. The creation of a Secondary World in the romance, a strange world where extrarational phenomena are the rule, where events unfold according to narrative logic rather than rational logic, is a privileged mode for doing this. To attempt it with the language of realism alone is to use an element of the very identity that created the alienated contents of the other world in the first place, and the result of the attempt to negate alienation in this manner will be continued and increased alienation. What Le Guin calls "false fantasies, rationalized fantasies," those stories in which the "tension between good and evil, light and dark, is drawn absolutely clearly," are stories in which the "author has tried to force reason to lead him where reason cannot go."[41] Reason cannot go there because reason excluded "there" from itself in order to *be* reason. If reason wanted to go there it would have to cease being reason. This is precisely what happens in romances. Fantasies, says Le Guin, "short-circuit verbal reasoning." In *The Farthest Shore,* when Ged takes on Sopli as a guide, Arren protests:

> "I would not quarrel with you, my lord," he said as coldly as he could. "But this—this is beyond reason!"
> "It is all beyond reason. We go where reason will take us."[42]

Ged's answer is Le Guin's prescription to the writer who would write "real" fantasies. A writer's moral responsibility, she believes, is to write "real" fantasies (what I call dialectically complete romance quests, journeys that take us where reason cannot go), rather than getting "entangled in the superficialities of the collective consciousness, in simplistic moralism, in projections of various kinds, so that you end up with the baddies and goodies all over again."[43] The way to "speak absolutely honestly and factually" to a reader, says Le Guin, is "to talk about himself. Himself, his inner self, the deep, the deepest Self."[44] Along with Frye, Le Guin is well aware that the message of romance is *de te fabula.*

III

We can conclude this examination of the poetics and rhetoric of the romance by looking at one of its subgenres, science fiction, the form of most of Le Guin's work. As a subgenre or a mode of romance, science fiction contains the dialectical potential already described, but while retaining the psychological, metaphysical, and ethical categories inherent in the romance, science fiction centers its attention on cognitive categories. Although some writers and critics of science fiction would like to establish some strict boundaries between fantasy (or romance) and science fiction, Le Guin does not. Romance is, after all, a form that ultimately transcends categorical horizons. In an autobiographical essay, Le Guin described her first efforts in science fiction as "fairytales decked out in space suits," and on another occasion, she compared her modes of fantasy and science fiction to the two hemispheres of the same brain, emphasizing that even if distinctions between them are possible, the two are in fact two parts of a single whole: they are complementary.[45]

A widely accepted definition of the science fiction genre—one that Le Guin herself accepts—is Darko Suvin's:

> SF is...a literary genre whose necessary and sufficient conditions are the presence and interaction of estrangement and cognition, and whose main formal device is an imaginative framework alternative to the author's empirical environment.[46]

Science fiction's "main formal device," clearly, is the same as the romance's: the alternative imaginative framework in science fiction corresponds to the nonprobable or enchanted world in the romance. Suvin's emphasis on estrangement signals his awareness that science fiction, like the romance, is a genre defined as much by its rhetorical strategies as by its poetics. Science fiction, through its estrangement techniques, reminds us that our world, our empirical environment, is not eternally fixed by unalterable scientific law. As Thomas Kuhn has shown in *The Structure of Scientific Revolutions,* a scientist's empirical world is constituted by the paradigms he and his colleagues accept, and these paradigms operate only until they are replaced by new paradigms (a process not unlike the dialectic in the romance), which can account for the anomalous data that could not be explained by the old paradigms. In a sense, a scientist is not really aware of the paradigms that control his thought until he is faced with accounting for the unexplained events which have no meaning in the obsolete categorical schemes. The phenomenological notion of "world," described by Jameson as "the framework for a description of the distinctive features of this or that world structure, [which can] not itself figure within that description as one of the latter's components,"[47] resembles Kuhn's concept of the paradigm, but only to a point. World in the ordinary sense, as an object of representation or a concrete physical environment, cannot—since Heisenberg, at any rate—exist independently of world in the technical phenomenological sense, as the framework used to describe a world. Romance, that literary form which is an "event in which the world-ness of world reveals itself," has had a tacit awareness of that all along, and only the most diehard mechanical materialist would deny the interpenetration of the two senses of the word "world."

The starting point of the romance dialectic is a world or an identity which believes itself to be self-sufficient, a world based on the idea of *substance,* not *relation.* The *sine qua non* of this sense of self-sufficiency is someone or something to absorb whatever is alienated, whatever threatens self-sufficiency. Similarly, the starting point in science fiction is a scientifically explained empirical environment that appears to be self-sufficient. But just as the romance carries the hero and the reader into a different world where they discover alien things and beings and forces, science fiction carries us into other worlds where we discover not only aliens but also alien scientific laws. The alien worlds in science fiction can be distinguished from the secondary worlds in fairy tales and fantasies, two other subgenres of the romance, by their emphasis on cognitive rather than magical modes of thought. But the distinction between science and magic, or between science and myth, should not be made too rigidly, for the more rigidly it is made, the easier it is for magic to become science and science to become magic.[48] Science and myth and magic are complementary in Le Guin's fiction. The point to insist on is not the qualitative distinctions that one can make between the different worlds in subgenres of the romance; rather we should concentrate on *relationships* between the so called "zero world" we operate in from day to day, and the "other" worlds in all forms of the romance. That relationship is responsible for the moment of vision from enchanted ground, the event that characterizes, more than any other, the special purpose of the romance plot.

Science fiction, says Suvin, is a "creative approach tending toward a dynamic transformation rather than a static mirroring of the author's environment."[49] Unlike realism, romance does not af*firm* or con*firm* the self-sufficiency of the author's environment by trying to mirror it. Instead, romance *estranges* (and science fiction cognitively estranges) the apparently self-sufficient identity or world by re-presenting its complementary alienation or its complementary other world. Thus what appeared normal appears strange, what had been alienated is brought home. When estrangement is carried through its dialectical synthesis, normal and strange, identity and alienation, are seen as they really are, interrelated and complementary parts of a whole. Literalization of metaphor is a method science fiction uses to do this. We go on quests to alien worlds in order to recover-discover our native world.

In an essay exploring the manifold meanings and relationships of the German words *entfremdung* (alienation) and *verfremdung* (estrangement) (an essay that not only stands behind Suvin's definition of the science fiction genre but also could serve as one of the best glosses on the theories of the romance genre I have mentioned), Ernst Bloch writes, "the roundabout way of estrangement is, after all, the shortest route away from alienation to self-confrontation—[it is] that exoticism that looks homeward." Although Bloch's main focus is on Brechtian drama and *Verfremdungseffekt*, his words about the recognition scenes in Brecht are a precise restatement of the purpose or *telos* of the romance:

> the beholder achieves insight by means of the estrangement-effect which can turn into its dialectical opposite—the recognition, or "Aha!" experience; insight into what is closest to the beholder grows out of his amazement at being confronted with what is farthest away ... wherever it leads to recognition, estrangement is concerned with the "tua fabula narratur."[50]

IV

"Our curse is alienation," writes Le Guin in "Is Gender Necessary?" (an essay on her intentions and methods in *The Left Hand of Darkness*); our curse, she says, is

> the separation of Yang and Yin. Instead of a search for balance and integration, there is struggle for dominance. Divisions are insisted upon, interdependence is denied. The dualism of value that destroys us, the dualism of superior/inferior, ruler/ruled, owner/owned, user/used, might give way to what seems to me, from here, a much healthier, sounder, more promising modality of integration and integrity.[51]

This observation is made from a position Le Guin calls "here." One could easily discover Le Guin's "here" in Taoism. Her remark about the separation of yin and yang in this passage is only one of the many references to Taoist ideas in all forms of her work, fiction, nonfiction, poetry, and prose. Her description of the "striking moral dialectic" in fairy tales, quoted earlier, is another. Whenever she uses the word "way," or its cognates "path" or "road"—and she uses them quite often—they are sure to have most of the meanings and implications, ethical and metaphysical, that the Chinese character *Tao* has. In her reply to the essays in the special issue of *Science-Fiction Studies* devoted to her work, she wrote, "the central image/idea of Taosim [the *t'ai chi,* the yin-yang symbol] is an important thing to be clear about, certainly not because it's a central theme in my work. It's a central theme, period."[52] There is an intimate connection between some form of belief and the romance. For Frye, Christian redemption and the *telos* of the romance are virtually synonymous, and Jameson notes that the "romance unfolds beneath the sign of destiny."[53]

Another way to discover where Le Guin's "here" is, is to assume that "here" is just where it says it is: right here, right now, where we all are, home, present time. Because we are too alienated from it to see it, however, because we lack the necessary vision, because we have conceptual blind spots, it does not exist for us: we do not feel at home. Because it does not exist for us, it is "nowhere," the English word for More's Greek neologism *utopia.* "Utopia," says Frye, "in fact and etymology, is not a place; and when the society it seeks to transcend is everywhere, it can only fit into what is left, the invisible nonspatial point at the center of space. The question 'Where is utopia?' is the same as the question 'Where is nowhere?' and the only answer to that question is 'here.'"[54] Frye's statement contains an implicit distinction between utopia as a place and utopia as a possibility, a distinction similar to Jameson's between "world" as an object of representation (a place) and "world" as a mode of perception (a possibility). Utopias, Suvin reminds us, are "verbal artifacts before they are anything else"; and the verbal mode appropriate to the utopia as an imaginative alternative, an "as if," is the subjunctive.[55] The verbal mode of Le Guin's perception from "here" is subjunctive ("dualism ... might give way"), so Le Guin's "here" is, in the light of all this, utopia.

In order to get "here," a real place where hope and promise and possibility and integration and integrity exist, we have to go "there," to an imaginary place in another world that exists subjunctively. We have to see the "world-ness of world reveal itself" in an estranged environment in order to see it in an alienated world. And as we know from the dialectical process at the heart of the romance, the vision and integration we search for is right here. When we discover it, we will recognize that we are recovering it: "true voyage is return" reads the inscription on Odo's tombstone in *The Dispossessed.*

Along with discovering the possibility of utopia, or perhaps on the way toward the discovery, we can recover and dealienate other things, like the true nature of our own sexuality; this is what happens as we travel imaginatively to Gethen in *The Left Hand of Darkness.* Le Guin emphasizes the fact that this story is about "here" in her "Introduction" to the novel:

> Yes, indeed the people in it are androgynous, but that doesn't mean that I'm predicting that in a millennium or so we will all be androgynous, or announcing that I think we damned well ought to be androgynous. I'm merely observing, in the peculiar, devious, and thought-experimental manner proper to science fiction, that if you look at us at certain times of the day and in certain weathers, we already are [androgynous].[56]

In "Is Gender Necessary?" Le Guin elaborates on the "thought-experimental manner proper to science fiction":

> I was not recommending the Gethenian sexual set-up: I was using it. It was a heuristic device, a thought-experiment. Physicists often do thought experiments. Einstein shoots a light-ray through a moving elevator; Schrödinger puts a cat in a box. There is no elevator, no cat, no box. The experiment is performed, the question is asked, in the mind. Einstein's elevator, Schrödinger's cat, my Gethenians, are simply a way of thinking. They are questions, not answers; process, not stasis. One of the essential functions of science fiction, I think, is precisely this kind of question-asking: reversals of an habitual way of thinking, metaphors for what our language has no words for as yet, experiments in imagination.[57]

And just to drive the point *home* that science fiction is concerned with "here," she adds,

> The purpose of the thought-experiment, as the term was used by Schrödinger and other physicists, is not to predict the future—indeed, Schrödinger's most famous thought-experiment goes to show that the "future," on the quantum level, cannot be predicted—but to describe reality, the present world.[58]

Like the romance, Schrödinger's thought experiment, his placing a cat in a box with radioactive matter, Geiger counter, and cyanide, an event in which the paradigms of quantum theory are laid bare, is an event in which the world-ness of world reveals itself. Thus, a literary genre and one kind of scientific method are complementary, even cooperative modes of understanding, or, in Le Guin's words, "ways of thinking...experiments in imagination." Unlike the discoveries in quantum mechanics, though, the discoveries made in the romance are recoveries. "We find ourselves facing what is yet to be in what was long forgotten," Ged tells Arren in *The Farthest Shore,* to which we can add Frye's observation that the "recreation of the possible future or ideal constitutes the wish-fulfillment element of the romance, which is the normal containing form, as archaism or the presentation of the past is the normal content."[59] But in a real sense, the containing form and the content of the romance are complementary, even cognate, for the paradox that lies at the heart of the form is that we move forward *only* by returning.[60]

This means that the romance's temporal "then" and "now" have the same relationship as do the spatial "there" and "here," and that history as well as psychic geography is a proper concern of the genre. The last stage of Hume's tripartie pattern, Higher Harmony, can recover the Equilibrium of the first stage *only* through a struggle in which the Equilibrium is transformed into a world whose temporal and spatial horizons transcend the dualistic or polarized oppositions which emerged from the Equilibrium. This process is depicted on a cosmic scale in Le Guin's Hainish future history: the Fore-Eras of Hain disintegrate into fragmentation; some worlds are then collected into a federation, the League of All Worlds; then the arrival of the Shing brings the destruction of the League and begins the Age of the Enemy; and finally, the worlds are gathered again, this time into an Ekumen.

Reality for Le Guin is dialectical—"process, not stasis" is her description of her own thought—she believes that there is a "law of mutual attraction," a law of elective affinity, of "*cooperative* relationship" in both art and life that "tends to bring things into a complexly ordered and harmoniously functioning whole."[61] As a character in one of her short stories says, "sentience or intelligence isn't a thing, you can't find it in, or analyze it out from, the cells of a brain. It's a function of the connected cells. It is, in a sense, the connection: the connectedness."[62] This metaphysic, which may very well be a product of a mind schooled in the reading and writing of romances, might be generalized as "existence is a function of relationship."

The Left Hand of Darkness mediates this metaphysic for Western readers as it embodies it in aesthetic form with the romance quest. The nominal goal of Genly Ai's mission to Gethen is to invite that world to join the 83 worlds in the Ekumenical Scope, to create a relationship between part and whole. But as his name (containing puns on "I" and "eye") indicates, the real goal of his quest is a discovery of self, a discovery that his own existence as an I is a function of his relationship with a Thou. This event, which culminates on the enchanted ground of the Gobrin Ice, involves his realization that sexuality is not a dualism of male and female, but an integrated whole in which masculinity and feminity are so inextricably involved with each other that they cease to exist as independent entities. At the moment that synthesis occurs, Genly Ai discovers a relationship with another person and finds himself capable of love for an alien Other, Estraven, the "other alien."[63] Having made these discoveries (which we make with him), Genly Ai is like the protagonist of the fairy tale, whom Le Guin describes as "the one who sees what is appropriate to be done, because he or she sees the *whole,* which is greater than evil or good." What is appropriate for Ai to do is to *do nothing.* This is the ethical imperative of Taoism, *wu wei,* usually translated as "inaction."[64] "Because of the alien who lay ill," Ai says of himself, "*not acting,* not caring, in a room in Sassinoth, two governments fell within ten days."[65] With the Sarf faction in Orgota and the Tibe ministry in Karhide gone, Gethen joins the Ekumen. Genly Ai's personal discoveries are thus parallel with and a symbol of social, political, and even metaphysical discoveries of relationship, affinity, and complementarity.

Although feminists have criticized Le Guin for choosing a male protagonist, she was, I think, right to do so, for the dialectic of the romance (and science fiction estrangement) almost makes it imperative. She chose a male, she says,

> because I thought men would loathe the book, would be unsettled and unnerved by it.... Since the larger percentage of science fiction readers are male ... I thought it would be easier for them if they had a man—and a rather stupid and bigoted man actually—to work with and sort of be changed with.[66]

Le Guin knows that it is male consciousness that is largely responsible for the sexual dualism in her empirical environment. She knows that a man cannot "*be* a man," as high school football coaches and army drill sergeants implore him to be, unless he alienates his femininity. What Le Guin had to estrange when she wrote *The Left Hand of Darkness* was the world of sexual dualisms—and many other dualisms too—on which Genly Ai's (and our) essential nature and identity (partial and fragmented as they are) are based. Sitting across from Estraven at a table, Genly Ai reflects:

> Though I had been nearly two years on Winter I was still far from being able to see people of the planet through their own eyes. I tried to, but my efforts took the form of self-consciously seeing a Gethenian first as a man, then as a woman, forcing him into those categories so irrelevant to his nature and so essential to my own.[67]

"Self-consciously" seeing from an alienated identity merely affirms the alienation and separation. What Ai needs to do is search for and struggle with (not against) what he has alienated, with what he fears to admit to consciousness, fears, because to admit it to consciousness would change that consciousness, would destroy the identity he brought to Gethen. Journeying with Estraven through another world, the Gobrin Ice, on which the "categories so essential" to his own nature are estranged, is the only way for him to do this. And in a moment of vision, analogous to the lifting of a visor or helmet in chivalric romance, Ai gets "a view in." He *sees:*

> And I saw again, and for good, what I had always been afraid to see, and had pretended not to see in him: that he was a woman as well as a man. Any need to explain the sources of that fear vanished with the fear; what I was left with was, at last, acceptance of him as he was. Until then I had rejected him, refused him his own reality.[68]

Now that Ai has ceased to refuse Estraven his-her own reality, he has ceased to refuse *his own reality;* the sources of his fear of seeing Estraven, his alienated identity, disappear as it is negated, absorbed, and transcended in a new identity. *Aufheben* completes the dialectic and Genly Ai has arrived "here."

Had Le Guin chosen a militant feminist for a protagonist, she would have perpetuated the dualism and division. She does include a female ethnologist, a double of sorts for Ai. Ong Tot Oppong, a member of the first Ekumenical landing party on Gethen, had reported that

> the first Mobile, if one is sent, must be warned that unless he is very self-assured, or senile, his pride will suffer. A man wants his virility regarded, a woman wants her femininity appreciated, however indirect and subtle the indications of regard and appreciation. On Winter they will not exist. One is respected and judged only as a human being. It is an appalling experience.[69]

In addition to being a superb piece of estrangement, this passage shows that the alienating divisions insisted upon infect the alienated as well as the alienator. One way to dealienate both, and return them to balance, integration, and harmony, is to use the romance quest, the dialectical thought-experimental method proper to science fiction.

Le Guin could, of course, have written a polemic against sexism and militarism, but she chose instead to write a *story* with a "rather stupid and bigoted man" as the protagonist and narrator, so that, by implication, her male audience, "rather stupid and bigoted," would have someone to identify with. She knows that telling them that they are stupid and bigoted would alienate them, but she also knows that the message of romance is *de te fabula.* She therefore spoke honestly to her male reader by talking "about himself. Himself, his inner self, the deep, the deepest Self." It is a measure of her compassionate radicalism that she chose to tell a story to her readers about themselves, to give them the chance to see what it is like "here," that place from which we might perceive the hope of a "much healthier, sounder, more promising modality of integration and integrity." In a serenely confident defense of her art, Le Guin concluded her acceptance speech for the 1973 National Book Award for children's literature by saying

> The fantasist, whether he uses the ancient archetypes of myth and legend or the younger ones of science and technology, may be talking as seriously as any sociologist—and a good deal more directly—about human life as it is lived, and as it might be lived, and as it ought to be lived. For after all, as great scientists have said and as all children know, it is above all by the imagination that we achieve perception, and compassion, and hope.[70]

2

Persuading Us To Rejoice and Teaching Us How To Praise: History, Fiction, and Ethics in *Orsinian Tales*

In 1951, the year Ursula Kroeber entered Columbia University to begin graduate work in French and Italian Renaissance literature, she invented an imaginary Central European country and wrote her first Orsinian tale. The country's name—Orsinia, or the Ten Provinces—and its creator's name have the same root: *orsino,* Italian for "bearish," and *Ursula* come from the Latin *ursa.* Le Guin explains rather dryly that "it's my country so it bears my name."[1]

After marrying Charles Le Guin in 1953, she abandoned her academic career to concentrate on writing. By 1961, she says in an autobiographical essay, she had completed five novels, four of them set in Orsinia, "as were the best short stories I had done."[2] When these novels and stories, classifiable as neither fantasy nor realism, were submitted to publishers like Knopf or Viking, or to magazines like *Harper's, Cosmopolitan,* or *Redbook,* they came back with the editor's remark, "this material seems remote." It *was* remote, says Le Guin:

> searching for a technique of distancing, I had come upon this one. Unfortunately it was not a technique used by anybody at the moment, it was not fashionable, it did not fit any of the categories. You must either fit a category, or "have a name," to publish a book in America. As the only way I was ever going to achieve Namehood was *by* writing, I was reduced to fitting a category. Therefore my first efforts to write science fiction were motivated by a pretty distinct wish to get published.[3]

But Orsinia did not go entirely unnoticed. A poem and a story set there were published in magazines in 1959 and 1961.[4] Yet just as a couple of Le Guin's minor Orsinian pieces were appearing in print, she discovered the science fiction writer Cordwainer Smith, rediscovered science fiction, which she had read as an adolescent, and, intent on getting published, started writing fantasy and science fiction for *Fantastic* and *Amazing* magazines. By 1963 she had begun her exploration of Earthsea and the Hainish worlds, and was on her way to Namehood. Now, of course, with numerous awards from both inside and outside science fiction, she has achieved Namehood. Twenty-five years after her Orsinian tales started collecting rejection slips, her *Orsinian Tales* (1976) received a nomination for the National Book Award for fiction.

I go into all this—the date of the earliest Orsinian tales, and their place vis-à-vis categories like "realism," "fantasy," and "science fiction"—to dispel the notion, put forward by a reviewer in a widely circulated science fiction fanzine, that *Orsinian Tales* is Le Guin's attempt to extend the range of her talents beyond the boundaries of fantasy and science fiction.[5] If anything, the opposite is the case. *Orsinian Tales* includes chunks of the bedrock that lie beneath Le Guin's other imaginary countries and worlds. Or, using another metaphor, I would suggest that a trip through Orsinia may lead us to those underground streams that nourish the imagination that created the Earthsea trilogy (1968-72), *The Left Hand of Darkness* (1969), and *The Dispossessed* (1974).

Some of these tales were written before Le Guin discovered-invented Earthsea and the Hainish worlds, some were written at the same time she was writing fantasy and science fiction, and they were all collected, arranged, and published after she has written the works that brought her Namehood. We cannot, therefore, try to understand *Orsinian Tales* as a discrete stage or step in Le Guin's development, for the parts and the whole were composed at different times. Accordingly, my approach here will be eclectic. In the first section, I will treat the book as a whole, discussing Le Guin's synthesis of complementary aesthetic and historical perspectives, and arguing that Le Guin's historical understanding is mediated by the literary form that structures most of her fiction, the circular journey or romance quest. Then, I will look at the country Orsinia as an imaginary construct whose fluid boundaries enclose both fantasy and realism, and also as a *paysage moralisé* which manifests the same qualities we find in Le Guin's other imaginary landscapes. In the final two sections, I will concentrate on parts rather than the whole, as I examine "Imaginary Countries" and *"An die Musik,"* two tales Le Guin wrote in 1960, before she turned to fantasy and science fiction, reading the first as the central tale in the collection, and the second as an early formulation of a problem that continues to be prominent throughout Le Guin's career, the conflict between her deep devotion to art and her strong commitment to ethical principles.

I

Orsinian Tales, Le Guin's second collection of short fiction, is radically different from *The Wind's Twelve Quarters* (1975), her first. In her "Foreword" to *The Wind's Twelve Quarters,* she explains that it is "what painters call a retrospective": the stories are assembled in the order they were written to give us an overview of her artistic development.[6] The tales in *Orsinian Tales,* however, are *not* arranged in the order of their composition, so this is not another Le Guin retrospective.[7] But if "restrospective" does not describe the collection, then another word from painting, "perspective," may indicate something about the nature of the tales and may help to reveal the ordering principles embedded in their arrangement.

After finishing any story, we step back from it as though stepping back from a painting, adjusting our vision to get an impression of its total design and meaning. This is aesthetic perspective, the desired effect of any technique of distancing. The distancing technique Le Guin uses in *Orsinian Tales,* the technique she developed in the fifties before she began writing for *Amazing* and *Fantastic,* is derived from Isak Dineson's tales and from Austin Tappan Wright's *Islandia.*[8] This technique does something more than create an aesthetic perspective; it creates a twofold perspective—aesthetic and historical.

Le Guin achieves aesthetic distance from her materials by writing *tales,* not stories (notwithstanding the publisher's dust jacket subtitle "A Collection of Stories"). *Orsinian Tales* does not belong in a class with Joyce's *Dubliners* and Anderson's *Winesburg, Ohio.* Rather, its title recalls the tradition that includes Scott's *Tales of My Landlord,* Hearn's *Tales Out of the East,* Dunsany's *A Dreamer's Tales,* and Dinesen's *Seven Gothic Tales* and *Winter's Tales.* A tale does not pretend to represent everyday reality as faithfully as a story does. A tale calls attention to itself as a work of art, closed off from the world. In its tendency to state a moral more overtly than a story usually does, it has affinities with fables, parables, and legends. A tale offers a clearer understanding of the shape and action of the moral order we dimly perceive in our sometimes disordered daily experience, and it does this because it detaches itself from the contingencies of a particular time and place. The very word *tale* has an archaic, distant tone missing from the common *story.* The discovery and delineation of moral laws, in fact, may be the most important goal of the teller of tales, and the pattern of those moral laws cannot be separated from the aesthetic forms which enable the artist to discover them and to communicate them to others. As ethical choices in our everyday lives are not free from history, those in a tale are bound by aesthetic forms. A tale offers a perspective that combines aesthetics and ethics in a single vision.

Yet at the same time that Le Guin creates this aesthetic perspective, she negates it by regrounding her tales in history, seemingly contradicting, yet really complementing the ahistorical qualities of the tale with precise historical connections. Le Guin sets her tales in an imaginary country, but that country is in *Mitteleuropa,* not *Faerie:* Orsinia is in the "sick heart" of modern Europe and knows at first hand what Mircea Eliade, a native of Romania, calls the "terror of history."[9] Le Guin therefore evokes as the larger setting of her tales some of the darkest, most chaotic, and most violent history available. Like Hardy's Wessex, Faulkner's Yoknapatawpha County, and Wright's Islandia,

Le Guin's Orsinia may be imaginary, but it is profoundly affected by real historical forces.

At the end of each tale we discover a date; these dates, ranging from the Early Middle Ages (1150) to the recent past (1965), locate each tale at a precise moment in Orsinia's (and Central Europe's) history. They invite us to step back from our involvement with a character's experiences, to insert those experiences in a definite historical context, and to understand them in a historical perspective. It is significant that the dates are at the *end* of each tale; they appear *at the very moment* we are stepping back to see aesthetically. At that moment, history and aesthetics, two modes of seeing and knowing and understanding, become one.

The process of reading the eleven pieces in *Orsinian Tales*, then, is the process of forming and reforming this two-fold aesthetic and historical perspective, progressively enlarging our understanding of the relationships among individual tales and deepening our understanding of the relationships between any one moment in the lives of individual Orsinians and the whole web of Orsinian history. As we finish the collection, we realize that the two perspectives are not contradictory, but complementary; the one being the dialectical negation of the other, art and history combine to create a single vision. "Heroes do not make history," says the narrator of "The Lady of Moge"—"that is the historians' job."[10] *Orsinian Tales*, however, offers abundant evidence that the job is not the sole responsibility of historians: it is shared by artists.[11] Le Guin's tales are as historical as Scott's Waverly novels are, and her history is as much an aesthetic invention as are Dinesen's finely crafted tales. As Le Guin's art in *Orsinian Tales* redeems her history from meaningless contingency and hopeless determinism, her history redeems her art from amoral escapism.

Le Guin's arrangement of the tales embodies a complex organic vision of history. If they are not arranged as they were written, neither are they arranged as history courses are, to give the impression that chronology and historical causality are somehow synonymous. Nor are they randomly mixed up just to give us the exercise of reconstructing Orsinia's history. Le Guin's ordering of the tales guides us through the history of Orsinia so that we move forward *only* by circling back to the past. We understand any present moment (actuality) only as we understand it to be an organic part of its past and future. After beginning in 1960 ("The Fountains"), we return in 1150 ("The Barrow"), move forward to 1920 ("Ile Forest" and "Conversations at Night"), then on to 1956 ("The Road East"), back to 1910 ("Brothers and Sisters"), forward beyond 1956 to 1962 ("A Week in the Country"), back to 1938 *("An die Musik")*, forward to 1965 ("The House"), back to 1640 ("The Lady of Moge"), and finally forward to 1935 ("Imaginary Countries"), coming to rest, at the end of the collection, at the chronological *center* of these eleven tales. Five are set before 1935, and five after 1935. This is not the only way in which "Imaginary Countries" is the central tale in *Orsinian Tales.*

The pattern of this movement through these tales that *are* Orsinia's history—a synthesis of circularity and linearity, a series of returns which are also advances—is not only the configuration of Le Guin's sense of history; it is also the aesthetic structure that informs most of her fiction. The romance quest which is at once a return to roots and an advance is Ged's path (way, Tao) in Earthsea. It is the route taken by Genly Ai and Estraven from Karhide over the Gobrin Ice to "The Place Inside the Blizzard" and back to Karhide, and the form of Shevek's journey from Anarres to Urras (the home of his ancestors) and back home again to Anarres. In *Orsinian Tales,* this pattern is present not only in the shape of the whole collection. It is present also in individual tales. For example, Freyga, Count of Montayna, returns to pagan sacrifice then advances the cause of Benedictine monks; Dr. Adam Kereth returns to Orsinia after "defecting" at Versailles; and Mariya returns to her husband Pier Korre in Aisnar after searching for independence and freedom from marriage in Krasnoy.

These circular journeys are in one way or another versions of the Romantic quest for home, freedom, and wholeness.[12] What Le Guin's characters learn on their quests is that freedom and wholeness are not to be found in self-regarding individualism, but in cooperative partnership, and further, that freedom from historical necessity comes not from escaping history, but from returning to roots. This is the moral message that emerges and takes shape when we see Le Guin's fiction from the perspective created by her distancing techniques. It is the ethical principle discovered by Sanzo Chekey and Alitsia Benat, by Stefan Fabbre and Bruna Augeskar, and by Mariya and Pier Korre. In Le Guin's fantasy and science fiction it is discovered by Ged and Vetch, Tenar and Ged, Arren and Ged, Genly Ai and Estraven, George Orr and Heather Lelache, Shevek and Takver. In *The Dispossessed,* we find Le Guin's most concise statement of the principle, chiseled into Odo's tombstone: "to be whole is to be part: / true voyage is return." It is the ethical foundation of Le Guin's fiction, even as it is aesthetic form and historical consciousness.

Ethics, art, and history, along with religion, philosophy, politics, and science, are what Joseph Needham calls "moulds of understanding."[13] Each one, taken by itself, offers a limited and limiting mode of comprehending and experiencing the world. *Orsinian Tales* is one of Le Guin's attempts to formulate a unified mould of understanding that integrates artistic, ethical, and historical modes. Convinced that the worlds we experience, from subatomic to cosmic levels, whether material or imaginative, are all integrated parts of an ordered whole, a continuous process, Le Guin has from the beginning of her career tried to fashion fictional techniques to explore and to understand that order. The hybrid of realism and fantasy in *Orsinian Tales,* the fantasy of the Earthsea trilogy, and the science fiction of the Hainish novels are all different means to the same end: a realization of the unity of the world we live in. The practical end, unity, and the formal means, a circular journey, are cognate. In one sense, Le Guin uses different genres; but in another sense, those genres are merely distinct, though not radically different, constellations of moulds of understanding. Just as artist and historian in Le Guin collaborate in *Orsinian Tales,* artist and scientist work together in her science fiction.

One of her storytellers, Genly Ai, weaves together his own story with extracts from Estraven's journal, an anthropological report, and Gethenian legends, folktales, religious texts, and myths. Each presents only a partial view of the truth. Together they collaborate to come closer to Truth. For Genly Ai and Ursula Le Guin, the real and the fantastic, fact and value, art and history, myth and science are neither separate nor even separable realms and modes of discovery, they are complementary and internally related parts of the same realm. "How can you tell the legend from the fact?" asks the narrator of *Rocannon's World.* Le Guin's fiction denies the walls we build with different moulds of understanding. It denies by negating the reification and dehumanization that a fragmented and compartmentalized way of life produces, and then, completing the dialectical process, affirms and celebrates the whole which is greater than the parts. Like the music Ladislas Gaye hears at the end of *"An die Musik,"* "it denies and breaks down all the shelters, the houses men build for themselves, that they may see the sky" (p. 145).

II

The Italian sociologist and economist Vilfredo Pareto was perturbed by the shifting and sometimes contradictory meanings of Marx's words and concepts:

> If you raise some objections against a passage in *Capital,* a passage whose meaning seems to you incontestable, someone can quote another, whose meaning is entirely different. It is the fable of the bat all over again. If you embrace one meaning, someone tells you
>> I am a bird; see my wings;
>> Long live the flying things!
> And if you adopt the other, someone tells you
>> I am a mouse; long live the rats;
>> Jupiter confound the cats![14]

Much of the same can be said—indeed has been said, though in a positive rather than a negative sense—about the ideas and concepts in Le Guin's fiction. In his essay on the Earthsea trilogy, T.A. Shippey may not argue that Le Guin's words are, like bats, both birds and mice, but he does note that Le Guin's story embodies an "argument" against "conceptual barriers" that result from "the very sharpness and hardness of modern concepts."[15] Not only does Le Guin make "covert comparisons between 'fantastic' and 'familiar,'" says Shippey, she also shifts the meanings of familiar concepts: at times magic in Earthsea seems to be a science, at other times an art, and at still other times, it is ethics. The "oscillation between concepts" that Shippey sees in the Earthsea trilogy is not peculiar only to Le Guin's juvenile fantasy; it permeates nearly everything she has written, from her individual sentences to her major themes, images, and even characters. Were Pareto alive, he might consider Le Guin's Gethenians just as bat-like as Marx's concepts: if he tried to see them as women, they would become men, and if he tried to see them as men, they would become women. Le Guin wants to teach readers like Pareto (and characters like Genly Ai) to think both-and (or even, perhaps, neither-nor) rather than either-or. She started doing just that in the fifties and sixties when she was writing her Orsinian tales.

Long before Le Guin wrote a sentence like "The king was pregnant" in *The Left Hand of Darkness,* she was writing sentences like this one in *Orsinian Tales:* "On a sunny morning in Cleveland, Ohio, it was raining in Krasnoy and the streets between grey walls were full of men" (p. 108). This sentence first situates us in a familiar time and place, then erases the distinctions we make between a real country like the USA and an imaginary country like Orsinia. Cleveland and Krasnoy do not exist in the same world. Or do they? Le Guin's sentence creates a new world, neither our familiar one, nor an entirely fantastic one, but a world which is both realistic and fantastic. The point of this sentence is not that one thing is real and the other is imaginary: the point is that they are both in the same sentence. The world of Le Guin's fiction, built from sentences like this as surely as our world is built from rock and stone and trees, is not a realm of well defined, discrete things and places and times and ideas. Rather, it is a realm where categories and perspectives are fluid, a world which is an ordered process in which nothing, except change itself, can be taken for granted as certain. In Earthsea, "the everchanging does not change,"[16] and in Orsinia, the country's location, its political history, even its geology, are all in flux.

Orsinia can be placed on two different maps. Darrel Schweitzer says that "in *Orsinian Tales* Le Guin seems to be trying to do a *Dubliners* set in an unnamed central European country (clearly Hungary, complete with a revolution against foreign conquerers in 1956)."[17] Le Guin's brother Karl Kroeber, on the other hand, tells us "not to seek in Bulgaria for the setting of 'Brothers and Sisters.' The curious growthless plain of limestone quarries is not East of the Sun and West of the Moon, just a little south of Zembla and north of Graustark."[18] Though Kroeber is mostly right in placing Orsinia on the same map with Nabokov's distant northern kingdom in *Pale Fire* and McCutcheon's Balkan kingdom, rather than in a totally fantastic realm ("East of the Sun and West of the Moon"), and though Schweitzer is mostly wrong in identifying

Orsinia with Hungary, neither of these two mappers takes full account of Le Guin's "oscillation," as Shippey might call it, between Joycean naturalism and the escapism of McCutcheon's *Graustark* or Hope's *The Prisoner of Zenda*. Literary naturalism and Ruritanian romances were contemporary phenomena at the turn of the century when many writers and readers were making clear distinctions between realism and romance. Le Guin's fictional techniques dissolve those distinctions. The boundaries between the real and the fantastic disappear when we understand them to be complementary and internally related parts of the imaginary.[19]

Le Guin herself says that Orsinia is an "invented though nonfantastic Central European country."[20] Le Guin's invented worlds, whether set in Europe or in the Hainish universe, still contain accurate naturalistic facts, history in the first instance, science in the second. To make the transition from writing Orsinian tales to writing science fiction was no major step for Le Guin; she replaced one social science (history) with another (anthropology), integrated some elements from the hard sciences, and mastered a new set of literary conventions. Some of the Orsinian tales, in fact, were written at the same time she was writing the Hainish novels and the Earthsea trilogy.

There are, certainly, ample naturalistic facts in *Orsinian Tales* to justify looking for Orsinia on a map of Europe. We visit Versailles, hear of Croatian microbiologists, get a glimpse of the conflict between Teutonic paganism and Christianity in the early Middle Ages. We see the social and economic dislocation caused by late nineteenth-century industrialization, watch the suffering of a disabled World War I veteran, and hear about an insurrection in Budapest in October 1956. But just when we become secure with our identifications between the fictive and the real, the things we see change (like Pareto's bat), and places appear on no map of Europe. Conversely, when we suspend belief and get comfortable in Krasnoy or Sfaroy Kampe or Aisnar, we learn, with a clerk-composer (who has a sister in Prague), that Hitler is meeting Chamberlain in Munich in September 1938. One city in Orsinia seems to have a foot in both worlds: Brailava could be as real as Bratislava, Czechoslovakia, or it could be as imaginary as Sfaroy Kampe. The point, however, is this: we must not read *Orsinian Tales* the way three blind men read an elephant. To avoid seeing either a tree trunk or a wall or a rope, we must see the whole, be sensitive to the *relationships* among parts which characterize an organic whole. Relationships, not discrete things, are the subject of all of Le Guin's fiction. In "A Week in the Country," Stefan Fabbre recalls the story of a Hungarian nobleman who lives through the wars between Hungary and the Ottoman Empire. The wars were real, the story is a legend, and Stefan Fabbre is a product of Le Guin's imagination. They are all related. "How can you tell the legend from the fact?"

The political entities in Central Europe, like the boundaries between the familiar and the fantastic, have been fluid, and this is probably one reason that Le Guin chose Central Europe as the location of Orsinia. Orsinia's name does more than play on its creator's name; it echoes names like Bohemia, Silesia, Moravia, Galicia, and Croatia. The singular fact of political experience for these peoples is that while they have tenaciously preserved their nationality, they have never had lasting political independence. Orsinia shares with these countries a position on the battlegrounds of European and Asian imperialism, from Attila to the present. Orsinia may have come under Hapsburg domination in the sixteenth century (Isabella, "the Lady of Moge," has a Spanish-sounding name) and was probably threatened by the Ottoman Empire in the sixteenth and seventeenth centuries. In the eighteenth century Austria and Prussia could have fought a war in Orsinia; in the nineteenth century, Napolean's armies probably crossed over Orsinian soil, and up to World War I, Orsinia was probably part of the Austro-Hungarian Empire. Then in the twentieth century, after a short-lived political independence, Orsinia was probably overwhelmed from the west by Hitler, and then a few years later, from the east by Stalin. This long historical nightmare of violent political change and oppression by authoritarian states only brings into sharper relief one of the major themes, if not *the* major theme, of these tales: the struggle of the individual to win a sense of freedom and wholeness in a prison-like society, and his heroic efforts to maintain a sense of identity and self-respect. It is but a short step from this to the thematic center of *The Dispossessed.*

Le Guin's imaginary countries are not finished creations in which the landscape, geological or moral, is set for all time. The glaciers on Gethen, the earthquakes on Anarres, as well as Orsinia's limestone bedrock, are notable instances of geological flux. As Genly Ai and Estraven are ascending a glacier (a fluid solid) past the active volcanoes Drumner and Dremegole to reach the Gobrin Ice, Estraven records in his journal,

> We creep infinitesimally northward through the dirty chaos of a world in the process of making itself.
> Praise then Creation unfinished (p. 227).

Orsinia's topography may not change as dramatically as Gethen's, but it is nevertheless also in flux, it too is "in the process of making itself." One of the striking features of the Orsinian landscape is the Karst, the setting of "Brothers and Sisters." Karst topography is characterized by rocky barren ground, caves, sinkholes, underground rivers, and the absence of surface streams and lakes, resulting from the work of underground water on massive soluble limestones. Originally the term "karst" was applied to the Kras, a limestone area along the

Adriatic coast of Yugoslavia. (The principal city in Orsinia, Krasnoy, may take its name from the Kras.) There are no hymns like "Rock of Ages" in Orsinia. The rocks dissolve in water.

Like all of Le Guin's imaginary landscapes, Orsinia is a *paysage moralisé.* The moral and psychological resonance of the settings and landscapes in Le Guin's science fiction has already been recognized.[21] What she does in the Hainish worlds and in Earthsea is anticipated in *Orsinian Tales.* Like the chasm beneath the Shing city in *City of Illusions,* like the forests in "Vaster than Empires and More Slow" and in *The Word for World is Forest,* like the islands and seas of the Earthsea Archipelago (another solid-liquid combination), the Karst in "Brothers and Sisters," the forest in "Ile Forest," and the mountains in "The Barrow," as well as the decaying house and garden on the Hill in Rákava in "Conversations at Night," are both images and symbols: they are at once themselves even as they refer beyond themselves to moral and psychological values and meanings. If Orsinia's bedrock can be dissolved and reconstituted, so can moral values. Dr. Adam Kereth steals freedom and is then drawn back to Orsinia by mere fidelity. Count Freyga sacrifices a Christian priest and then aids Christian monks. Dr. Galven Ileskar, who believes that murder ought to be an unpardonable crime, loves a murderer who turns out to be his brother-in-law, and brother, too.

The thematic significance of the fluidity of Le Guin's political, topographical, and moral landscapes is this: her human actors are free to choose and to be responsible for their choices. No less than the rocks in her landscapes, Le Guin's characters are "in the process of making themselves." Neither reality nor ethics is handed to them on adamantine tablets (though some of them may think they are); whole cultures as well as individuals dissolve and reconstitute themselves as they change and grow. This happens repeatedly in her science fiction. Terrans and Tevarans cease to exist as independent cultures in *Planet of Exile,* Gethenian cultures are on the brink of a major change in *The Left Hand of Darkness,* and reality itself is repeatedly reconstituted by George Orr's effective dreams in *The Lathe of Heaven.* It goes without saying that the society on Anarres in *The Dispossessed* is a society in the process of making itself which offers the individual the most freedom to make himself (thereby remaking the society), as long as it does not petrify. Faxe the Weaver speaks for Le Guin in *The Left Hand of Darkness* when she-he says "The only thing that makes life possible is permanent, intolerable uncertainty: not knowing what comes next" (p. 71). Life is making choices; if we knew what comes next, we could not choose.

But what certainties can Le Guin offer in the midst of all this flux? Only human relations: fidelity, constancy, and love. In "A Week in the Country,"

Stefan Fabbre and Kasimir Augeskar, on their way to visit the Augeskar's summer home, exchange these words in a train compartment:

> "So here we are on a train to Aisnar," Kasimir said, "but we don't know that it's going to Aisnar. It might go to Peking."
> "It might derail and we'll be killed. And if we do come to Aisnar? What's Aisnar? Mere hearsay."—"That's morbid," Kasimir said .... —"No, exhilarating," his friend answered. "Takes a lot of work to hold the world together, when you look at it that way. But it's worthwhile. Building up cities, holding roofs up by an act of fidelity. Not faith. Fidelity" (pp. 109-10).

What at first strikes us as merely an academic discussion by two students to pass the time takes on new meanings by the end of the tale. After Stefan falls in love with Bruna Augeskar, after he hears Joachim Bret sing an English lute song,

> You be just and constant still, Love may beget a wonder.
> Not unlike a summer's frost or winter's fatal thunder:
> He that holds his sweetheart dear until his day of dying
> Lives of all that ever lived most worthy the envying (p. 120),

after he sees Kasimir killed by the secret police, and after he is tortured—after all that, when Bruna comes for him, he knows that there is "no good letting go, is there .... No good at all" (p. 129). Fidelity—being just and constant still— and love hold the world together in ways Stefan had not imagined. And the more precarious existence becomes, the more necessary fidelity becomes. In "Conversations at Night," Sanzo Chekey and Alitsia Benat are little more than beggars, and their hope, like Stefan's and Bruna's, lies in the personal fidelity that holds their world together:

> "Lisha," he [Sanzo] said, "oh, God, I want to hold on .... Only it's a very long chance, Lisha."
> "We'll never get a chance that isn't long."
> "You would."
> "You are my long chance," she said, with a kind of bitterness, and a *profound certainty* ....
> "Well, hang on," he said .... "If you hang on, I will" (pp. 58-59, my emphasis).

"Betrayal and fidelity were immediate to them," Le Guin says of the Augeskar family in "A Week in the Country" (p. 121). Like many Le Guin characters, the Augeskars live out on the edge. They live near the Iron Curtain in a political climate that makes their existence as perilous as the Gethenians' is in their barely habitable natural climate. It is worth remembering that Le Guin says that *The Left Hand of Darkness* is "a book about betrayal and fidelity."[22]

Betrayal and fidelity are as immediate to Genly Ai and Estraven when they trek across the Ice and when they seek aid from Thessicher, as they are to the Augeskars in Orsinia. Probably the best example in Le Guin's fiction of personal fidelity against a background of flux and uncertainty comes in *The Dispossessed*. Just as Shevek is coming into Chakar to rejoin Takver and Sadik after a four-year separation, an earthquake hits the region. He finds Takver's domicile, and knocks. She answers the door:

> She stood facing him. She reached out, as if to push him away or to take hold of him, an uncertain, unfinished gesture. He took her hand, and then they held each other, they came together and stood holding each other on the unreliable earth.[23]

Just a moment before, Shevek had thought that "the earth itself was uncertain, unreliable. The enduring, the reliable, is a promise made by the human mind." Human relations are no different on Orsinian soil.

A good analogue, perhaps a source, for Le Guin's use of landscape in *Orsinian Tales* is another *paysage moralisé*, Auden's "In Praise of Limestone":

> If it form the landscape that we, the inconstant ones,
>   Are consistently homesick for, this is chiefly
> Because it dissolves in water....
> It has a worldly duty which in spite of itself
>   It does not neglect, but calls into question
> All the Great Powers assume; it disturbs our rights....
>   when I try to imagine a faultless love
>   Or the life to come, what I hear is the murmer
> Of underground streams, what I see is a limestone landscape.[24]

Le Guin knows Auden's work, and may have read "In Praise of Limestone" at the time she was inventing her Orsinian Karst.[25] Even if Le Guin was not directly influenced by Auden, there are elective affinities here, and these might be explained by the fact that both Auden and Le Guin have been influenced by Rilke.[26] Like Rilke, both Auden and Le Guin rely on concrete settings and naturalistic landscape detail to express emotions and moral values. When Dr. Kereth returns to his hotel in Paris after having "stolen" freedom at Versailles, "kingly he strode past the secret police agent in the lobby, hiding under his coat the stolen, inexhaustible fountains" (p. 4).

In a review of Rilke's *Duino Elegies*, Auden wrote that Rilke is

> almost the first poet since the seventeenth century to find a fresh solution [to the poet's problem of] how to express abstract ideas in concrete terms .... He thinks in physical rather than intellectual symbols .... Rilke thinks of the human in terms of the nonhuman, of what he calls Things *(Dinge)*, a way of thought which, as he himself pointed out, is more characteristic of the child than of the adult.[27]

What Auden says of Rilke applies to Le Guin, and may help to account for the artistic superiority of the Earthsea trilogy over the science fiction. Science fiction, as many have pointed out, is a literature of ideas. Le Guin succeeds as well as anyone in finding concrete images for the abstract ideas of modern science, but this success falls short of what she accomplishes in her juvenile fantasy, and in many of the pieces in *Orsinian Tales.* In her "Response" to the Le Guin issue of *Science-Fiction Studies,* Le Guin says that she

> can't even think one stupid platitude without dragging in a mess of images and metaphors, domes, stones, rubble [Rilkean *Dinge?*].... This lamentable concreteness of the mental processes is supposed, by some, to be a feminine trait. If so, all artists are women. And/or vice versa.[28]

Or children. Whenever Le Guin succeeds in expressing human values and abstract ideas (freedom) in vividly sketched landscapes, or with a "mess of images and symbols" (fountains), she creates superior art.

In his discussion of Auden's moral landscapes and "psychic geography," Monroe K. Spears notes that "for Auden, as for Rilke, the distinction between inner and outer worlds is tenuous and interpenetration is constant."[29] He could say the same of Le Guin, for the Earthsea trilogy is as much about Le Guin's own inner world as an artist as it is about Ged. Le Guin herself admits as much in "Dreams Must Explain Themselves," an essay recounting the genesis and growth of the Earthsea trilogy:

> Wizardry is artistry. The trilogy is then, in this sense, about art, the creative experience, the creative process. There is always this circularity in fantasy. The snake devours its tail. Dreams must explain themselves.[30]

In the same sense that Ged *is* Le Guin, Orsinia *is* Ursula; the "true name" of her country, a pun on her own name, is one more instance of this "circularity of fantasy." And that circularity can be seen clearly in the last and central tale in *Orsinian Tales,* "Imaginary Countries."

III

"Imaginary Countries" is a family portrait. Baron Severin Egideskar, his wife, and their three children Stanislas (fourteen), Paul (seven), and Zida (six) are in the last few days of their annual stay at "Asgard," their summer home in the country. The baron will return to his chair as Follen Professor of Medieval Studies at the University of Krasnoy. Josef Brone, his research assistant, has been with them throughout the summer, helping the professor with the documentation for his history of the Ten Provinces (Orsinia) in the Early

Middle Ages. Rosa, the maid, and Tomas, the caretaker, complete the group. The family that sat for this portrait is the A.L. Kroeber family, who used to spend summers at "Kishamish" in the Napa Valley, 60 miles north of Berkeley, where Kroeber was Professor of Anthroplogy at the University of California. Like Kroeber, who spent his summers in the thirties working on an encyclopedic study in comparative cultural anthropology *(Configurations of Culture Growth),* Egideskar is at work on a "history [that] was years from completion" (p. 172). And like Ursula Kroeber, born in 1929, Zida Egideskar is six years old in 1935, so "Imaginary Countries" is, among other things, a portrait of the artist as a young girl.[31]

Le Guin has written a tale about the family of a professor who is writing a history of Orsinia, a country she invented. The professor has a daughter who is a portrait of the girl who grew up to invent an imaginary country where, in 1935, a professor is writing a history. . . and so on. The snake devours its tail. In addition to recognizing the uroboros, though, we might as easily see Chinese boxes. Le Guin includes in a collection of tales set in an imaginary country a tale entitled "Imaginary Countries," which includes characters who live from time to time in imaginary countries. "Imaginary Countries" is the central tale in the collection in the same sense that the point at which the snake's tail disappears into its mouth is central. It is central in the way that the intersection of two mirrors that produce an infinitely regressing image is central.

So "Imaginary Countries" is central in *Orsinian Tales* in more ways than just being the middle tale chronologically. If we read Le Guin's *Orsinian Tales* as Ursuline tales, then our reading of them becomes at once a journey into Orsinia's history and a journey into the history of Le Guin's invention of Orsinia's history. The work created and the creative work become one. Just as Le Guin's arrangement of the tales directs us back into Orsinia's past even as we move forward into the collection, "Imaginary Countries" returns us to the roots of the imagination that created the book we have finished reading. The last tale concludes the collection at the same time it looks forward to the creation of the collection by showing us a portrait of the artist as a young girl. When Le Guin placed "Imaginary Countries" at the end of *Orsinian Tales,* she was saying, in effect, "In my beginning is my end" and "In my end is my beginning" (the first and last lines of T.S. Eliot's "East Coker"). *Orsinian Tales,* then, has the same organic structure that *The Dispossessed* has. The alternating chapters on Anarres and Urras are put together so that when we come to the end of Shevek's story on Anarres, he is ready to begin the trip to Urras that opens the novel, and when we come to the end of Shevek's story on Urras and his return to Anarres, we see him ready to leave Anarres. Le Guin would probably accept what another Romantic, Coleridge, says about the function of poetry:

> The common end of all *narrative,* nay of *all,* Poems is to convert a *series* into a Whole: to make those events, which in real or imagined History move on in a *strait* Line, assume to our Understandings a *circular* motion—the snake with it's Tail in it's Mouth.[32]

Orsinian Tales does this for the imaginary history of Orsinia at the same time it does it for the real history that is Le Guin's career as a writer.

It could be that Egideskar, who writes narratives of "real" history, as well as his creator, who writes narratives of imagined history, would agree with Coleridge. An observer of history as sensitive as the baron would have seen that the idea of Progress, the ever-ascending "strait Line" of history that was born in the Enlightenment, was not working in the ethics and politics of the twentieth century. By studying early medieval times he may be trying to understand history not in strictly linear terms (chronology and causality), but in circular terms as well (returns and rebirths). The baron could not be unaware of the goings on to the west of Orsinia in the thirties. Nazi barbarism, in fact, may be the silent subject of his history of Orsinia in the Early Middle Ages. Among the events he is studying and interpreting would be incidents like the one Le Guin describes in "The Barrow," set in 1150. His assistant Josef Brone reads from "the Latin chronicle of a battle lost nine hundred years ago" (p. 172); one of the incunabula Josef and the baron pack in a trunk probably contains the "bad Latin for [the Benedictine] chronicles of Count Freyga and his son," mentioned at the end of the "The Barrow" (p. 14). Count Freyga lived at the time when pagan ethics and Christian ethics clashed; although he is nominally a Christian, he reverts to sacrificing a priest to "Odne the Silent" to relieve his terrifying anxiety about his wife and unborn child. The baron lives at a time when a nominally civilized culture is reverting to barbarism. Understanding medieval Orsinia, going to historical roots, may help Egideskar understand twentieth-century Europe.

Some readers may think that the baron, who calls his wife Freya and his summer home Asgard, is implicated in the revival of Norse myth used by the Nazis to legitimate their ideologies. That would be doing the baron a disservice, for he does know the difference between a unicorn's hoofprint and a pig's (p. 177), and there is as much difference between a true myth and a false myth as there is between a unicorn and a pig.[33] The baron faces the problem that any serious student of history and culture sooner or later faces: he is part of what he is trying to understand. He needs a technique of distancing. He can get it by spending his summers away from Krasnoy, by participating in his family's imaginary countries, and by studying the history of Orsinia in the Early Middle Ages. In order to get free of the distorting fog of subjectivity and ideology, he needs an Archimedes point from which he can get "a view in"; he needs to see from a place "a very long way from anywhere else."[34] The baron, that is to say, encounters the same problems as a historian that Le Guin faces as a writer, and this is yet another way in which "Imaginary Countries" is the central tale in *Orsinian Tales*. In a book that is in many ways about history, we have a portrait of a historian: still another instance of the circularity of fantasy.

But "Imaginary Countries" is more than the central tale in the collection. Earlier I said that a trip through Orsinia may take us to the underground streams that nourish the roots of the imagination that created Earthsea and the

Hainish worlds. Coming at the end of the trip, "Imaginary Countries" brings us as close as we are likely to come to those streams, Le Guin's childhood experience of Norse myth and folklore.

Written in 1960, after Le Guin had been exploring Orsinia in novels and tales for a decade, and before she turned to stories that fit publishers' categories, "Imaginary Countries" is a tale in which Le Guin returned to the myths that informed her childhood play and nourished her imagination.[35] Like "the Oak" in Stanislas's "kingdom of the trees," the whole body of Le Guin's fiction can be seen as Yggdrasil, the Norse world-tree, with its roots in Orsinia and its branches and leaves in the far away galaxies of the Hainish universe. When Josef Brone follows Stanislas into "the Great Woods," Stanislas guides him to "the Oak":

> It was the biggest tree [Josef] had ever seen; he had not seen very many. "I suppose it's very old," he said; looking up puzzled at the reach of branches, galaxy after galaxy of green leaves without end (p. 173).

In this tale, which precedes by three years Le Guin's invention-discovery of the Hainish universe, she was already using the language of science fiction with Norse myth. As we will see in the next chapter, that is exactly how she created the Hainish worlds. In "The Dowry of Angyar" (retitled "Semley's Necklace" in *The Wind's Twelve Quarters*), she wove together the Einsteinian notion of time-dilation with the Norse myth of Freya and the Brisingamen Necklace. That story became the germ of *Rocannon's World*, her first novel, and from that the rest of the Hainish novels followed. The Earthsea trilogy evolved in much the same way.

After Le Guin started writing science fiction, she returned to Yggdrasil again and again. In *Planet of Exile*, Rolery gazes at a mural representing Terra and "the other worlds":

> The strangest thing in all the strangeness of this house was the painting on the wall of the big room downstairs. When Agat had gone and the rooms were deathly still she stood at this picture till it became the world and she the wall. And the picture was a network: a deep network, like the interlacing branches in the woods, like interrunning currents in water, silver, gray, black, shot through with green and rose and yellow like the sun. As one watched their deep network, one saw in it, among it, woven into it and weaving it, little and great patterns and figures, beasts, trees, grasses, men and women and other creatures, some like far-borns and some not; and strange shapes, boxes set on round legs, birds, axes, silver spears with wings and *a tree whose leaves were stars* (my emphasis).[36]

Here is an actual landscape (spacescape?) painting (which incidentally, describes Le Guin's fiction as well as any critical article has—it is just one more of the many self-interpretive elements in her fiction), a *paysage moralisé*, representing an imaginary landscape, the Hainish worlds, seen through the

eyes of a native of Gamma Draconis III, a person whose ways of seeing have been shaped by the landscape of her native world, itself another of Le Guin's *paysages moralisés*. The tree in this painting, "the Oak" in "Imaginary Countries," and all the other trees in Le Guin's fiction from the rowan tree (which, like Yggdrasil, is an ash) in the opening scene of *The Farthest Shore,* in Le Guin's "Inner Lands," to the forests on Athshe in *The Word for World is Forest,* in "Outer Space"—they all have the same roots.

Like the painting we see through Rolery's eyes, Le Guin's prose landscapes are full of *things.* Could it be that her artistry in representing abstract concepts derives from her childhood moulds of understanding, moulds like those of Zida Egideskar, who builds a unicorn trap from "an egg crate decorated with many little bits of figured cloth and colored paper.... a wooden coat hanger.... an eggshell painted gold.... a bit of quartz.... a breadcrust" (pp. 176-77)? Like Zida's unicorn trap, Le Guin's fiction is built by an artisan from a "mess of images and metaphors, domes, stones, rubble" to catch imaginary beasts, imaginary people, imaginary countries, androgynes, mythic archetypes, truth. Zida Egideskar is indeed a portrait of the artist as a young girl.

When Josef Brone asks Stanislas what he does in the "Great Woods," Stanislas answers, "Oh, I map trails" (p. 173). That answer is profoundly meaningful, for it describes what Le Guin herself does in her fiction. Her discovery-invention and mapping of imaginary countries has been her artistic solution to the epistemological problem that confronts everyone in the human sciences: like anthropologists, historians, psychologists, sociologists, and students of art, Le Guin is part of the social and cultural situation she wants to write about. In this position, objectivity and truth seem impossible ideals, especially when the writer's culture debases language and fictional forms, the writer's only tools for discovering truth. Because Le Guin is an artist, this philosophical/ideological/political problem presents itself to her as an artistic problem requiring an artistic solution. And because artists are supposed to tell the truth, it is an ethical problem. Inventing imaginary countries and mapping them has been Le Guin's solution to her artistic/ethical problem. Lies are the way to truth. The real subject of Le Guin's fiction is not life in any of her imaginary countries, in Orsinia or on Gethen or Anarres or Gont or Havnor; these are metaphors, landscapes, *Dinge,* thought experiments, what Kafka (in a letter to Max Brod) calls "strategic considerations":

> It sometimes seems to me that the nature of art in general, the existence of art, is explicable solely in terms of such 'strategic considerations,' of making possible the exchange of truthful words from person to person.[37]

Seen in this light, "Imaginary Countries" is not just the central tale in *Orsinian Tales;* more than that, it is central to the whole body of Le Guin's writing, and still more than that, to the act of writing itself.

IV

Even if Le Guin's strategic considerations do make possible the exchange of truthful words, what if no one wants to publish them? What good are truthful words if they are not exchanged? What's the use of writing? What's the use of art? Questions like these may have been in Le Guin's mind around 1960 when she wrote *"An die Musik."*[38] Like Ursula Le Guin herself, who had been writing Orsinian novels and tales for ten years without seeing them in print, Ladislas Gaye (whose name faintly echoes his creator's) has been writing songs and a Mass for ten years and has little hope of ever hearing them performed. If "Imaginary Countries" includes a portrait of the artist as a young girl, then *"An die Musik,"* written at the same time, includes an oblique portrait of the artist as a grown woman. Like the Earthsea trilogy, it is "about art, the creative experience, the creative process." *"An die Musik,"* however, is much more than self-portraiture, for it raises questions about the relationship between art and politics—questions fundamental not only to any serious discussion of Le Guin's later works, but fundamental also to any serious discussion of the social role of art in the twentieth century.

The tension between "public and private imperatives"[39] in Earthsea and the Hainish worlds is a reflection or a projection of an ethical conflict in Le Guin herself, and that conflict—between her duty as an artist to serve her art and her commitment to a social and political ideal—is at the center of *"An die Musik,"* and continues to be prominent in her later fiction, even when an artist is not the central character. A theoretical physicist like Shevek or a mathematician like Simon in "The New Atlantis" is as much an artist as are the musicians that appear throughout Le Guin's fiction. Le Guin does, of course, define the problem in radically different ways in *"An die Musik"* early in her career and in her later works like *The Dispossessed* and "The New Atlantis." But beneath the changing counterpoint of art and politics runs a *cantus firmus.* Her conception of the purpose of art has remained constant and steady. With Auden, she believes that the end of art, its final cause, its *raison d'être,* is to persuade us to rejoice and to teach us how to praise. Answering Tolstoy's question "What is Art?" Le Guin defines the job of art with one word: "celebration."[40]

If Le Guin's trilogy of imaginary countries—Orsinia, Earthsea, and the Hainish worlds—manifests the same circularity that her fantasy trilogy does (as I think it does), then we can apply her injunction "dreams must explain themselves" to the whole body of her fiction. In order to begin an exploration of the problematic relationships in her later fiction between creativity and politics, between the demands of the imagination and the demands of everyday life, or, more broadly, between the individual and society, we can do no better that return to *"An die Musik,"* her first published story. It is the first of many works in which Le Guin dramatizes the problems she herself faces whenever she sits down to write. This is not the place to make a comprehensive survey of the ways Le Guin has handled these issues in all of her fiction; that would be a major study in itself. What follows is a careful look at one of her earliest formulations.

As she would do in *The Left Hand of Darkness* when she constructed a thought experiment to explore sexuality, in *"An die Musik"* Le Guin creates a character—a composer with an "absolutely first-rate" talent (p. 249)—and places him in a setting—Foranoy, Orsinia in 1938, a "dead town for music...not a good world for music, either" (p. 254)—in order to ask three related questions: (1) should an artist, as a private individual, ignore the demands of his family to meet the demands of his art; (2) should an artist use his public voice to serve art or a political cause; and (3) what is the function of art.

When Le Guin puts Gaye in a cramped three-room flat, and gives him a bedridden mother, an ailing wife, three children to support on his wages as a clerk in a ballbearing factory, and makes him a talented composer with a compulsion to rival Berlioz and Mahler by writing a grandiose Mass for "women's chorus, double men's chorus, full orchestra, brass choir, and an organ" (p. 249), she formulates the question in such stark either-or terms that Gaye's conflicting ethical duties are simply irreconcilable. At the same time, she dramatizes each of these claims on Gaye so skillfully that neither can be denied. Gaye cannot abandon his Mass because, as he tells Otto Egorin, "'I've learned how to do what I must do, you see, I've begun it, I have to finish it'" (p. 253), and he cannot abandon his family because he is "not made so" (p. 251). If neither obligation can be denied and if their conflicting claims are so polarized that they cannot be reconciled, then Gaye's moral dilemma cannot be resolved; it can only be transcended, and then only for a moment. Moreover, by setting the tale in 1938, Le Guin polarizes the artist's public duties as severely as she polarizes his private ones. His only choices are to write apolitical music (*Lieder* or a Mass) or socialist realism (a symphony "to glorify the latest boiler-factory in the Urals" [p. 255]).

Le Guin's formulation of Gaye's moral/aesthetic dilemma is thoroughly dualistic: it rests on the belief that a devotion to art, like the devotion to a religious creed, is absolutely incompatible with everyday life. In *"An die Musik"* art is religion; if it traffics in social issues, it debases itself. Just as Jesus Christ called on his disciples to abandon all family ties if they wanted to follow Him (Matt. 10:34-39; Mark 3:31-35; Luke 14:25-26), Egorin, who believes that "If you live for music you live for music," suggests to Gaye that he "throw over...[his] sick mother and sick wife and three brats" if he wants to write his

Mass and hear it performed (p. 251). And then quoting Christ directly, he tells Gaye,

> "You have great talent, Gaye, you have great courage, but you're too gentle, you must not try to write a big work like this Mass. You can't serve two masters [Matt. 6:24; Luke 16:13]. Write songs, short pieces, something you can think of while you work at this Godforsaken steel plant and write down at night when the rest of the family's out of the way for five minutes.... Write little songs, not impossible Masses" (p. 252).

But Gaye, like Kasimir Augeskar, another Orsinian musician, is an "enemy of the feasible" (*Orsinian Tales,* p. 121). He must write the Mass. He will continue to serve art and his family, Godly art and a Godforsaken steel plant, knowing that the tension might tear him in two. All he wants from Egorin is the recognition of his identity as a musician, for that would give him the strength and freedom he needs to endure the conflict he can neither escape nor resolve.

Finally exasperated by "the arrogance, the unreasonableness...the stupidity, the absolute stupidity" of artists (p. 253), yet recognizing Gaye's talent and wanting to encourage him to write and then to produce some of his work, Egorin gives Gaye a volume of Eichendorff's poetry. "'Set me some of these,'" he tells Gaye, "'here, look, this one, "Es wandelt, was wir schauen," you see—that should suit you'" (p. 253). It is one of Eichendorff's religious lyrics:

Es wandelt, was wir schauen,
Tag sinkt ins Abendrot,
Die Lust hat eignes Grauen,
Und alles hat den Tod.

Things change, whatever we look at,
Day sinks into sunset glow,
Desire has its own horror,
And everything dies.

Ins Leben schleicht das Leiden
Sich heimlich wie ein Dieb,
Wir alle müssen scheiden
Vor allem, was uns lieb.

Into life steals sorrow
As secretly as a thief,
We must all be separated
From everything that loves us.

Was gäb' es doch auf Erden,
Wer heilt' den Jammer aus
Wer möcht' geboren werden,
Hielt'st du nicht droben haus!

What is there of value on earth,
Who could endure the misery,
Who would want to be reborn,
Dost Thou not promise a home above!

Du bist's, der, was wir bauen
Mild über uns zerbricht,
Daß wir den Himmel schauen—
Darum so klag' ich nicht.

It is Thou, who, whatever we build,
Gently breakest down over us
That we may see Heaven—
And so I do not complain.[41]

Why should this "suit" Gaye? Egorin sees Gaye's personal dilemma as hopeless and wants to offer him the consolation that things change: "'Es wandelt.' Things do change sometimes, after all, don't they?" (p. 253). He wants to offer Gaye some way of enduring the suffering he cannot escape. The religious belief of Eichendorff, a Roman Catholic, is Egorin's solution to Gaye's personal problems as an artist.

Egorin can offer no consolation whatever to Gaye to help him out of his public dilemma. Because his conception of art forces him to separate it from politics, Egorin's attitude toward the possiblity that art can change things in 1938, can make something happen, is completely defeatist:

> "Gaye," said Otto Egorin, "you know there's one other thing. This world now, in 1938. You're not the only man who wonders, what's the good? who needs music, who wants it? Who indeed, when Europe is crawling with armies like a corpse with maggots, when Russia uses symphonies to glorify the latest boiler-factory in the Urals, when the function of music has been all summed up in Puzzi playing the piano to soothe the Leader's nerves. By the time your Mass is finished, you know, all the churches may be blown into little pieces, and your men's chorus will be wearing uniforms and also being blown into little pieces. If not, send it to me, I shall be interested. But I'm not hopeful. I am on the losing side, with you. . . . music is no good, no use, Gaye. Not any more. Write your songs, write your Mass, it does no harm. But it won't save us . . . ." (pp. 254-55).

Perhaps because she has a hindsight Egorin does not have, and perhaps because she does not share his views on the relationships between art and politics, Le Guin does not share his defeatism. As we discover at the end of the tale, Gaye does not share Egorin's defeatism either. Music does save him, though not in the sense Egorin has in mind.

In the final scenes, Le Guin brings all the questions about the artist and art together, forces Gaye's tensions to the breaking point, and then resolves them not by answering any of the questions she has raised, but by arranging an epiphany which transcends the questions. On the afternoon of the day that Chamberlain meets Hitler in Munich to give him the Sudetenland, Gaye is trying to finish his setting of *"Es wandelt"* and his wife is demanding that he do something about their son Vasli who has been caught with some other boys trying to set a cat on fire. Gaye's cry "let me have some peace" (p. 257) is both his and Europe's: private and public merge. A moment later, European politics, the coming war, his family problems, and his Mass all converge as he consoles Vasli, with the sound of his mother's radio coming from the next room:

> All cruelty, all misery, all darkness present and to come hung round them. . . . In the thick blaring of the trombones, thick as cough sirup, Gaye heard for a moment the deep clear thunder of his Sanctus like the thunder between the stars, over the ege of the universe—one moment of it, as if the roof of the building had been taken off and he looked up into the complete, enduring darkness, one moment only (p. 257).[42]

In the evening, as he sits at the kitchen table with his wife, who is mending and listening to the radio (full of news of Munich, no doubt), Gaye tries to recapture the accompaniment to the last verse of *"Es wandelt"* so he can write it down and send it to Egorin in Krasnoy. At the moment when "the total impossibility of writing was a choking weight in him," at the moment when he thinks "nothing would ever change," he hears Lotte Lehmann on the radio singing Schubert's *Lied "An die Musik."*[43] The barrier between inner and outer worlds evaporates as he initially mistakes the music on the radio for the unwritten music in his mind:

> He thought it was his own song, then, raising his head, understood that he was actually hearing this tune. He did not have to write it. It had been written long ago, no one need suffer for it any more. Lehmann was singing it,
> Du holde Kunst, ich danke dir.
> He sat still a long time. Music will not save us, Otto Egorin had said. Not you, or me , . . . not Lehmann who sang the song; not Schubert who had written it and was a hundred years dead. What good is music? None, Gaye thought, and that is the point. To the world and its states and armies and factories and Leaders, music says, "You are irrelevant"; and, arrogant and gentle as a god, to the suffering man it says only, "Listen." For being saved is not the point. Music saves nothing. Merciful, uncaring, it denies and breaks down all the shelters, the houses men build for themselves, that they may see the sky (p. 258).

Gaye's epiphany rises not only from the identification of inner and outer music; it also depends on the conjunction of the words in the last stanza of Eichendorff's *"Es wandelt"* and the words in the lyric set by Schubert, Schober's *"An die Musik."* Here is Schober's poem:

Du holde Kunst, in wieviel grauen Stunden,	O kindly Art, in how many a grey hour
Wo mich des Lebens wilder Kreis umstrickt,	when I am caught in life's unruly round
Hast du mein Harz zu warmer Lieb' entzunden,	have you fired my heart with ardent love
Hast mich in eine bessre Welt entrückt!	and borne me to a better world!
In eine bessre Welt entrückt.	Borne me to a better world!
Oft hat ein Seufzer, deiner Harf' entflossen	Often, has a sigh from your harp,
Ein süsser, heiliger Akkord von dir,	a chord, sweet and holy, from you
Den Himmel bessrer Zeiten mir erschlossen	opened for me a heaven of better times;
Du holde Kunst, ich danke dir dafür!	O kindly, Art, for that I thank you!
Du holde Kunst, ich danke dir.	O kindly Art, I thank you.[44]

Gaye has been suffering, trying to write the music for the last stanza of Eichendorff's poem, which Le Guin renders as "It is Thou in thy mercy that breakest down over our heads all we build, that we may see the sky: and so I do not complain" (p. 257). In the afternoon, Gaye had heard the thunder of his Sanctus like thunder between the stars "as if the roof of the building had been taken off." Now, in the evening, as he hears his own unwritten tune in Schubert's, Gaye also hears Eichendorff's and Schober's lyrics simultaneously, the first inside his head and the second outside, sung by Lehmann on the radio. He experiences the synchronicity of a poem addressed to God and a poem addressed to Art: Eichendorff's God, who breaks down what men build that they may see heaven, is incarnated in Schober's kindly Art, realized by Schubert and performed by Lehmann, opening for Gaye a heaven of better times (not eternity). "Arrogant and gentle as a god," music, not God, "breaks down all the shelters, the houses men build for themselves, that they may see the sky." It fires his heart with love and carries him to a better world. Art renews the possibility of utopia. The paradox at the core of Gaye's epiphany is religious: what he suffers for releases him from suffering for it. Music does save him. Le Guin arranges Gaye's salvation from the conflict of "public and private imperatives" as she merges inner and outer worlds in a palimpsest of art and religion, immanence and transcendence.

Gaye's epiphany does not, however, unravel the Gordian knot of his ethical dilemmas. It cuts right through them. Otto Egorin, who believes that "music is no good, no use... not any more," has a defeatist attitude because he retains vestiges of a belief that music *is* of some good, that it is of some use. Gaye's flash of insight saves him from defeatism by wiping out entirely the question of the success or failure of an artist's attempts to do some good. The world's states, it armies, its factories, and its Führers are all simply irrelevant; politics and economics are of no concern to the artist. The function of art is not to save anything or to make something happen or to change the world. Its function is to deny the world, to detach people from politics and history so they can receive visions of a better world, and perhaps redeem politics and history with that vision. Art mediates a negative dialectic; it removes the obstacles that block the way to a better world, but it does not bring that world into being. That is the historical task of the artist's audience.

So, as he sits in Foranoy, Orsinia, in September 1938—as Hitler is meeting Chamberlain and as "Europe is crawling with armies like a corpse with maggots"—Gaye concludes that "music saves nothing." A few months later, after Chamberlain had returned to London proclaiming "peace with honour... peace for our time," W.B. Yeats died. Auden, who had wrestled throughout the thirties with the problem of the artist's duty, came to a position in his elegy on the death of Yeats that is nearly identical with Gaye's:

> For poetry makes nothing happen: it survives
> In the valley of its making where executives
> Would never want to tamper, flows on south
> From ranches of isolation and the busy griefs,
> Raw towns that we believe and die in; it survives,
> A way of happening, a mouth.

If poetry makes nothing happen, what then is the proper duty of the poet? What should he do in a world where

> In the nightmare of the dark
> All the dogs of Europe bark,
> And the living nations wait,
> Each sequestered in its hate;
>
> Intellectual disgrace
> Stares from every human face,
> And the seas of pity lie
> Locked and frozen in each eye.

Auden's answer is

> Follow, poet, follow right
> To the bottom of the night,
> With your unconstraining voice
> Still persuade us to rejoice;
>
> With the farming of a verse
> Make a vineyard of the curse,
> Sing of human unsuccess
> In a rapture of distress;
>
> In the deserts of the heart
> Let the healing fountains start,
> In the prisons of his days
> Teach the free man how to praise.[45]

This is, I would argue, what Le Guin does, not only in *"An die Musik,"* but throughout *Orsinian Tales* and the rest of her fiction as well. With "all cruelty, all misery, all darkness present and to come" hanging about him, Gaye hears his Sanctus and looks into "the complete, enduring darkness." In each volume of the Earthsea trilogy, Le Guin journeys into the "nightmare of the dark," to the "bottom of the night," and emerges to rejoice and to praise. Genly Ai and Estraven go into "The Place Inside the Blizzard" and Shevek's quest takes him into a cellar with a dying man. Each of the Orsinian tales describes a similar journey into darkness. And there is, moreover, a sense in which every story Le Guin tells is an Orsinian tale: they all bear her name. In that sense, the trip into darkness that most of her characters make is a trip she herself makes as an artist whenever she writes a story. Along with some other modern writers Le Guin shares a common ancestor: Orpheus.[46] Sometimes the map of her journey is historical, as in *Orsinian Tales;* sometimes it is psychological and ethical, as in the Earthsea trilogy; sometimes it is political, as in *The Word for World is Forest* and *The Dispossessed.* It is always an aesthetic journey. In each case, the message Le Guin returns with is a version of the invocation Estraven murmers every night as he goes to sleep: "Praise then darkness and Creation unfinished."

If we could abstract from Le Guin's practice the ideas that define for her the proper duty of an artist, if we could formulate a statement of the ethics that guides her when she practices her art, it would probably come close to Rilke's definition of the artist's role:

> Art cannot be helpful through our trying to keep and specially concerning ourselves with the distresses of others, but [only] in so far as we bear our own distresses more passionately, give now and then a perhaps clearer meaning to endurance, and develop for ourselves the means of expressing the suffering within us and its conquest more precisely and clearly than is possible to those who have to apply their powers to something else.[47]

Le Guin has consistently occupied herself with her own inner life. She has always written fantasy, searching not in the outside world, but in her own creative unconscious, for the subjects of her fiction. The course of her development from the early sixties when she wrote "Imaginary Countries" and *"An die Musik"* into the middle seventies when she wrote *The Dispossessed* and "The New Atlantis" has been a series of attempts to develop for herself the means of expressing her own suffering (which, of course, can be ethical and political as well as psychological) and its conquest more precisely and clearly. She would probably agree with Rilke's repeated assertion that we are "only just where we persist in praising."[48] But she also feels the need to blame. The strength of her convictions and her ethical principles—and even her outrage at some of the conditions of modern life—demands that. When her fiction blames, however, as *The Word for World is Forest* does, it is less just.

Ultimately, the real subject of *"An die Musik"* and the rest of Le Guin's fiction that explores ethical problems is not a group of ethical questions. These are means, not ends. Her purpose is to ask them, not to answer them. The real subject of *"An die Musik"* is celebration; the tale is a celebration of Gaye's devotion to his art, and beyond that, a celebration of art itself. That is the meaning of its title. Like Estraven, Shevek, Kasimir, and many other Le Guin characters, Gaye is "an enemy of the feasible." Le Guin places so many obstacles between him and his music not merely to wrestle with questions about the duty of the artist and the function of art, but to dramatize more vividly Gaye's capacity to endure and survive, and to pursue an ideal without compromising either himself or his goal. Like Auden's "In Memory of W.B. Yeats," which, in Samuel Hynes's words, "transforms calamity into celebration by an act of the imagination, and so affirms the survival of art in a bad time,"[49] *"An die Musik"* and *Orsinian Tales* are acts of imagination that transform the calamity of history that is Central Europe into a celebration of the individual's ability to survive bad times.

3

The Complementarity of Myth, Magic, and Science in Le Guin's Fantasy and Science Fiction

I have wondered if there isn't some real connection between a certain kind of scientific-mindedness (the explorative, synthesising kind) and fantasy-mindedness. Perhaps "science fiction" isn't really such a bad name for our genre after all. Those who dislike fantasy are very often equally bored or repelled by science. They don't like either hobbits, or quasars; they don't feel at home with them; they don't want complexities, remoteness. If there is any such connection, I'll bet that it is basically an aesthetic one.

—Ursula K. Le Guin

It seems that if one is working from the point of view of getting beauty in one's equations, and if one has a really sound insight, one is on a sure line of progress.

—Paul A.M. Dirac

When Darko Suvin introduced the essays in the special Le Guin issue of *Science-Fiction Studies,* he wrote that he was sorry that he "couldn't find anybody to integrate the Earthsea trilogy with Le Guin's SF."[1] Within a year, George Edgar Slusser's *The Farthest Shores of Ursula K. Le Guin* appeared and offered one way of understanding the relationship between Le Guin's fantasy and her science fiction. Slusser argues that Le Guin wrote the trilogy in a period of "bifurcation": on the one hand, she explored and developed her characteristic themes in "a fantasy setting which bears no resemblance with our contemporary world; on the other, she examined the need to come to grips with the pressing problems of the day.... During these experimentive years" between *The Left Hand of Darkness* (1968) and *The Dispossessed* (1974), says Slusser, the Earthsea trilogy (1968-72) "provided a counterweight" to the pessimism and despair of science fiction novels like *The Word for World is Forest* (1972).[2]

I think Slusser's mimetic and thematic approach concentrates too much attention on the divisions between Le Guin's fantasy and science fiction, and thus neglects the complementary relationships between them. I will use a genetic approach to emphasize the connections; my goal, like Falk-Ramarren's in *City of Illusions,* is "not really that of creating a unity, only of comprehending it."[3] In order to understand Le Guin's fiction as an "organized unity in which all individuation and diversity survive . . . as distinctions without division,"[4] I will look at the three stories that Le Guin wrote in the early sixties that are the genesis of the Earthsea trilogy and the Hainish cycle, and will argue that not only these stories, taken individually, but also the body of fiction that grew from them, taken as a whole, *and* the process by which it grew, have the form of a spiral journey back home, the *Bildungsreise* characteristic of Romantic thought and imagination. The science fiction novel that Slusser opposes to the Earthsea trilogy, *The Word for World is Forest,* turns out to be more securely rooted in "The Word of Unbinding," the earliest Earthsea story, than in any of the four novels that preceded it in the Hainish cycle.

Like the romance plots that inform most of her fiction, Le Guin's imagination moves in circles, synthesizing divergent elements. The science in the Hainish novels and the magic in the Earthsea trilogy are not the diametrical opposites we customarily take them to be; rather, they are complementary and compensatory modes of understanding. In the same way that there is a spot of yin in the yang half of the *t'ai chi* symbol, and a spot of yang in the yin half, Le Guin's science is as fantastic as her fantasy is scientific. The middle section of this chapter will illustrate this by exploring the relationships between myth and science in "Semley's Necklace," a science fiction story, and by showing how the magic in the Earthsea fantasies is a weaving together of myth and science. This chapter's discussion of complementarity concludes with an analysis of "Schrödinger's Cat," a science fiction fable that conflates two readings of reality, one a famous *Gedankenexperiment* from quantum mechanics, the other a Greek myth, in order to see some of the most fundamental problems in the history of philosophy in a new light, to get "a view in."

I

Le Guin invented-discovered both Earthsea and the Hainish worlds in 1962-63 when she wrote three stories that turned out to be the "germs," as she calls them, of the Earthsea trilogy and the Hainish novels. Two of the three stories, "The Word of Unbinding" (*Fantastic,* January 1963) and "The Rule of Names" (*Fantastic,* April 1963), gave her the setting (an archipelago) and a subject (magic) for the Earthsea fantasies, while the third story, "The Dowry of Angyar" (*Amazing,* September 1964), gave her the hero (Rocannon) and the setting (Formalhaut II, and the League of Worlds) for the first novel in the Hainish cycle. Throughout the next nine or ten years, Le Guin explored and mapped these two Secondary Worlds, working sometimes in one, sometimes in the other, and occasionally in both at the same time.

Le Guin put down deep roots when she wrote those three stories, for they nourished a decade of intense creativity. In 1964-65, she wrote, but never published, "a longish story about a prince" from Havnor, the central island in the Earthsea Archipelago;[5] in those years she also wrote the first three Hainish novels: *Rocannon's World* (1966), *Planet of Exile* (1966), and *City of Illusions* (1967). Continuing her simultaneous exploration of these two worlds in 1967-68, she wrote *A Wizard of Earthsea* (1968) and *The Left Hand of Darkness* (1969); they were published within five months of each other. While *A Wizard of Earthsea* and *The Left Hand of Darkness* were appearing in the USA in 1968-69, Le Guin was in England writing *The Word for World is Forest* (1972, and separately, 1976). In 1970 she was working on *The Tombs of Atuan* and *The Lathe of Heaven* at the same time; these two novels appeared in magazines in the winter and spring of 1971, and were published in hardcovers by Atheneum and Scribner's in June and October 1971, respectively. And then in September 1972, three months after Atheneum published *The Farthest Shore,* Scribner's announced its forthcoming publication of *The Dispossessed.*[6] Because *The Dispossessed* was finally published by Harper & Row in 1974, it has appeared to occupy a separate place in Le Guin's *oeuvre.* In time of conception and execution, however, it is as close to *The Farthest Shore* as *The Left Hand of Darkness* is to *A Wizard of Earthsea.*

This brief sketch of Le Guin's writing and publishing in the decade 1963-73 indicates that we cannot separate the Earthsea trilogy from Le Guin's other writing and treat it as though it were written in a period of bifurcation and experimentation between *The Left Hand of Darkness* and *The Dispossessed.* In fact, any separation of Le Guin's writing into only two strands, or into two parallel worlds, is to oversimplify and misrepresent with linear images a process more adequately described with circular images. As I pointed out in chapter 2, Le Guin was writing and rewriting stories set in Orsinia as she was exploring Earthsea and the Hainish worlds; she was *returning* to the country she discovered-invented in the early fifties even as she was *advancing* her travels into the two imaginary countries she invented-discovered in the early sixties.

All three of the stories with which Le Guin began her explorations of Earthsea and the Hainish universe depict the failure of a solitary individual's quest for home. Festin seeks home in his native forests and Blackbeard and Semley seek it in jewels owned by their ancestors. Like the novels that grew from them, these stories are romance quests. The heroes of the novels, unlike the questers in the germinal stories, are successful in varying degrees because they realize that *the means and end of their quests is community*—a relationship with another person or persons who are radically, culturally, or sexually "Other." *The Dispossessed* expresses this most fully. Shevek and Takver and Bedap and Efor, like their predecessors Rocannon and Mogien,

Jakob and Rolery, Genly Ai and Estraven, Sparrowhawk and Vetch, Tenar and Ged, Arren and Sparrowhawk, and George Orr and Heather Lelache, realize that they get on better "with a little help from their friends." Le Guin's novels thus add a social dimension missing from her early stories and from the traditional Romantic *Bildungsreise* (educational journey) into Nature and back home again. Still, the plot of nearly every piece of fiction Le Guin writes is the distinctively Romantic spiral journey back home. What M.H. Abrams identifies as the characteristic philosophies and forms of imagination of the Romantic Age are all deeply embedded in Le Guin's fiction and thus help constitute her world view: the self-moving and self-sustaining system, immanent teleology, unity lost and unity regained, progress by reversion, spiral journey back home, and the literary plot of the circular or spiral quest.[7] Not only are these embedded in Le Guin's fiction; they are also present in the shape of her development as a writer. The three stories I will be concentrating on in the first parts of this chapter—"The Word of Unbinding," "The Rule of Names," and "Semley's Necklace" (Le Guin's preferred title for "The Dowry of Angyar")—form the starting points for Le Guin's spiral journeys in Earthsea and the Hainish universe.

II

In "Dreams Must Explain Themselves," Le Guin offers us a "history of the discovery of Earthsea." Describing herself as an explorer rather than an inventor, she says that she did not deliberately invent Earthsea, nor did she plan it; she found it in her subconscious, and then began to explore it.[8] The first published report of her discovery is "The Word of Unbinding," the story of a middle-aged wizard named Festin who has withdrawn from human society on his island in order to learn patience by talking to trees, "whose roots are in profound communication with running water."[9] His goal, presumably, is to find a way to be at home with himself, to get in touch with the deepest springs of his own being. For six months he ceases all doing, speaking to no one and casting no spells. But Festin's urge to commune with Nature, his attempt to go home again to "his own woods" (p. 72), fails. Voll the Fell and his trolls, evil powers that destroy forests and fields, enslave men, and imprison any wizard or mage who resists, block Festin's Romantic solution to his middle age malaise. The plot of "The Word of Unbinding," if it can be said to have a plot, is the story of Festin's repeated failures to escape from a dungeon guarded by one of Voll's trolls. After exhausting his repertoire of spells of Projection and Transformation, and after discovering that even the "magic of going home" fails (p. 76), Festin finally freely chooses the inevitable (death) by uttering the "word of unbinding" (p. 77). Freed from the dungeon and from Being itself, he can thus face Voll on his own terms. After chasing Voll down the "far slope of the hill of being" (p. 78) into the "heart of the country which has no seacoast" (p. 79), where nothing changes, Festin forces Voll back into his body, which immediately returns to its grave. He must then guard "this place where death had found a way back into the other land" (p. 79).

Festin's search for the roots of being and of life leads him through doing into nonbeing and death. Intending to communicate with running water, he ends in a dry stream bed, forgetting "the sound of rain on the leaves of the forests of life" (p. 79). Festin, Le Guin's first Earthsea hero, dies in order to learn what a later character in the Hainish universe already realizes before he dies: in *The Left Hand of Darkness* Estraven knows that his "one way home was by way of dying."[10] And like Festin, Estraven freely chooses the ultimate necessity when he skis into the foray guns of the Karhide border guards.

As a study of the relationship between life and death, between being and doing, freedom and necessity, spirit and matter—themes which have become central in Le Guin's work—"The Word of Unbinding" is more psychomyth or psychodrama than a story with a well developed character and plot. The symbolic settings—the *paysage moralisé* of the land of the dead, which may owe much to Rilke—carry the story's meaning. Even so, the story is rich with discoveries that Le Guin developed more fully in those later works in which her heroes go on a quest with another person. As she points out in the headnote to the story in *The Wind's Twelve Quarters,* the imagery of the land of the dead foreshadows the end of *The Farthest Shore.* What she calls her "obsession with trees," apparent throughout her work, makes its first appearance in this story.[11] But "The Word of Unbinding" is germinal for more than just the Earthsea trilogy: it anticipates *The Word for World is Forest,* her fifth Hainish novel, as well as the third Earthsea novel. Just as Voll the Fell and his trolls destroy Festin's forest home and enslave his people, Davidson and the Terran loggers destroy Selver's forest home and enslave the Athsheans; Selver, like Festin, has to fight the forest destroyers on their own terms; he must learn their ways with weapons. As a middle-aged hero who is forced into action and self-discovery, Festin is an early, naive version of later Le Guin heroes like Rocannon, Estraven, Selver, the Archmage Sparrowhawk, and Shevek, all of whom face a mid-life, crisis and must make moral decisions which in the end, after pain and loss, create the possibility of a world in which they can "be at home with themselves in their otherness as such," as Hegel says, and, more importantly, to be at home with the Other in a community.[12]

III

Le Guin's first Earthsea story does not give us a clear idea of the geography of the Archipelago and the Reaches (although the Reaches are mentioned once, Festin's island is not named). Comparing herself to the first discoverers of Antarctica, she says that she did not know whether she had discovered an island or the tip of a continent.[13] Nor does the story develop magic as fully as does the second Earthsea story, "The Rule of Names." If "The Word of Unbinding" is symbolic, "The Rule of Names" is imagistic: much of the story is made up of marvelously detailed set-pieces of descriptions of daily life on Sattins, an island Le Guin populates not with faceless evil and trolls, but with "characters" in the old sense of the word: Goody Guld and her nephew Birt would be at home in a lowlife comic interlude in one of the Waverly novels. More than mere set-pieces, though, the first few scenes carefully prepare for the dramatic demonstration of "the rule of names" in the confrontation between Blackbeard and Mr. Underhill/Yevaud. In one of the first stories-within-a-story that she would write, Le Guin has Blackbeard explain to Birt that he is a descendant of the Sealords of Pendor, "mighty men, in the old days before the League" (p. 87). But they were not mighty enough to withstand the attacks of the dragon Yevaud, who drives the people of Pendor from the island and rather conventionally (the dragons in the trilogy do not act so much like traditional Occidental dragons) hoards the treasure of the House of Pendor, including "the great emerald, the star of the hoard, Inalkil the Greenstone" (p. 88). After a League is formed, it clears the Archipelago of piracy, then launches a fleet to attack Pendor and recover the hoard for the League's treasury. But Yevaud evades them ("evade," perhaps being his "true name"), leaving a false trail that Blackbeard picks up and follows to Sattins. With total self-sufficiency and self-righteous bluster, Blackbeard tells Birt, "'I am the Sealord of Pendor, oaf, and I will have the gold my fathers won, and the jewels my mother wore, and the Greenstone! For they are mine" (p. 89). Although Blackbeard has learned Mr. Underhill's true name, he has not learned that Yevaud is a dragon; in a recognition scene which is also a reversal, he dies as he discovers the truth.

One of the distinctive qualities of Le Guin's prose style in the Earthsea trilogy makes its appearance in "The Rule of Names": her uncanny knack for interweaving the familiar and the strange, for investing ordinary events with aura.[14] When Blackbeard arrives on Sattins Island, he poses as a peddlar with a "small mixed cargo of cloth and sandals and piswi feathers for trimming cloaks and cheap incense and levity stones and fine herbs and great glass beads from Venway" (p. 84). It is just this kind of detail—Rilkean *Dinge*—that makes Le

Guin's fantasy (and her science fiction, too) so compelling. As Peter Dickinson, a British writer of fantasy, has remarked,

> If you're writing fantasies, you're like somebody who is trying to lay a carpet where there's a terrifically strong draught coming up between the floor boards; the carpet keeps billowing up and you've got to tack it down with detail all the time.[15]

Le Guin's carpets are well tacked down.

Another important element in the trilogy, dragons, first appears in "The Rule of Names." The history of the dragon Yevaud provides us with an excellent opportunity for studying the relationship between a germinal story and a fully developed novel, and throws some light on the way Le Guin's writing has developed. In her headnote to "The Rule of Names" in *The Wind's Twelve Quarters,* she rather coyly explains that

> readers familiar with the trilogy will notice.... that the history of the dragon Yevaud is somewhat obscure. (he must have been on Sattins Island some decades or centuries *before* Ged found him, and bound him, on the Isle of Pendor.) But this is only to be expected of dragons, who do not submit to the unidirectional, causal requirements of history, being myths, and neither timebinding, nor timebound (p. 71).

It may be true that dragons do not submit to the unidirectional, causal requirements of history (little else in Le Guin's fiction does), but this one, Yevaud, does submit to the requirements of the dialectical logic of Ged's Romantic *Bildungsreise.* Yevaud *has* to be on Pendor when Ged is sent to Low Torning in the Ninety Isles. When Le Guin planned *A Wizard of Earthsea,* she cast Ged's coming of age in the form of a story which is, she says, "essentially a voyage, a pattern in the form of a long spiral."[16] What Abrams identifies as "a distinctive figure of Romantic thought and imagination—the ascending circle, or spiral . . . a circuitous journey back home,"[17] is the inevitable aesthetic form for Ged's journey toward selfhood and wholeness, a process easily identified with Jungian individuation. Beginning his clockwise spiral journey from Gont, Ged sails to Roke, then swings up to Low Torning and Pendor, tries to get back to Roke but is impelled by his destiny up to Isskil, then across to Gont (home again), and on out toward the Open Sea where the conflict between Ged and his Shadow is *aufgehoben.* His struggle with Yevaud on Pendor, and not elsewhere, is as necessary for the completion of that journey as are his return home to Ogion and his visit to Vetch on Iffish (see the maps of Earthsea for this).

But why Yevaud and not some other dragon? Why not leave Yevaud on
Sattins and bring in another dragon to Pendor from Selidor or The Dragons'
Run? Because, possibly, the course of Le Guin's literary career, her own
Bildungsreise, follows the same pattern that her heroes' journeys do. Each new
book she creates is at once a circling back to an earlier work to pick up a
character or an image or a plot structure or a way of handling point of view,
even as it is, at the same time, an advance into new territory. If we consider
Yevaud subject to the dialectical process that is the pattern of Le Guin's career,
his history becomes less obscure. Just as Ged had to return home to Ogion
before he could advance to meet his Shadow, Le Guin returned to "The Rule of
Names" to advance the plot of *A Wizard of Earthsea.* Thus the Romantic
paradigm of a circular return which is also an advance is not only the informing
structure of the parts and wholes of her fiction, but is is also the design of the
whole body of her fiction as it grows and evolves.

In "A Citizen of Mondath," Le Guin explains that her writing "has been a
matter of keeping on pushing out toward the limits—my own, and those of the
medium."[18] For each push at the limits, though, there has been a
complementary return to the sources. One of her larger pushes, *The Left Hand
of Darkness,* is also a return; it is almost a point by point retelling of
Rocannon's World.[19] And like *Planet of Exile, The Left Hand of Darkness*
portrays love between a black Terran and a lighter-skinned alien. Genly Ai's
clockwise journey from Horden Island through Erhenrang, Sassinoth,
Mishnory, Pulefen Farm, over the Ice and then back through Sassinoth and
Erhenrang, ending in Kerm Land (Estraven's home), not far from Horden
Island, where he began, is a journey nearly homologous with Ged's in Earthsea.
The idea of the Shadow of Gethen, moreover, is as important as it is in
Earthsea. So a push at the limits of the Hainish cycle does not preclude a return
to sources in Earthsea. Conversely, a push at the limits of the Earthsea trilogy
includes a return to the Hainish cycle: *The Tombs of Atuan* is about how a
white-skinned young woman comes of age with the aid of a dark-skinned alien
man, just as *Planet of Exile,* written six years earlier, showed a white-skinned
young woman coming of age with the help of a black-skinned alien. Just as
Jakob Agat entered Rolery's mind with mindspeech, Ged enters Arha's
labyrinth, patently a symbol of her unconscious. Another Hainish novel, *The
Word for World is Forest,* reaches back to the first Earthsea story, "The Word
of Unbinding," echoing its title as well as its themes, and, like *Planet of Exile,*
contains three points of view, as does the science fiction novel that followed it,
The Lathe of Heaven. Finally, *The Dispossessed* (a circular journey if ever
there was one), which returns the Hainish cycle to the Pre-League days, ends
with a conversation between Shevek and Ketho, first mate of the Hainish
starship *Davenant.* The *first* Hainish novel, *Rocannon's World,* opens with a
conversation between Ketho, curator of the League museum in Kerguelen on

New South Georgia, and Rocannon. Like Yevaud, Ketho (if he is the same person in both novels) may not be subject to the unidirectional, causal requirements of history.

It is possible to read each one of Le Guin's novels as the quest of an artist-hero; it is also possible to read her entire body of fiction as we read *The Prelude* and other Romantic epics: as the growth of the artist's mind. From this perspective, we should be able to see Le Guin's fiction as an "organized unity in which all individuation and diversity survive . . . as distinctions without division" and not as a unidirectional stream that bifurcates. In 1961 Le Guin returned to science fiction, which she had left behind in the late forties as she went on to Radcliffe and Columbia and Orsinian tales in the fifties. In the seventies she returned to her Orsinian tales, publishing them after she had been making a name for herself by writing fantasy and science fiction for over a decade. The relationships between Orsinia, Earthsea, and the Hainish worlds are thus considerably more complex than images of parallelism or counterweights would indicate.

But to circle back to "The Rule of Names"—one thing (in addition to the trolls) that Le Guin did not bring forward from that story into the Earthsea trilogy is the League. If, as she explains in *The Wind's Twelve Quarters,* "trolls became extinct in Earthsea at some point" (p. 71)—her roundabout way of saying that she tapped her own creative unconscious and did not have to rely on the Norse collective unconscious for imagery—then the League, by an analogous explanation, may have been teleported from her Inner Lands to her Outer Space, there to find a home as The League of Worlds in the Hainish universe, which Le Guin discovered as she wrote "Semley's Necklace." Besides sharing the League, "The Rule of Names" and "Semley's Necklace" have other things in common. Both stories open with the point of view of the owners of the jewels the heroes quest for, and both stories are failed quests, making the same ethical judgments about arrogance and self-sufficiency. "Semley's Necklace" draws on Earthsea as it creates the Hainish universe.

IV

When Le Guin assembled *The Wind's Twelve Quarters,* she placed "Semley's Necklace" first because it is, she says in her headnote, "the most characteristic of [her] early science fiction and fantasy works, the most romantic of them all" (p. 1). "Semley's Necklace" is characteristic in that it combines fantasy and science fiction, myth and science. It is one of those early stories Le Guin elsewhere calls her "fairytales decked out in space suits."[20] But "Semley's Necklace" is more than a characteristic and romantic early story; it was the germ of *Rocannon's World,* the first of six science fiction novels set in Le Guin's Hainish future history.

"Semley's Necklace," as it appears in *The Wind's Twelve Quarters,* was first published as "Prologue: The Necklace" in *Rocannon's World* (1966). "Prologue: The Necklace," in turn, is the revision of "The Dowry of Angyar" (1964). In her account of the genesis of *Rocannon's World* in her "Foreword" to *The Wind's Twelve Quarters,* Le Guin says,

> I had done with Semley when I had finished ["The Dowry of Angyar"], but there was a minor character, a mere bystander, who did not sink back obediently into obscurity when the story was done, but kept nagging me. "Write my story," he said. "I'm Rocannon. I want to explore my world" (pp. vii-viii).

Le Guin responded to Rocannon's nagging by writing parts I and II of what is now *Rocannon's World.* When her manuscript reached Ace books, it was not long enough to fill one-half of an Ace Double, so she revised thoroughly "The Dowry of Angyar," added the opening paragraphs on fact and legend, and attached it to *Rocannon's World* as "Prologue: The Necklace."[21]

By describing "Semley's Necklace" as the germ of *Rocannon's World,* Le Guin invites us to consider that novel and the subsequent stories and novels in the Hainish cycle as an organic growth from the story. "Semley's Necklace," then, would be the formal and thematic source of the Hainish cycle, the root of the more complex and developed plots and statements in the later works. This does not mean that "Semley's Necklace" is the first of several serial-linear episodes set on Hainish worlds. Rather, it means that "Semley's Necklace," although complete in itself, contains tensions and raises questions that its plot resolves only temporarily. "Semley's Necklace" is an aesthetic whole that synthesizes divergent elements, yet it is like the synthesis in any open-ended dialectical process; its internal tensions produce contradictory elements that require a new synthesis. Rocannon is one such element: he does not sink back into obsurity, but nags for further development.

"Semley's Necklace" opens with one of the most conventional situations in science fiction: the encounter with an alien. The original version of the story begins with Rocannon reading from his *Handy Pocket Guide to Intelligent Life-forms.* (At the same time Le Guin invites us to identify with Rocannon's point of view, seeing through his eyes as he reads, she also signals us not to trust too fully someone who uses a guidebook with so many telling adjectives in its title. *The Left Hand of Darkness* opens with a much more subtle use of the same technique). A stunningly beautiful woman (Semley) and four "dwarves" have come to the League museum in Kerguelen, capital of New South Georgia (a member world in the League of Worlds), and stand before Ketho and Rocannon. Rocannon has encountered the "dwarves" before, but because the League contacts with their home have been selective, he had no idea what or who the woman might be. So he consults his guide book and determines that she is an Angya escorted by four Gdemiar from Fomalhaut II, several light years away. Looking up from his book, Rocannon says, "Well, now at least we know what she is." Ketho, profoundly impressed by her beauty, replies, "I wish there were some way on knowing *who* she is . . . ."(p. 3). There is a way, but it is not available to Rocannon and Ketho. Le Guin offers it to us as she shifts from Rocannon's point of view to Semley's, and tells Semley's story, for she knows intuitively what Hannah Arendt explains in *The Human Condition:* "*who* somebody is or was we can only know by knowing the story of which he is himself the hero . . . . everything else we know of him . . . . tells us only *what* he is or was."[22]

In the opening paragraphs of this germinal story, Le Guin uses a narrative technique and establishes a theme that she will return to again and again: the relationship between different kinds of knowledge or ways of knowing, and the use of multiple points of view to explore those relationships. On the one hand there is "what-knowledge," the product of an advanced technology based on rational, objective, scientific, and conscious thought. On the other hand, the "who-knowledge" we get from a story is grounded in intuitive, subjective, artistic, and unconscious modes. In "Semley's Necklace" these two modes are literally light years apart, even when they meet in the museum as Rocannon and Semley face each other; without a common language, they cannot communicate. But if the characters in the story cannot understand each other, the story itself gives us, its readers, ways of seeing the connections between them: the story itself is the mediation between the two modes of knowing, the metalanguage that can synthesize seemingly irreconcilable opposites into complementary aspects of a whole. Le Guin will use myth in *The Left Hand of Darkness* to the same effect. This is precisely one of the functions of storytelling: "the way of art," says Le Guin, "is . . . to keep open the tenuous, difficult, essential connections between the two extremes."[23] Le Guin's principal tool for that integrative task is, as I argued in chapter 1, the romance quest.

Although "Semley's Necklace" contains all the trappings of a quest, it is not a romance. It is a tragedy. Like the other heroes and heroines of the romance, though, Semley has experienced a loss of social status, and is acutely aware of her deteriorating identity as a pure descendant of the first kings of the Angyar. *Who* she is has become problematic for her; she does not feel at home. After her marriage to Durhal, her pride turns to envy and resentment as she discovers that she is not able to "outshine other women" (p. 6), especially those who defer to her because of her superior birth and rank, but who nevertheless display greater riches. The Angyar, described in Rocannon's guide book as a "feudal-heroic culture" (p. 3), have accumulated wealth as the Vikings did, in raids and wars on their neighbors, just as the Sealords of Pendor do in "The Rule of Names," just as the Kargad Empire does in *A Wizard of Earthsea*. But since the League has been taxing the Angyar, they sit in their Revelhalls in "idle shame" (p. 4), their warlike spirits and their cultural identities broken. Semley remembers that her great-grandmother had worn a massive sapphire set in a solid gold necklace—lost now for three generations—and she hopes that by recovering it she will be able to restore the lost glory of her ancestral identity, just as Blackbeard had hoped to restore himself as a Sealord of Pendor by retrieving Inalkil the Greenstone. "Think, Durossa," Semley says to her sister-in-law, "if I could come into Hallan Revel and sit down by my husband with the wealth of a kingdom round my neck, and outshine the other women as he outshines all men!" (p. 6).

Impulsively brushing aside Durossa's suggestion that Durhal's pride is in his wife and not in what she wears, Semley leaves her three-year-old daughter with Durossa and sets out on a quest to recover the precious object she hopes will reestablish and reconfirm her identity. She flies to her father's home on a windsteed (a horse-sized flying cat) but finds him in a drunken stupor amid the ruins of his castle and of no assistance. The "magic of going home" is as futile for Semley as it was for Festin. She visits the Fiia, an elfish people living an idyllic life in sunshine and happiness (Frye's "idyllic world"); they advise her against her quest. Single-mindedly intent on getting the necklace, she disregards their warnings and flies on to the caves of the Gdemiar, a race of dwarf-like people who made the necklace, sold it to Semley's ancestor, and are rumored to have stolen it back. Just as many questers cross a threshold into another world, enchanted or demotic, Semley enters a "cave-mouth, a toothless, yawning mouth from which a stinking warmth sighed out" (p. 12), the entrance to "the Realm of Night" (p. 13) (clearly, Frye's "demotic world," characterized by alienation). Semley is no less insistent than Blackbeard, though she is more polite, as she asks the Gdemiar for the Eye of the Sea (Seaheart in the original version). The Gdemiar, who had traded it to the League for an automatic-drive spaceship, agree to guide Semley to the necklace, knowing that the trip will take sixteen years, yet telling her that it will last "but one long night" (p. 16). They have recognized that Semley's single-minded commitment to recovering the necklace leaves her vulnerable to manipulation and they maliciously anticipate an opportunity to dupe and to take advantage of an arrogant and beautiful Angya. In due course, she receives the necklace from Rocannon (from Ketho in the original version), returns to her home planet, flies back to Hallan on her windsteed, only to discover Durhal has been dead for nine years, her sister-in-law Durossa is an old woman, and her daughter Haldre is as old as she is. These revelations overwhelm Semley; dropping the necklace on the stone floor, she runs into the forest, lost in madness. Like Blackbeard's quest, hers has not let to a recovery of identity, but to complete alienation and disaster.

V

When Ted White reprinted the story in *The Best from Amazing,* he introduced it with this headnote:

> the idea as such is now new. We've all played with the notion of time-dilation, with the Einsteinian principle of the contraction of time as one approaches the speed of light. But Ursula K. Le Guin—in a story which became the root of her first novel, and thus the entire series which has culminated in her superb *The Left Hand of Darkness*—has distilled this common concept into the purity of myth.[24]

White's remarks, which embody a widely held belief that science fiction is the mythology of the modern world, and which imply that a science fiction writer makes myths from the materials of twentieth-century science, do not accurately describe what Le Guin is doing in "Semley's Necklace." On different occasions, when she was discussing the role of myth in science fiction, Le Guin has explained that in "Semley's Necklace" she was retelling a Norse myth, the story of Freya and the Brisingamen Necklace. So the purity of myth is clothed in science fiction, not distilled from it.[25] Better than metaphors of extraction and purification or covering and disguising, however, the idea of chiasmus describes what Le Guin is doing in "Semley's Necklace": myth and science are crossed with each other as the nerves from our eyes to our brains are, making left into right and right into left, or, they are crossed as homologous chromosomes are during meiosis, producing exchanges and recombinations of genres.

    In the Norse story, Freya, the lascivious goddess of summer and love, leaves Asgard in a chariot drawn by cats, wanders into Midgard, and in a cave encounters four dwarves making the Brisingamen Necklace. The beauty of the necklace so impresses Freya that she has to have it at any price. The dwarves have all the gold and silver they want, and therefore reject her offer of hard currency. They are interested in Freya herself. So Freya exchanges her favors for the necklace, and returns to Asgard only to find that her husband Odur is gone. Broken by her loss, she runs from Asgard looking for him, dropping tears of gold (or flowers in some versions) wherever she goes. Like the Greek myth of Persephone's marriage to Pluto, Freya's story is connected with the end of summer; the tragic simplicity of her fate is rooted in the inevitability of seasonal change.

    The Gdemiar, who have "grey-white skins, dampish looking like the skins of grubs" (p. 11), are Le Guin's version of the subterranean nocturnal dwarves who grew from maggots in the corpse of the giant Ymir, just as the Fiia are her version of the airy and benevolent elves of Norse myth and legend. The windsteeds have their source in the cats which pull Freya's chariot (crossed, perhaps, with something like Pegasus), and the necklace Semley quests for resembles not only the Brisingamen Necklace, but also the various rings in Norse myth and legend which exercise a baleful influence on their possessors and ultimately return to their makers, myths revived by Wagner in the nineteenth century and by Tolkien in the twentieth. Four dwarves receive Freya's favors; four Gdemiar escort Semley to Kerguelen, pawing and fondling her along the way. In addition to borrowing and transforming specific elements from Norse myth, Le Guin preserves the flavor of Norse poetic style with kennings: Semley's father is "gray and swollen as the web-spinner of ruined houses" (p. 8), and Semley herself is "Halla's bride, Kirien-lady, Windborne, and Semley the Fair" (p. 9). This orphic style contrasts sharply with the pedestrian speech of Ketho and Rocannon, and reinforces the divisions between the two worlds.

But it is less important to know Le Guin's sources than it is to understand the relationship between the myth and its science fiction setting. Le Guin said in an interview that her job as an artist "is not to use myths, but to be used by myths.... The real thing is to find the native symbology of your own creative unconscious... and try to integrate it in terms comprehensible to others, and aesthetically solid." Norse myths, she continued, "are part of my 'childhood lore,' they shaped my imagination."[26] So Freya's story is part of the native symbology of Le Guin's creative unconscious, which she integrated with the idiom of science fiction, terms comprehensible to twentieth-century readers. In a sense, Norse myth is a heuristic device, a catalyst for freeing Le Guin's own creativity; she circled back to her "childhood lore," a circular return which was also an advance. What makes Semley's tragedy "aesthetically solid" is the tragic irony Le Guin creates from the intersection, the crossing and interaction of the myth and its science fiction setting, and from the mutually estranging interplay of the two points of view in the story. Frye says that the normal containing form of the romance is a possible future while archaism is the normal content; the science fiction and the myth in "Semley's Necklace" seem to fit this notion, and Le Guin consciously exploits the clash between the two. In a review of a Russian science fiction novel, she writes,

> The genre [of *Hard to be a God*] is one familiar to American SF readers: Terran observers of the future, bound to noninterference, among (extraterrestrial) human beings whose society and culture resemble that of medieval Europe. A double estrangement, and the best of both worlds—the romance of future technology, plus the romance of feudalism. Something similar has been done by several American authors... including myself.[27]

But the science fiction in "Semley's Necklace" does not "contain" the myth, as Frye's formulation would suggest; rather, it is braided together with it, woven in and out of it. Because the two points of view estrange each other, and because we hold them both in our minds as we read the story, each event has at least two dimensions, mythic and scientific, unconscious and conscious. After we read (through Rocannon's eyes) the coldly "scientific" description of the races on Fomalhaut II, we then experience them mediated through Semley's eyes as we participate in her intense desire to recover the Eye of the Sea. And while we subjectively experience "one long night" with Semley, we objectively know that it is sixteen years long. With one "part" of our minds, we are actors in the story, and with another "part," we are spectators: acting with Rocannon, we watch Semley in the museum; acting with Semley, we arrive in the museum to watch Rocannon. The ironies are reciprocal. Fact and myth and scientific law and tragic fate are intertwined so that (to shift the metaphor) the story becomes a Möbius strip: the two sides or "parts" may seem to be different, yet they are in fact the same. Through *coincidentia oppositorum,* the chiasmus becomes a figure-eight.

This is more a description of the potential of Le Guin's method; in practice, in this story, one side is decidedly weaker than the other. Rocannon the objective intellectual is a "mere bystander"; his main function is to embody the scientific point of view, to be a vehicle for introducing the notion of time-dilation so that Semley's mythic fate becomes rationally credible for readers who have come to expect scientific explanations. Crossed with relativity physics, a myth about seasonal change is readily accepted by readers who might otherwise dismiss it as a "mere story."

Just as Le Guin uses physics to translate Semley's fate for modern readers, she uses another science, anthropology, to translate mythic and fairy tale figures into the individuals, races, and cultures which give Semley's story a vividly imagined background. In the process of inventing the settings and cultures in which Semley enacts her quest, Le Guin placed her in a complex web of relationships on Fomalhaut II, and made the initial exploration of a theme which is developed more fully in the Hainish cycle: the relationship of part and whole.

Semley is a member of a culture which is part of a world of many separate cultures which in turn become part of the colonial empire of the League. When the League begins taxing the Angyar and developing the technological skills of the Gdemiar with only the most superficial knowledge and understanding of their cultural patterns and relationships, it upsets the balance of Fomalhaut II and thus dislocates the culture of which Semley is a part. Semley's quest is her response. It is reactionary in that she wants to recover a necklace which is a symbol of the old ways before the coming of the League when Angyar lords conquered fiefs, dressed their women in jewels, and bought husbands for their daughters with dowries of "heroic loot" (p. 4). Semley's quest is a denial of the new relationships with the League, a denial of something she is ignorant of. In a series of dialectical reversals, Semley's effort to deny the League carries her into the future. She does not understand, and because of her pride as an Angya does not want to understand, her culture's relationships with the Gdemiar and the League. The goal of her quest, like the goal of Blackbeard's quest, is self-aggrandizement, and the failure of her quest is a pointed ethical judgment of her motivation. Her sixteen-year-long journey is Le Guin's metaphor for the judgment that Semley's self-absorption and pride, her tragic flaws, cut her off from relationships with those around her, remove her from history, and form a breach between herself and her world that leads to madness. She ceases to be part of the whole.

The thematic statement that runs throughout the Hainish cycle, and the Earthsea trilogy as well, and is articulated first in "Semley's Necklace" is this: if people act without an understanding and appreciation of the web of relationships in which they are a strand, they will find their actions producing effects and consequences which are the opposite of those intended. But if one acts in harmony with the whole, he will be at home with himself and his world. And it seems that the only way one ever gets knowledge of the whole is to go on a quest, to go "there" in order to discover "here," to discover and confront the Other in order to find the Self.

But all the responsibility for Semley's failure to understand her part in the web of relationships on her world and between her world and the League cannot be assigned to her alone. She is also a victim of the manner in which the League cavaliery exploits Fomalhaut II without understanding the people there. In the Norse myth, Freya's tragedy is as natural as seasonal change. In "Semley's Necklace," Le Guin has translated a myth of the end of summer into a story about the personal costs of cultural and militaristic imperialism. Ketho and Rocannon, mere bystanders, are in the story to represent the League's ignorance of its colonial subjects. Rocannon has to consult his guide book, a parody of ethnological knowledge, merely to identify *what* Semley is. *Who* she is is completely beyond his grasp because he does not know any of her culture's *stories* (and, as I will argue in chapter 4, that is why Genly Ai collects Gethenian narratives: he wants to know *who* Estraven is so that he can find out who he is by telling "the story of which he is himself the hero"). Not knowing who Semley is, Rocannon greets her with a silly gesture he calls his All-purpose Intercultural Curtsey. He corrects Ketho when he hears him using the label "trogs" for the Gdemiar, and then nearly uses the same racial slur when he says, "I wish we could talk to her without these tr— Gdemiar as interpreters" (p. 19).

When Le Guin constructed the complex situation in which Semley's quest is played out, she created tensions and raised questions that the tragic resolution of the plot holds together only momentarily. The background of Semley's tragedy, the conflict between the feudal-heroic world of Angyar and the technological-militaristic world of the League, remains. If Le Guin were a writer with a tragic vision, she could rest there, for tragedy confirms the status quo as it bows to the inevitability of fate. But she is a Romantic, and therefore sensitive to the possibilities and potentialities that may be latent in the present situation. At the end of "Semley's Necklace" Rocannon is aware of a blind spot in the League's understanding of its colonial races and cultures. Twice Le Guin has Rocannon admit his lack of understanding: "I never feel I really understand these hieratic races," he says of the Gdemiar; and as Semley walks away from him, he feels as though he has "blundered through the corner of a legend, of a tragic myth, even, which I do not understand" (p. 21). Rocannon's new awareness of the League's limitations, combined with the erotic awe and curiosity Semley elicits from Rocannon, raise possibilities and expectations that are neither fulfilled nor dissipated at the end of the story.

What Le Guin needed after finishing "Semley's Necklace" was a structure capable of carrying the creative growth that resulted from her planting Freya's story in the conventions and traditions of science fiction. So after she finished with Semley, she responded to Rocannon's nagging by sending him to Fomalhaut II as the leader of an ethnographic survey team. Nowhere in the original version of "Semley's Necklace" does Le Guin identify Rocannon as an ethnologist. But when Rocannon nagged himself into existence as a fully fledged ethnologist, Le Guin had a ready vehicle for exploring the details only hinted at in "Semley's Necklace." As an ethnologist, he can explore the cultures glimpsed only briefly in "Semley's Necklace," he can in his own person as scientist and romance hero represent a combination of "what-knowledge" and "who-knowledge," and he can sublimate his desire to know more about Semley and her world in a romance quest that will bring together the two points of view that had been light years apart when they first met in the League museum. More than that, he will learn mindspeech, a new form of communciation, and will communicate his discovery of the "Last Art" to the rest of the League, giving it a way of breaking down the walls that separate worlds and cultures. Communication creates community.

VI

"Bacon's attempt to rehabilitiate *magia* as natural science in its operative aspect proved quite abortive."[28] Not so Le Guin's attempt in the Earthsea trilogy, at least not for Robert Scholes: "no one," says Scholes, "has ever made magic seem to function so much like science as Ursula Le Guin." Scholes quotes Ged's words to Yarrow, Vetch's sister, on the sources of power,

> It is no secret. All power is one in source and end, I think. Years and distance, stars and candles, water and wind and wizardry, the craft in a man's hand and the wisdom in a tree's

root: they all arise together. My name and yours, and the true name of the sun, or a spring of water, or an unborn child, all are syllables of the great word that is very slowly spoken by the shining of the stars. There is no other power. No other name,[29]

and then asks,

Is this magic? Religion? Science? The great gift of Ursula Le Guin is to offer us a perspective in which these all merge, in which realism and fantasy are not opposed, because the supernatural is naturalized—not merely postulated but regulated, systematized, made part of the Great Equilibrium itself.[30]

The perspective Scholes is talking about here is just one facet of Le Guin's overall perspective, just one constellation of her moulds of understanding. Like her distancing technique in *Orsinian Tales,* which dissolves the barriers between realism and fantasy as it synthesizes aesthetics, history, and ethics, and like her perspective in "Semley's Necklace," which crosses myth with science, Le Guin's perspective in the Earthsea trilogy demonstrates the complementarity of myth and legend, magic, science, and religion (in a general sense: Taoism).

Le Guin's artistry in "Semley's Necklace" is a process of weaving together a Norse myth and a principle of physics; in her fantasy trilogy, she projects and objectifies that creative process as the institution of magic in Earthsea, and that institution is simultaneously and similarly woven from two major strands. On the one hand there is the warp of myth and legend: the Celtic and Teutonic lore about magic which Le Guin has been absorbing since she was a child. On the other hand there is the weft of science: the anthropological investigations and theories of magic which she has also been absorbing since she was a child growing up in the Kroeber household. Complementing the literary and imaginative image of magic she received from Colum, Asbjornsen, Andersen, the Eddas and Sagas, Dunsany and Tolkien, is a scientific image of actual magic from Frazer and Malinowski, the two anthropologists who seem to have contributed the most to Le Guin's picture of magic in Earthsea.

One of the famliar elements in Le Guin's magic is the 600 Hardic runes that every wizard must learn to read; anyone coming to Le Guin's trilogy from Tolkien's would be at home with them. But Le Guin's wizards, unlike Tolkien's aged and solitary men of wisdom and power, are members of a social institution (except Ogion, perhaps, who is more Taoist hermit-sage than wizard). The institution shares much with Celtic druidism.[31] Like the druids, who were a nonhereditary order headed by a leader elected to serve for life, the wizards and mages of Earthsea are a society which elects an Archmage to rule over them. Becoming a druid meant undergoing a protracted period of oral instruction in subjects like astrology, geography, physical science, and natural theology. The school for wizards on Roke in Earthsea, like the colleges for druids reputed to have existed in Ireland, provides just this kind of training for would-be mages. The druids were renowned as shape-changers, as are the wizards in Earthsea, who can change themselves into animals or birds. The druids were supposed to have resisted Christian missionaries with mists and fogs, and were credited with saving Paris from Viking marauders in A.D. 845: they enveloped them in a fog and then the Parisians easily cut down the baffled invaders. Ged uses this spell to save his home town Re Albi from the Kargad warriors and to save Arren from pirates.

The vital significance of the Innermost Grove for all of Earthsea is a reflection of the importance of trees for the druids. The Romans knew very well that tree-worship was the heart and soul of druidism: when Suetonius Petronius wanted to eliminate the power of the druids, he defoliated their sanctuaries on Angelsea in A.D. 58. Although Le Guin shrouds the Immanent Grove in mystery, she clearly indicates that it means as much to Earthsea as the sacred groves of oak meant to the druids:

> What is learned in the Immanent Grove is not much talked about elsewhere. It is said that no spells are worked there, yet the place itself is an enchantment. Sometimes the trees of that Grove are seen, and sometimes they are not seen, and they are not always in the same place and part of Roke Island. It is said that the trees themselves are wise. It is said that the Master Patterner learns his supreme magery there within the Grove, and if ever the trees should die so shall his wisdom die, and in those days the waters will rise and drown the islands of Earthsea (*WE*, p. 87).

In *The Farthest Shore*, Le Guin gives us a fuller picture of the Grove. We learn that "the Grove does not move. Its roots are the roots of being. It is all the rest that moves" (*FS*, p. 12).

Most of this lore, along with much more on weather working, the shadow, and the magic power of names, is collected in Frazer, which Le Guin came to quite early on. She says she read *Leaves from the Golden Bough*, a children's edition "culled" by Lady Frazer, as other children would read Beatrix Potter's animal fables; and then, "as a kid," she went on to read *The Golden Bough* itself.[32] Frazer surely contributed to Le Guin's notion of magic as a kind of science, and probably influenced or reinforced some of the ideas that form the general framework of her fiction: the seasonal changes that are the background for almost all the turns of plot in her romances, and the waste land that she dramatizes in *The Farthest Shore*.

But Le Guin has not accepted Frazer's condescending attitude toward his subject (he described *The Golden Bough* as "a dark, a tragic chronicle of human error and folly, of fruitless endeavor, wasted time, and blighted hopes"[33]); she has instead adopted some of the ideas about magic that Malinowski, one of Frazer's disciples, derived from his fieldwork in the archipelagos of the western Pacific. Frazer says in his "Preface" to

Malinowski's *Argonauts of the Western Pacific* that "magic is a power of supreme importance either for good or evil";[34] Ogion tells Ged that "every word, every act of our Art is said and done either for good, or for evil"(*WE*, p. 35). This is but one of the many echoes of Malinowski's book in Le Guin's trilogy. Malinowski, in fact, may have had something to do with Earthsea being an archipelago: Le Guin did not have a clear picture of what her imaginary country was like until after she gave "serious consideration [to] magic," she says, and that could have included looking into Malinowski.[35] The Long Dance in Earthsea, "one music binding together the sea-divided lands" (*WE*, p. 69), does for the several peoples of Le Guin's archipelago what the Kula does for the cultures Malinowski studied. It

> welds together a considerable number of tribes, and it embraces a vast complex of activities, interconnected, and playing into one another, so as to form one organic whole.... All around the ring of Kula there is a network of relationships... the whole forms one interwoven fabric.[36]

Malinowski's organicism and his weaving metaphor would be attractive to Le Guin; her cosmology of Equilibrium and Balance in Earthsea may derive as much from Malinowski's study of the Kula as it does from Taoism.

Unlike some anthropologists, Mauss and Lévi-Strauss for example, Malinowski is more interested in the relationships between magic and science than the similarities between magic and religion; he follows Frazer in seeing it as a pseudo-science:

> Magic is akin to science in that it always has a definite aim intimately associated with human instincts, needs, and pursuits.... Like other arts and crafts, it is also governed by a theory, by a system of principles which dictate the manner in which the act has to be performed in order to be effective.... Both magic and science develop a special technique. In magic, as in the other arts, man can undo what he has done or mend the damage which he has wrought.... Thus both magic and science show certain similarities, and, with Sir James Frazer, we can appropriately call magic a pseudo-science.[37]

Le Guin's magic is very close to this. In Earthsea, evil is something woven by men alone, and can be unraveled only by another man. The School for Wizards on Roke is devoted to teaching the system of principles which govern the use of magic. For both Malinowski and Le Guin, magic is a thoroughly humanistic and secular activity, based not on rites but on the magic word. Magic, says Malinowski,

> is a specific power, essentially human, autonomous and independent in its action. This power is an inherent property of certain words [whose] action is direct and not mediated by any other agency.... The native is deeply convinced of this mysterious, intrinsic power of certain words; words which are believed to have their virtue in their own right, so to speak; having come into existence from primeval times and exercising their influence directly.[38]

The Old Speech, or Eldest Tongue as it is sometimes called, has been in existence in Earthsea since primeval times, indeed since the demiurge Segoy created the world with a speech act. When he knows these words, the "true names" of things, the mage can control them and change them. Like the natives Malinowski studies, Le Guin herself is "deeply convinced of the mysterious, intrinsic power of certain words." They are the tools of her craft. For her, she says, "as for wizards, to know the name of an island or a character is to know the island or person."[39]

According to Malinowski, magic "bridges over the gap" between the realm of myth and everyday reality.[40] It is "not only human in its embodiment, but also in its subject-matter . . . it is not directed so much to nature as to man's *relation* to nature."[41] Magic, then, is an activity that connects the timeless world of myth with present actuality, or, using words familiar to European thought, we could say that magic bridges over the gap between the unconscious and consciousness even as it connects subject and object. It is an activity that makes possible a coherent relationship between humanity and nature, between perceiving mind and perceived object. In this sense, in terms of its purpose, it is no different from art and science. "The force of magic," says Malinowski, "resides within man and can escape only through his voice."[42] This is to say that the individual magician uses language, like an artist or a scientist, to shape the relationship between self and other in two senses: in one sense it binds the Other within and the Other without, and also binds the realm of spirit and the realm of matter. Magic, like art, is an integrating and synthesizing activity. In Le Guin's cosmology these two realms are one: Ged can communicate with dragons (which he calls dreams and which Le Guin calls myths) as easily as he can control rocks. Their true names are words in the same language. He can be both Dragonlord and builder of "the deep-founded sea wall of Nepp" (*FS,* p. 9).

There are, surely, many more sources for Le Guin's magic, but these two, the Celtic-Teutonic from the extreme northwest corner of the Eurasian landmass, and the Melanesian from the extreme southeast corner, the first mythic and the second scientific, seem to be the most important. A brief survey of the curriculum of the School of Wizards on Roke will illustrate how Le Guin has woven them together on a frame of ethics. After an apprentice mage has learned to read and write the Six Hundred Runes of Hardic, he goes to Roke where his instruction begins with myth and legend, ends with physics, and is crowned with metaphysics and mysticism.

He studies with the Master chanter and the Master Windkey, learning from the first the legends, songs, and myths of Earthsea, and from the second meteorology and sailing, the "arts of wind and weather" (*WE,* p. 55). "Mage and sailor are not so far apart," Le Guin tells us; "both work with the powers of sky and sea, and bend great winds to the uses of their hands" (*FS,* p. 39). From the Master Herbal he learns botany, medicine, and medical ethics: "heal the wound and cure the illness, but let the dying spirit go" (*WE*, p. 95). The Master Hand teaches entertainment and conjuring, "sleight and jugglery and the lesser arts of Changing" (*WE*, p. 55), as well as giving Ged a lesson on the ethical uses of power:

> Illusion fools the beholder's senses; it makes him see and hear and feel that the thing is changed. But it does not change the thing. To change this rock into a jewel, you must change its true name. And to do that, my son, even to so small a scrap of the world, is to change the world. It can be done. Indeed it has been done. It is the art of the Master Changer, and you will learn it, when you are ready to learn it. But you must not change one thing, one pebble, one grain of sand, until you know what good and evil will follow on that act. The world is in Balance, in Equilibrium. A wizard's power of Changing and Summoning can shake the balance of the world. It is dangerous, that power. It is most perilous. It must follow knowledge, and serve need. To light a candle is to cast a shadow (*WE*, pp. 56-57).

He could as easily be speaking to an atomic physicist. Because "magic consists in . . . the true naming of a thing" (*WE*, p. 59), the Master Namer has a central place in the education of a mage. In *A Wizard of Earthsea*, Le Guin shows him teaching geographical place names, and in *The Farthest Shore*, he is teaching botanical names. Like the other Masters, he too teaches ethics:

> In the world under the sun, and in the other world that has no sun, there is much that has nothing to do with men and men's speech, and there are powers beyond our power . . . . A mage can control only what is near him, what he can name exactly and wholly. And this is well. If it were not so, the wickedness of the powerful or the folly of the wise would long ago have sought to change what cannot be changed, and Equilibrium would fail. The unbalanced sea would overwhelm the islands where we perilously dwell, and in the old silence all voices and all names would be lost (*WE*, pp. 60, 61).

The Master Changer teaches not only the "true spells of Shaping" (*WE*, p. 67), but also the wider implications of changing anything:

> if a thing is really to be changed into another thing, it must be renamed for as long as the spell lasts, and . . . this affects the names and natures of things surrounding the transformed thing (*WE*, p. 67).

Once again, the teaching of a skill involves lessons in the ethical use of that skill. The Master Summoner teaches nothing less than physics:

> only true magic, the summoning of such energies as light, and heat, and the force that draws the magnet, and these forces men perceive as weight, form, color, sound: real powers, drawn from immense fathomless energies of the universe . . . . [He] showed them why the true wizard uses such spells only at need, since to summon up such earthly forces is to change the earth of which they are a part (*WE*, p. 68).

Finally, the student wizard enters the Immanent Grove to learn from the Master Patterner. All along his instruction has been studded with ethical lessons based on a metaphysics of organicism and integration and balance. Now he enters the Immanent Grove and apparently experiences that ultimate reality of Being into which all contraries and dualities merge. Perhaps in the Immanent Grove the mage hears the one word Segoy spoke when he created the world, that "great word that is very slowly spoken by the shining of the stars" (*WE,* p. 185). Whatever happens there—and Le Guin wisely leaves it all shrouded in mystery—we know that ultimate Being in Earthsea, the *Urgrund,* is immanent, not transcendant, and that creation is a dynamic process ever continuing, ever unfinished. The education of a mage, then, which began with instruction in the myths and legends of Earthsea, concludes with physics and metaphysics; the scientific conception of magic culminates in one of the more abstract and formalistic of sciences and the mythic conception of magic culminates in the mysticism of tree-worship. Le Guin affirms not only Nicholas of Cusa, a mystic *(coincidentia oppositorum),* but also Niels Bohr, a physicist *(contraria sunt complementa).*

VII

"Schrödinger's Cat" may seem, on a first reading, radically different from both "Semley's Necklace" and the Earthsea trilogy, but it too weaves together myth and science in complementary patterns, even as it creates an entirely different world.[43] Unlike the landscapes in Le Guin's outer space and in her inner lands, unlike Orsinian geography, the world we experience as we read "Schrödinger's Cat" resembles neither the conventional imaginary landscapes of fantasy and science fiction nor any familiar landscape we have experienced or might experience. There are, to be sure, allusions to Michelangelo, Bach, and Schumann; there are references to Democrats, Episcopalians, Methodists, and Baptists; there is an account of Erwin Schrödinger's famous *Gedanken-experiment,* "performed" originally in 1935, and a large fragment of the myth of Pandora's Box; and, finally, there are cans of sardines and pork and beans. But even if these people and things are familiar, the context in which we find them is entirely strange and anomalous: the whole world outside the house to which the narrator has retreated is heating up and speeding up. Recalling Jameson's distinction between the technical and popular senses of the word *world,* we might say that while the *world* in the normal sense of nature, people, and things is familiar, the *world* in the phenomenological sense as a *Gestalt,* the "supreme category that permits all experience or perception in the first place," is strange. In "Schrödinger's Cat," our normal categories of time and logic and causality do not apply. In most of her fiction, Le Guin positions invented cultures and beings and things in an environment which has been created according to familiar conventions or rules or paradigms, but in "Schrödinger's Cat" she seems to place familiar things in a world that exists wholly outside the horizons of our normal world. Instead of estranging a familiar conceptual framework by putting strange things in it, Le Guin seems to be estranging the familiar things in our world by putting them into a strange frame. Thus the relationship between the two senses of *world* is reciprocal; they are internally related and relative to each other.

If the two senses of *world* are relative to each other, so also are our notions of strangeness, our cateogries of reality and fantasy, objective and subjective, subject and object. The strange frame of "Schrödinger's Cat," therefore, may not be the world outside the house, but rather may be in the house itself: the narrator's consciousness and its contents. We know from the relativity theory that our perception of time and velocity is relative to the time frame in which we are moving. To the extent that biological processes and heat (the velocity of molecules) are functions of time, they would be relative also. Thus if it appears to the narrator that the world inside the house is cooler and that things move more slowly there, then those impressions may be the result of the *narrator's* speeding up. Like Semley, who returns from "one long night" of near lightspeed travel to find her daughter sixteen years older than she was "yesterday," the narrator of "Schrödinger's Cat" may be in a time frame moving faster than the world around her (him?—we never know for certain). If that is the case, then the outside world with its increasing heat (kisses like a branding iron) and its accelerated biological process (children growing up before your eyes) would *appear* to be moving faster. Moreover, the suggestion at the end of "Schrödinger's Cat" that the narrator is mad—she recognized before the glue of her mandolin melted that the note she had been hearing on "the mandolin strings of the mind" was A, "the note that drove Robert Schumann mad" (implying that her mind has become unglued?)—parallels Semley's madness at the end of "Semley's Necklace." In one sense, then, "Schrödinger's Cat" may be a retelling of "Semley's Necklace," this time wholly from the subjectivity of the time traveler's point of view. But all of this may be merely the metaphorical mechanics of science fiction, the literalization of metaphor and the concretizing of subjective perceptions in aesthetic imagery which we should not read literally. Even so, one gets the impression that the tenors of some metaphors come from one world while the tenors of others come from another world.

Indeed, one could just as easily account for the differences between the world outside the house and the narrator's world by reading the house as a metaphor for a dream world separated from the outside waking world. Dreamers may have the impression of living if not in a timeless world, then in a world that moves more slowly than their waking worlds. Even in our waking moments time passes more quickly at one "time," and more slowly at other "times." This reading would explain the dream-like qualities of the narrative, the sudden shifts and interruptions, the coincidences, and the overdramatizations, in sum, the absence of normal causality. The narrator's punning ambiguities about telling stories and sleeping and dreaming seem to support this:

> the impulse to narrate remains. Many things are not worth doing, but almost anything is worth telling. In any case, I have a severe congenital case of Ethica laboris puritanica, or Adam's Disease. It is incurable except by total decephalization. I even like to dream when asleep, and to try and recall my dreams: it assures me that I haven't wasted seven or eight hours just lying there. Now here I am, lying, here. Hard at it.

Is the narrator merely lying, there (making things up, telling a story), or is she lying here before us (asleep), while we see the world from her dream world?

The point of all this uncertainty is just that: Uncertainty. We could press an interpretation of the story in scientific terms, but that would displace the dream elements into the background. On the other hand, we could foreground the dreamy qualities of the narrative, sacrificing a full understanding of the purely scientific elements. We are in a position similar to the physicist's as he tries to observe the velocity and momentum of an electron at the same time: only one can be measured accurately. And what better position to be in while reading a story that deals with just these anomalies of quantum mechanics that arise from the relationships between the observing subject with his tools and the observed object? Only when we try to "measure" the story with our critical tools do we need an Uncertainty Principle. If *contraria sunt complementa* is a useful motto for physicists, it is equally useful for readers. In "Schrödinger's Cat," literal and figurative, outside and inside, the language of science and the language of dreams—these are by no means mutually exclusive, but are rather complementary parts of an imaginative whole, the story itself, a metalanguage that incorporates apparently separate languages.

Although "Schrödinger's Cat" is one of Le Guin's shortest stories, it has a density and a range of meaning that are as allusive and complex as what we encounter in difficult modern poetry. It takes us to the heart of epistemological and ontological questions raised by the modern revolutions in physics at the same time that it engages pressing moral problems in its search for Hope in a world where marriages (Le Guin's "central, consistent theme") are "coming apart" and where people are reified into "hopelessly tangled" and chaotic fragments of themselves. Yet for all its complexity, "Schrödinger's Cat" has a classical simplicity: the implied equation of Pandora's Box and the box in Schrödinger's thought experiment has an elegance that matches the beauty Dirac and other physicists try to get in their equations. More than any other story Le Guin has written, it displays self-consciously the "thought-experimental manner proper to science fiction." Itself a thought experiment, the story contains a thought experiment that is one part of an aesthetic connection between an explorative, synthesizing scientific-mindedness and a fantasy-mindedness. Its yoking together of a Greek myth and quantum theory, a chiasmus of science and fantasy, is, Le Guin would say, "simply a way of thinking," a question, not an answer. "One of the essential functions of science fiction," said Le Guin as she compared it to the thought experiments of Einstein and Schrödinger, "is precisely this kind of question-asking: reversals of an habitual way of thinking, metaphors for what our language has no words for as yet, experiments in imagination." The question-asking Le Guin has in mind here is the same process George Steiner has recently described:

> our asking is, in Hegel's incisive terminology, an *Aufhebung*. Asking is an action, a possible bringing into view and into being of perspectives in which the question is seen to be trivial or falsely posed. Or, at its rare best, to ask is to provoke not the answer one actually fears or aims at, but the first contours of a new and better asking—which is then a first kind of answer.[44]

This is precisely what happens in "Schrödinger's Cat," whose plot, like the plots of Le Guin's romances, culminates in a moment of vision in which contradictions are *aufgehoben,* a moment that brings into view new perspectives. Like Le Guin's other science fiction, "Schrödinger's Cat" generates a "view in" as it reverses habitual ways of thinking.

The person who barges into the narrator's cool retreat accepts the orthodox Copenhagen interpretation of quantum theory, and wants to use the narrator's cat to prove that "if you desire certainty, any certainty, you must create it yourself!" Apparently unaware of the contradiction, he wants certain knowledge of uncertainty; he wants to prove Einstein wrong: he wants "to know for *sure* that God *does* play dice with the world."[45] The narrator raises the same epistemological questions that Eugene Wigner raised, but "Rover" brushes them aside.[46] He does not want the issue complicated by involving the observer in his system. He wants to keep things restricted to the box and confined within the categorical boxes of his binary thinking. Either the cat will be dead or not dead. When the narrator flings back the lid of the box and the cat is not there, Rover's questions are *aufgehoben.* A new perspective has come into view, a perspective much larger than the one permitted by Rover's categorical boxes: Non-Being transcends both life and death and certainty and uncertainty. Because the answer he aimed at is not provoked by his questions, Le Guin is telling us, his questions have been falsely posed. There are always more than two alternatives. And then when the roof of the house is lifted off "just like the lid of a box," the *Aufhebung* of Rover's questions is itself *aufgehoben.* If the "unconscionable, inordinate light of the stars" that floods into the house carries our minds beyond the box of the house, beyond our Earth, our solar system, even beyond our galaxy, then we might also think of boxes larger than our universe. When Le Guin removed the cat from the box she was not only doing a conjuring trick, an inversion of pulling a rabbit out of a hat. Since this is a science fiction story, she may be suggesting that the cat is in an alternate universe. This hypothesis is not as fantastic as it might seem. The multiple universe interpretation of quantum theory—the "EWG metatheorem" proposed by Elliot, Wheeler, and Graham—would give that hypothesis scientific credibility. The EWG metatheorem posits not only the existence of "simultaneous, noninteracting, but equally real worlds"; it says there are $10^{100}+$ of them![47]

If physicists can soberly conjure other worlds into existence and then support their theories with mathematical equations, the only language in which these ideas can be expressed, then their questioning of reality parallels the questionings of science fiction writers, who likewise hypothesize other worlds and then use stories, the only language in which their ideas can be expressed, to communicate with an audience. It is at this point that the incomplete myth of Pandora takes on significance. If Hope is blocked from a world (in the popular sense of the word) by the categorical boxes that constitute that world as they make perception of it possible (world in the technical sense), then a new and larger perspective that includes other worlds (in both senses of the word) means that a world without hope is not the only answer, and certainly not the final answer. Science fiction can create those other, alternate worlds (again, in both senses of the word) and therefore can change the way we ask questions of this world. If the perspectives that constitute a world without Hope are *aufgehoben* by a new asking, by the estranging techniques of science fictional thought experiments, then we will see that grief and loss, fear and *Angst,* are not the final human condition, but on the contrary are only the answers to a specific and limited kind of questioning.

The narrator enters her cool retreat grieving over a loss; she seems "to have no other self, nothing further, nothing that lies outside the borders of grief." What she has lost and cannot remember, the Nothing that lies outside the borders of her grief—Hope itself—constitutes the horizons of her world by its absence as surely as it would by its presence. While the cat is in the box, the narrator muses:

> Nothing happened. Nothing would happen. Nothing would ever happen, until we lifted the lid of the box.
> "Like Pandora," I said in a weak whisper. I could not quite recall Pandora's legend. She had let all the plagues and evils out of the box, of course, but there has been something else, too. After all the devils were let loose, something quite different, quite unexpected, had been left. What had it been? Hope? A dead cat? I could not remember.[48]

The world does not happen, or at least does not make sense, unless and until we look at it. *Esse est percipi,* as Berkeley said. Recalling Michelangelo's "Last Judgment," the narrator thinks of the fellow "who has clapped his hands over his face in horror as the devils drag him down to Hell." But she notes that he has covered only one eye: "the other eye is busy looking. It's all he can do, but he does it. He observes. Indeed, one wonders if Hell would exist if he did not look at it." Significantly, just as the narrator cannot remember what was left in Pandora's Box, she does not refer to the top half of the painting. It is as though she too is looking with just one eye. The mandolin strings of her mind have a limited range of notes.

In *The Dispossessed,* published the same year (1974) as "Schrödinger's Cat," Shevek says that "the earth itself was uncertain, unreliable. The enduring, the reliable, is a promise made by the human mind." Similarly, in the world of total Uncertainty in "Schrödinger's Cat," Hope is something that exists in the human mind, or it exists nowhere. Having forgotten a myth, the narrator has lost hope and is thus confined within the boundaries of her grief. The value free language of science cannot predict the future, at least on the quantum level. The multivalent languages of myth, however, determine the moral attitude toward the future that we adopt in the present, and if we forget parts of that language, we alienate ourselves from significant parts of reality. Recovery of that language is then a moral task, as seeing with both eyes is a moral imperative. Seeing with only one eye the devils, and evils in the world, we capitulate to despair and thereby help bring about the very conditions that we fear. But if we see with both eyes, along with an inner imaginative eye, if we use the complementary languages of myth and science when we interrogate the world, we make room for moral choice. "I shall miss the cat," says the narrator at the end of the story; "I wonder if he found what it was we lost?" If the cat is nowhere *(u-topia),* in an world simultaneous with this one but equally real, then he may have found it. The message of "Schrödinger's Cat" is the message of Le Guin's "ambiguous utopia" *The Dispossessed:* for a full view of present reality, this world, we must see with hope as well as grief and fear, we must include utopia on our maps of this world. Because Hope is absent from the narrator's world, it is all the more present in our minds as we read the story, whose theme then appears as the theme of much of Le Guin's fiction: the necessity of Hope. Demogorgon's words at the end of Shelley's *Prometheus Unbound* may be the best gloss on this story as well as Le Guin's work as a whole:

> To suffer woes which Hope thinks infinite;
> To forgive wrongs darker than Death of Night;
>   To defy Power which seems Omnipotent;
> To love, and bear; to hope, till Hope creates
> From its own wreck the thing it contemplates;
>   Neither to change nor falter nor repent:
> This, like thy glory, Titan! is to be
> Good, great and joyous, beautiful and free;
> This is alone Life, Joy, Empire and Victory.[49]

VIII

Myth and science are usually regarded as two mutually exclusive languages, each with its own vocabulary, grammar, and syntax, each with its own way of seeing the world, each constituting its own world. What Heisenberg says of scientific work in physics applies, *mutatis mutandis,* to one who uses myth or any other specialized language to understand nature:

> We have to remember that what we observe is not nature in itself but nature exposed to our method of questioning. Our scientific work in physics consists in asking questions about nature in the language that we possess and trying to get an answer from experiment by the means at our disposal. In this way quantum theory reminds us, as Bohr has put it, of the old wisdom that when searching for harmony in life one must never forget that in the drama of existence we are ourselves both players and spectators. It is understandable that in our scientific relation to nature our own activity becomes very important when we have to deal with parts of nature into which we can penetrate only by using the most elaborate tools.[50]

Like physicists, Le Guin asks questions of nature—the primary question being "who are we?"—as she experiments with one of the most elaborate tools human beings have developed, the story, not so much to get an answer as to provoke an *Aufhebung* that brings into view the first contours of a new and better asking. She knows that Mind and Nature are interdependent, perhaps even identical at some moments, and that the specialized tools made for exploring one will not yield results when they are used on the other. There are parts of nature—the imagination, the mind, the moral intelligence—which can be penetrated with the language of the night: the symbols and narrative logics of dreams and myths. Conversely, there are parts of nature that we know best with the language of the day: the concepts and logics of science and rationality. Recognizing that these several parts of nature are interdependent, that we are ourselves both players and spectators in the drama of existence, and that a view of the whole web of relationships in the drama requires complementary modes of thought and feeling, Le Guin has tried to fashion stories which, as they weave together the languages of myth and science, as they make connections between fantasy-mindedness and scientific-mindedness, become themselves a new language in which myth and science can communicate with each other. That language then becomes an elaborate tool in the search for harmony in life.

4

Le Guin's Hainish Future History: The Dialectic of Beginnings and Endings

What counts for total comprehension of the story of man's doings . . . is the concatenated masses of culture and the interrelations of these—interrelations of transmittal and absorption of content, along with regrouping and refashioning according to national and supranational style of civilization. It is in connection with the understanding of major drifts such as these that the concept is here submitted of an *Oikoumenê* consisting of a specific, preponderant, interwoven, definable mass of culture charged with a modern significance additional to the original [Greek] socio-geographical designation in which culture was at best only implicit.

—A.L. Kroeber

". . . all the men we've run into are in fact men. But the kinship goes back some five hundred and fifty thousand years, to the Fore-Eras of Hain. The Hainish settled a hundred worlds . . . ."

"The Powers of the Ekumen dream, then of restoring that truly ancient empire of Hain; of regathering all the worlds of men, the lost worlds?"

". . . Of weaving some harmony among them, at least. Life loves to know itself, out to its farthest limits. To embrace complexity is its delight. All these worlds and the various forms and ways of the minds and lives on them: together they would make a really splendid harmony."

"No harmony endures," said the young king.

"None has ever been achieved," said the Plenipotentiary. "The pleasure is in trying."

—Ursula K. Le Guin

If we go back to the forties—back to the years of global war when Le Guin was an adolescent—we will discover what I believe are the most important sources of the "rather erratic 'future history' scheme," as Le Guin calls it, that forms the background and framework for four science fiction stories and six science fiction novels she wrote between 1963 and 1973.[1] One of those sources is Issac Asimov's series of Foundation stories, first published between 1942 and 1949 in *Astounding Science Fiction,* one of the pulp magazines Le Guin was reading in the early forties. Later collected and published as *The Foundation Trilogy,* Asimov's serial combined space opera with macro-historical speculations about the course of galactic civilization in future millennia, and thereby established a set of conventions that no writer of science fiction in the fifties and sixties could easily escape. Another source is her father's anthropology, specifically his Huxley Memorial Lecture for 1945, "The Ancient *Oikoumenê* as an Historic Culture Aggregate," a macro-historical cultural theory about the single origin and centrifugal diffusion of "the millennially interrelated higher civilizations in the connected land masses of the Eastern Hemisphere."[2] Both Asimov and Kroeber were writing in the shadows of Spengler and Toynbee (and, in Asimov's case, of Gibbon), Asimov following them derivatively, Kroeber offering alternatives to a cyclic view of history.[3] Spengler and Toynbee, in turn, were responding to the early twentieth century and World War I by writing *Universalgeschichte* in the tradition stemming from Herder and Schiller and branching off into German and English Romanticism. Modern science fiction, it should be noted, is generally agreed to be an offshoot of Romanticism, having its origin when Mary Shelley wrote *Frankenstein* in the company of her husband and Lord Byron. Science fiction after the Second World War, then, including Le Guin's, recombines the romance, one of the major forms of Romantic prose, with the universal history, one of the major forms of Romantic philosophy. *"De nobis, fabula narratur,"* wrote Will Durant when he presented the third volume of his *Story of Civilization* in 1944; "of ourselves this Roman story is told."[4] The message of the *Universalgeschichte* is the message of the romance: *de te fabula.* It is surely no coincidence that wars should stimulate the creation of universal histories, for it is during wars that writers feel intensely the pressure of Plotinus' demand "And we, who are we, anyway?"

Asimov's concern is teleology; Kroeber's etiology: the former extrapolates and projects into the future, while the latter delves into the past, exploring for roots and origins. The one asks "where are we going?" while the other asks "where have we been?"; both are versions of "who are we?" Northrop Frye would see these two impulses in terms of myth:

> There are two social conceptions which can be expressed only in terms of myth. One is the social contract, which presents an account of the origins of society. The other is the utopia, which presents an imaginative vision of the *telos* or end at which social life aims. These two myths both begin in an analysis of the present, the society that confronts the mythmaker, and they project the analysis in time and space. The contract projects it into the past, the utopia into the future or some distant place . . . . The social contract, though a genuine myth which, in John Stuart Mill's phrase, passes off a fiction as a fact, is usually regarded as an integral part of social theory. The utopia, on the other hand, although its origin is much the same, belongs primarily to fiction . . . . the contract myth preserves at least the gesture of making assertions that can be definitely verified or refuted, [but] the utopia is a *speculative* myth; it is designed to contain or provide a vision of one's social ideas, not to be a theory connecting social facts together.[5]

Like many of Frye's formulations, this is persuasive because of its elegant neatness—and Asimov and Kroeber do indeed fit it very neatly—but, it is also, again like many of his theories, over generalized. Yet for all that, I introduce it as a heuristic device to identify the mythic archetypes buried in Asimov's ideological stereotypes and embedded in Kroeber's anthropological theory, and to prepare for a discussion of the mythic dimensions of Le Guin's Hainish future history, which, like her father's theory, deals with "major drifts" in a "specific, preponderant, interwoven, definable mass of culture."

Asimov's teleological myth issues in a utopia—a "civilization based on mental science," as he calls it in *Second Foundation,* the third volume of the trilogy—a utopia accurately characterized by Charles Elkins as an alienated humanity dominated by a "technobureaucratic elite";[6] yet buried in that ideologically motivated view of the future is a real desire to have some control over human destiny in the present (in the early forties, an understandable desire). Kroeber's etiological myth, on the other hand, returns us to "that first hearth of all higher civilization—in the Near Eastern area of the Neolithic Revolution, of the first farming and towns and kings and letters"; embedded in the hearth metaphor is the myth of a unified primal family and its dispersion, a creation myth that expresses a desire for wholeness and integration (again, in the early forties, an understandable desire).[7] For Asimov, for Kroeber, and, a generation later, during the Vietnam War, for Le Guin too, "the society that confronts the mythmaker" is riddled with deep divisions, is fragmented and alienated, and is at war. Le Guin has responded to that society by inventing a science fictional future history in which those two myths—the etiological creation myth, and the teleological utopian myth—are married. "Men die because they cannot join the beginning to the end," said Alcmaeon of Croton, a Presocratic physician and philosopher. Le Guin's marriage of myths of beginning and myths of ending suggests that she would agree with Alcmaeon, and would extend his idea beyond the life of an individual to cover whole cultures and the ecumene of which they are all a part.

Unlike Athena, Le Guin's Hainish future history did not spring from its creator fully formed, nor is it completely consistent; it has developed story by story and novel by novel, and it is, as she admits, "rather erratic." Instead of analyzing its final shape, I will trace its growth from its origins in "The Dowry of Angyar" (1964) through "The Day Before the Revolution" (1974). The development of Le Guin's future history—*its* history—may be understood best as a dialectical interplay between the conventions of pulp science fiction and the methods, attitudes, ideas, and values of anthropology. This development is, on a deeper level, a dialectical or complementary interplay between teleological and etiological myths, leading to a synthesis of *telos* and *aitia,* the creation of the present. Rather than expressing a contradiction, the two words *future* and *history* together define the present.

In the first third of the decade 1963-73 in which Le Guin's future history was taking shape, she was working largely within the science fiction conventions established by Asimov and others, but in 1966, when she drew on her father's anthropology to invent the Ekumen, she outgrew those conventions and began to concentrate on beginnings. Instead of extending the chronology of her Hainish future history forward, she wrote novels set progressively farther in the past.[8] Paradoxically, her return to origins and her creation of an anarchist utopia went together. Only when she turned back to her father's etiology did she advance toward utopia. At the same time that the form of her future history was influenced by sources in the early forties, it was being shaped by the narrative techniques she was developing as she matured as an artist in the sixties. Drawing on Mark Schorer, we could say that she used technique to discover the "intellectual and moral implications" of her material.[9] Before tracing that development, however, we should review briefly the "cosmogony of the future," as Donald Wollheim calls it, that Le Guin found when she returned to science fiction in the early sixties.[10]

I

Asimov's Foundation trilogy is the story of the fall of a 12,000-year-old Galactic Empire of 25,000,000 inhabitable worlds with a total population of 1,000,000,000,000. Earth is apparently the source of all this (space opera was written before "be fruitful and multiply" became dirty words). In the last years of the Galactic Era, Hari Seldon perfects a science called psychohistory, defined by his biographer Gaal Dornik as:

> that branch of mathematics which deals with the reactions of human conglomerates to fixed social and economic stimuli.... Implicit in all these definitions is the assumption that the human conglomerate being dealt with is sufficiently large for valid statistical treatment.... A further necessary assumption is that the human conglomerate be itself unaware of psychohistorical analysis in order that its reactions be truly random (I, 14).

Psychohistory is based on "the synthesis of the calculus of n-variables and of n-dimensional geometry... what Seldon once called 'my little algebra of humanity" (III, 93). Seldon predicts that the imminent fall of the Galactic Empire will be followed by a 30,000-year-long Dark Age; he therefore sets in motion "Seldon's Plan" to reduce this to 1,000 years, and succeeds. Bentham's hedonistic calculus never really caught on, but Seldon's psychohistory and Asimov's projection of Occidental history took the science fiction world by storm; Wollheim calls the Foundation trilogy "the pivot of modern science fiction" (p. 37), and science fiction fans have overwhelmingly confirmed his judgment.

"Because science fiction builds on science fiction," says Wollheim, "and one man's originations become the next man's [sic] accepted premises, the rise, reign, and fall of a galactic empire is...taken for granted in the many millennia-spanning novels" that followed Asimov's trilogy in the fifties and sixties (p. 41); this is, in the words of another historian of modern science fiction, the "consensus future history."[11] The Foundation novels established a set of assumptions, premises, and conventions that allow any reader of science fiction to "tell what is implied by the simple facts of a story's background" (p. 42). And the background implied by those simple facts is a version of the Western, middle class, technological vision of history that Asimov puts forth in the Foundation trilogy. Almost all the future histories invented during the years following Asimov's fit into a scheme, outlined by Wollheim as follows:

I.   Exploration of the Solar System: contact with intelligent species on other planets; colonization of the planets; colonial problems; problems of interplanetary commerce.

II.   Flights to the Stars: problems of time-dilation and faster-than-light (FTL) travel; discovery of life in other solar systems; encounters with and problems with alien intelligences; establishment of human colonies in other solar systems; renewed contact with Mother Earth; commerce—exploitation and otherwise.

III.   Rise of the Galactic Empire: contact and commerce between many human-colonized or alien worlds; treaties and defensive alliances to solve problems between worlds; presence of aliens who threaten the Galactic Empire; eventual triumph of a union or federation, "dominated usually from Old Earth" (p. 43).

IV.   Galactic Empire in Full Bloom: commerce and adventure; maverick worlds on the Galactic Rim; problem of extra-galactic alien enemies; political intrigue; robots vs. humans; exploration of the rest of the galaxy by official exploration ships, adventurers, or commercial pioneers.

V.   Decline and Fall of the Galactic Empire: intrigue, palace revolt, breakaway planets; rebellions and corruption, invasion by extra-galactic enemy; crumbling of commerce, distrust and fear, loss of contact with worlds farthest away from the center of the Empire; rebellious worlds withdraw into themselves as "empire/alliance/federation/ union becomes an empty shell or is destroyed at its heart" (p. 43).

VI.   Interregnum: reversion to prespaceflight conditions; savagery, barbarism, superstition; raids of one barbaric world on another; loss of knowledge, dissolution of centers of learning; attempts to save fragments of scientific knowledge and technological skills; loss of contact for thousands of years; humanity becomes indigenous to most inhabitable worlds, forgetting origins; evolutionary changes and mutations on isolated worlds.

VII.   Rise of Permanent Galactic Civilization: restoration of commerce; reexploration of lost worlds; restoration of technology to high levels and democratic politics; efforts to smooth over hostility between worlds that no longer recognize each other as kin; beating back new efforts to form new empires; eventual rise of galactic harmony; exploration of other galaxies and of the entire universe.

VIII. Challenge to God: galactic harmony at undreamed of high level; experiments in creation; harmony between galactic clusters; seeking out and confronting Creative Force or Being or God; sometimes merging with that Creative First Principle; end of the universe and end of time; beginning of a new universe and a new space-time continuum.

This class-bound, ethnocentric vision of *universal* history ignores the ways and values of not less than three-quarters of our world's cultures as it projects European and American values—essentially imperialistic, mechanistic, and masculine values—onto the galaxy (and a galaxy, our Milky Way at any rate, contains 100,000,000,000 stars and is over 22,000 light-years wide), and even onto the universe. Although Le Guin would surely reject almost all of the assumptions and premises on which this historical vision is based—she professes anarchistic, organic, and feminist values—she still had to work within the literary conventions that carried it when she started writing science fiction in the early sixties.

II

Le Guin gave up reading science fiction after her high school years and thus did not follow the development of this "cosmogony of the future" into a "consensus future history." Science fiction in those postwar years, she says, "seemed to be all about hardware and soldiers. Besides, I was busy with Tolstoy and things."[12] "And things" included degrees from Radcliffe and Columbia, a Fulbright to France to study Jean Lemaire de Belges, marriage, college teaching, children, and Orsinian tales. Then in 1961, a friend in Portland loaned her a copy of the *Magazine of Fantasy and Science Fiction;* it contained Cordwainer Smith's story "Alpha Ralpha Boulevard." Le Guin discovered that, compared to the science fiction she had read as an adolescent in the forties, "everything was different" in the sixties. Unlike the writers for the pulps, Smith "was using the language with delight."[13] She started reading science fiction again, and, not having much success with her Orsinian tales, began writing and submitting stories to science fiction magazines. She sold her first story in 1962, and in 1964 published "The Dowry of Angyar," the story that turned out to be the germ of her Hainish future history. By the middle of the seventies, she had published six novels and four stories set in this future history scheme:

Le Guin's Hainish Cycle[14]

	Date of Composition	Date of Publication	Position in Hainish Chronology
"The Dowry of Angyar" ("Semley's Necklace")	1963	1964	5
Rocannon's World	1963	1966	6
Planet of Exile	1963-64	1966	7
City of Illusions	1965	1967	8
"Winter's King"	1966	1969	10
The Left Hand of Darkness	1967-68	1969	9
The Word for World is Forest	1968-69	1972	3 & 4
"Vaster than Empires and More Slow"	1970	1971	
The Dispossessed	1971-73	1974	2
"The Day Before the Revolution"	1973	1974	1

It is unlikely that the Asimov-Wollheim tradition exercised any direct (positive) influence on the genesis of Le Guin's future history. Cordwainer Smith, however, whose "Instrumentality of Mankind" epic of the future was being developed at the same time as Asimov's Foundation series, but was far less influential in shaping the conventions of the Galactic Empire, may have been the catalyst, the writer who mediated the conventions to Le Guin and made them palatable to her. Smith's future history, while superficially similar to the Asimov-Wollheim scheme, is subtly different:

> In Cordwainer Smith's epic of the future, the Instrumentality of Mankind has all the hallmarks of both a political elite and a priesthood. Its hegemony is that, not of the Galactic empire so typical of less imaginative SF, but of something far more subtle and pervasive—at once political and spiritual. Its lords see themselves not as mere governors or bureaucrats or politicians, but as instruments of human destiny itself. [15]

How much Le Guin knew of the whole shape of Smith's future history in 1963 is uncertain; this description was made in 1975, nine years after his death. Nevertheless, the cultural values apparent in Smith's individual stories would have appealed to Le Guin. Unlike most American science fiction writers that preceded Le Guin, Smith was widely experienced in other cultures, expecially the Chinese, and this gave his work a tone that Le Guin, herself deeply involved in Chinese thought, would have found most attractive. [16] Absent from Smith's fiction is the aggressive ethnocentrism so pervasive in the Asimov-Wollheim tradition.

Le Guin tells us very little about the League in "The Dowry of Angyar." What she does reveal indicates that she was working both within, and at the same time criticizing, the Asimov-Wollheim vision of galactic civilization. We do know from Rocannon's *Handy Pocket Guide to Intelligent Life-forms*, for example, that the galaxy (presumably our Milky Way) is divided into at least eight areas, and that Galactic Area 8 includes at least 62 worlds inhabited by intelligent life-forms ("DA," p. 46). Fomalhaut II, world number 62, is not yet a member of the League ("DA," p. 61). The League classifies and catalogues the life forms on these worlds according to criteria which help to determine which races or species to enlist as allies in the coming war. The League has given the Gdemiar, one of the five species on Fomalhaut II, an automatic-drive NAFAL (not as fast as light) messenger-ship for travel to and from New South Georgia, a League member. "Pidgin-Galactic" is a *lingua franca* that makes inter-species communication possible ("DA," p. 60). We learn from Semley's narrative that

> the Strangers had come in their warships and put an end to the old ways and wars, exacting tribute for their greater war that was to be fought with some strange enemy, somewhere in the hollow places between the stars, at the end of time ("DA." p. 49).

All we know of Ketho and Rocannon is that they are League functionaries, the former a museum director, the latter of unknown profession (only in *Rocannon's World* is he identified as an ethnologist); their birthplaces are not given, so readers in 1964 would probably assume that they are Terrans. If they are representative of the League and its values, and there is no reason for them not to be, then the League is not only ignorant of the people it is exploiting; it regards them as things ("DA," p. 59-61). The League is, in short, racist and ethnocentric; in "handy pocket guides" it grants other people recognition only as potential extensions of itself.

When readers of science fiction magazines picked up their September issues of *Amazing Stories* in the autumn of 1964, and began reading them from beginning to end, they came upon Le Guin's story after finishing Edmund Hamilton's "Kingdom of the Stars," and before they started Ben Bova's "The Alien Worlds," an essay on the technological problems to be surmounted when we begin colonizing the planets in our solar system. Hamilton, credited by Wollheim with setting off the spark in the late twenties "that was ... to light up the greatest concept of the world of science-fiction ideas: the galactic civilization" (p. 30), was one of the fathers of the space opera. In a context like this, Le Guin's barest allusion to her story's background would call up in her readers' minds the whole "consensus future history" that had taken shape in the forties and fifties; they would quickly recognize that her League falls somewhere near the end of Wollheim's fourth stage, "Galactic Empire in Full Bloom." Aware or unaware of the conventions, Le Guin allowed her readers' generic expectations to flesh out her bare skeleton with the body generated by Asimov's Foundation trilogy. Since she gives so little information about the League, that was all they could do. Yet even as the first story in Le Guin's Hainish cycle appeared in a pulp magazine in the context of space opera and technological problem-solving, it uses the conventional machinery of science fiction only as a vehicle for Semley's story, which, as I pointed out in chapter three, is a retelling of a Norse myth. Because it is Semley's story, narrated from her point of view, our sympathies are with her, not with the League. Le Guin uses the convention of a galactic empire to criticize it for its disregard for people like Semley. It is here, in the germinal story of the Hainish cycle, that the dialectical interplay between science fiction conventions and myth generates Le Guin's history of the future.

III

In the two-year interval between the appearance of "The Dowry of Angyar" and *Rocannon's World*, the League publishing house issued a new edition of Rocannon's *Handy Pocket Guide.* It has become the *Abridged Handy Pocket Guide to Intelligent Life-forms* (this is one of the changes Le Guin made when she revised "The Dowry of Angyar" to make it into "Prologue: The

Necklace"). The amended title emphasizes more strongly the League's cavalier disregard for its subject peoples; the amended contents include *dates,* missing from the first edition of the *Guide.* Le Guin had begun to invent *history.* At the same time, she invented her first science fiction world. The description of Fomalhaut II extracted from the *League Handbook for Galactic Area Eight,* and placed at the beginning of Rocannon's story, is a well-worn convention not only in science fiction (Asimov, for example, uses extracts from the *Encyclopedia Galactica* in the Foundation trilogy), but also in the long tradition of fantastic narratives which include "documents" to create an air of factuality. It is as though science fiction writers were appropriating the methods for creating a contract myth ("which, in John Stuart Mill's phrase, passes off a fiction as a fact"), in order to transform a teleological myth into history.

The following selection from the League *Handbook* gives us an idea of how Le Guin's League operates:

> History: The planet was charted by the Eleison Expedition in 202, robot-probed in 218.
> First Geographical Survey, 235-36. Director: J. Kiolaf. The major landmasses were surveyed by air (see maps 3114-a, b, c, 3115-a, b.). Landings, geological and biological studies and HILF contacts were made only on East and Northwest Continents (see description of intelligent species below).
> Technological Enhancement Mission to Species 1-A, 252-54. Director: J. Kiolaf (Northwest Continent only).
> Control and Taxation Missions to Species I-A and II were carried out under auspices of the Area Foundation in Kerguelen, N.S.Ga., in 254, 258, 262, 270; in 275 the planet was placed under Interdict by the Allworld HILF Authority, pending more adequate study of its intelligent species.
> First Ethnographic Survey, 321. Director: G. Rocannon (*RW,* pp. 25-26).

This is all standard science fiction machinery (except, perhaps, for the ethnographic survey), even down to the "Foundation" in Kerguelen, New South Georgia, perhaps an allusion to Asimov's trilogy. Even so, Le Guin does not present a sympathetic image of the Foundation; it is the arm of the League that dominates and exploits colonial worlds; its activities are based on incomplete information, for Kiolaf ignored several areas of the planet. (With hindsight, we can see the seeds of Winter/Gethen here: Kerguelen and South Georgia are islands that figured in the early exploration of Antarctica, and the literature of Antarctic exploration would become a major element in *The Left Hand of Darkness.*)

The picture of the League Le Guin gives us in *Rocannon's World* is quite different from the one she hinted at in "The Dowry of Angyar." Not only does she invent a history for it; she also introduces ethnology to it: a new element joins the myth-science fiction dialectic. *Rocannon's World* is a weaving together of myth (Rocannon is a reincarnation of Odin), space opera (he saved

Fomalhaut II from evil invaders by calling in FTL bombers), and ethnology (Rocannon is no longer the faceless bystander he was in "The Dowry of Angyar," but is rather a "hilfer, an ethnologist of the High Intelligence Life Forms" [*RW*, p. 20]). It is clear from Rocannon's reflections on the League's policies, that the "Area Foundation" (i.e., the Asimov-Wollheim vision of the future) and the "AllWorld HILF Authority" (i.e., anthropology) have different values:

> ...to an aggressive people only technology mattered. And there...was the League's own weak spot. Only technology mattered. The two missions to this world in the last century had started pushing one of the species toward preatomic technology before they had even explored the other continents or contacted all intelligent races. He had called a halt to that, and had finally managed to bring his own Ethnographic Survey here to learn something about this planet, but he did not fool himself. Even his work here would finally have served only as an informational basis for encouraging technological advance in the most likely species or culture. This was how the League of All Worlds prepared to meet its ultimate enemy. A hundred worlds had been trained and armed, a thousand more were being schooled in the uses of steel and wheel and tractor and reactor. But Rocannon the hilfer, whose job was learning, not teaching, and who had lived on quite a few backward worlds, doubted the wisdom of staking everything on weapons and the uses of machines. Dominated by the aggressive, tool-making humanoid species of Centaurus, Earth, and the Cetians, the League had slighted certain skills and powers and potentialities of intelligent life, and judged by too narrow a standard.... Other races on other worlds could be pushed faster ahead, to help when the extra-galactic enemy returned at last.... What if the weapons of the Enemy were things of the mind? Would it not be well to learn a little of the different shapes minds came in, and their powers? The League's policy was too narrow; it led to too much waste, and now evidently it had led to rebellion. If the storm brewing on Faraday ten years ago had broken, it meant that a young League world, having learned war promptly and been armed, was out to carve its own empire from the stars (*RW*, pp. 32-33).

This is both conventional science fiction and a critique of it. The number of worlds involved, while not as large as Asimov's 25,000,000 is still larger than it would be in the later history of the League and the Ekumen; one hundred and one thousand are merely numbers that Le Guin tosses off as easily as rhymes like "steel and wheel and tractor and reactor." The "extra-galactic enemy" is little more than a stage prop, as is a rebellious world "out to carve its own empire from the stars." But the humanist critique of materialism from an ethnological point of view, which recognizes the self-destructive impulses of a culture devoted to technology and militarism, is Le Guin's own voice.

It is in *Rocannon's World* that Le Guin mentions Hain for the first time. That world, Rocannon explains to Yahan, is his birthplace:

> I was born on a world called Hain by my mother's people, and Davenant by my father's. You call its sun the Winter Crown.... By blood I'm entirely of my mother's race; my father, who was Terran, adopted me. This is the custom when people of different species, who cannot conceive children, marry. As if one of your kin should marry a Fian woman.... Terran and Davenanter are as alike as you and I. Few worlds have so many different races as this one. Most often there is one, much like us, and the rest are beasts without speech (*RW*, p. 74).

Now there is nothing in *Rocannon's World* to indicate with any certainty that Hain is the single source for all the races or species on worlds in the League; Le Guin was not yet actively interested in the *aitia* (Gk., responsibility, cause; the root of "etiology") of the cultures she had invented. That interest developed as she went along. The League is dominated by Centaurans, Terrans, and Cetians and is therefore much closer to the conventional Galactic Empire than it is to the Ekumen Le Guin invented later, replacing imperialism with anarchism. The seeds of Le Guin's later etiological interests, however, are latent in the very structure of *Rocannon's World*, whose plot carries the questing party first to the Ancient One and then to the Liuar, the undifferentiated sources of the Fiia and Gdemiar, and the Angyar and Olgyior, respectively. This impulse to return to roots, this journey into the realm of mythic origins, which drives and guides the plot of *Rocannon's World*, would become the pattern controlling the action not only of individual stories and novels later in the Hainish cycle, but also of the whole cycle itself. The techniques Le Guin uses in Rocannon's World thus led to discoveries. Patterns in a part of the cycle influence the shape of the whole cycle as it grows. The growth of Le Guin's Hainish future history is a creative hermeneutic circle. Discoveries in the parts influence inventions of the whole, and discoveries about the whole influence inventions in the parts.[17]

We know that Le Guin uses names with care and with a profound respect for their power, and we know that Hain, in the final version of Le Guin's future history, is the source of all the humanoid species on one hundred worlds in one corner of the galaxy. Buried in "Davenant," the Terran name for Hain, may be a hint that that world is indeed a source or a beginning. If "Davenant" comes from the French *avenement* (coming, advent), or French *avenir* (future, future ages), or both, then *d'avenant* may be Le Guin's French neologism meaning "from the beginning" or "of the future" (a synthesis of beginning and ending, of etiology and teleology); or, if "Davenant" comes from the French *avenant* (prepossessing, personable, comely), then *d'avenant* may mean "of the prepossessing [people]." Lepennon, as we will see in *The Word for World is Forest*, is a Hainish with these qualities, as is Ketho, the Hainish first mate on the starship *Devenant* in *The Dispossessed*.[18] The text of *Rocannon's World*, however, offers little support for these speculations; they exist, as it were, only as *potentia*, as material not represented by drawing on the map.

IV

Planet of Exile is the story of a stranded Terran colony. It would fit easily into Wollheim's sixth phase, "Interregnum," that time after the fall of the Galactic Empire when isolated worlds, long out of touch with the mother planet, either drift back into barbarism, or try tenaciously to preserve the knowledge, skills, and old ways of their ancestors. (As Le Guin developed her future history and filled in the prehistory before and the future beyond the League Era, she discovered that the League Years were themselves part of a larger Interregnum between the Hainish seeding of a hundred worlds and the Ekumen.) In the eleven-century interval between League Year 321 (*RW*, p. 26) and League Year 1405 (*PE*, p. 27), the League of All Worlds continued to prepare for the "War to Come" (*RW*, p. 28), and then apparently lost it sometime around the beginning of the ninth century.

Le Guin uses Rolery's curiosity to elicit from Jakob an expository chunk of the League's history, as the Terrans on Gamma Draconis III understand it:

> "I'll tell you if you want to hear, but it's not just a tale, Rolery. There's a lot we don't understand, but what we do know of our history is true."
>
> "I hear," she whispered in the ritual phrase, impressed, but not entirely subdued.
>
> "Well, there are many worlds out among the stars, and many kinds of men living on them. They made ships that could sail the darkness between the worlds, and kept traveling about and trading and exploring. They allied themselves into a League, as your clans ally with one another to make a Range. But there was an enemy of the League of All Worlds. An enemy coming from far off. I don't know how far. The books were written for men who knew more than we know...."
>
> "For a long time the League prepared to fight that enemy. The stronger worlds helped the weaker ones to arm against the enemy, to make ready. A little as we're trying to make ready to meet the Gaal, here. Mindhearing was one skill they taught, I know, and there were weapons, the books say, fires that could burn up whole planets and burst the stars.... Well, during that time my people came from their home-world to this one. Not very many of them. They were to make friends with your peoples and see if they wanted to be a world of the League, and join against the enemy. But the enemy came. The ship that brought my people went back to where it came from, to help in fighting the war, and some of the people went with it, and the ... far-speaker with which those men could talk to one another from world to world. But some of the people stayed on here, either to help this world if the enemy came here, or because they couldn't go back again: we don't know. Their records say only that the ship left. A white spear of metal, longer than a whole city, standing up on a feather of fire. There are pictures of it. I think they thought it would come back soon.... That was ten Years ago [600 League Years]."
>
> "What of the war with the enemy?"
>
> "We don't know. We don't know anything that happened since the day the ship left. Some of us figure the war must have been lost, and others think it was won, but hardly, and the few men left here were forgotten in the years of fighting. Who knows? If we survive, some day we'll find out; if no one ever comes, we'll make a ship and go find out...." (*PE*, pp. 42-43).

This passage sounds a new note in Le Guin's science-fictional historiography, a note that echoes the harmonies between tale and history in *Orsinian Tales*. While it still contains elements of space opera (star-bursting weapons and the "far-speaker" [the ansible]), it is not an extract from a document. Rather, it is a self-contained narrative, a "true" story that is "not just a tale," but a tale nevertheless. The one piece of documentary evidence that Jakob does include, an old picture, is brought to life through poetic diction: "a white spear of metal . . . standing on a feather of fire." This aestheticizing of a bare historical document anticipates Le Guin's more sophisticated use of "documents" in her historiography in later episodes in the Hainish history, especially "Winter's King" and *The Left Hand of Darkness*. Historical consciousness in *Planet of Exile* is mediated through art not only in this tale Jakob tells Rolery, but also in the murals in the Hall of the League in Landin (*PE*, pp. 27-28, 61-62).

Rolery's curiosity about the murals (which, as I noted in chapter 2, affect her to the point that she identifies with them), elicits some more history of the League, this time from Seiko Esmit:

> "What is that?" Rolery pointed, from a respectful distance.
> "A building—the Great Hall of the League on the world called Davenant."
> "And that?"
> "An erkar."
> "Can your people make such cars now?" . . .
> "No . . . . You see, we don't know all about erkars and many other things that used to belong to our people, because when our ancestors came they forbade them to use many things different from the things the native people used. This was called the Cultural Embargo . . . . It means, you see, that we were to live exactly as you live. In so far as we do not, we have broken our own Law" (*PE*, pp. 62-63).

Besides dropping a hint (and no more than a hint) that Hain-Davenant is the central world in the League, Le Guin invents the Law of Cultural Embargo, indicating that ethnology has played a greater role in the League's policies than it did before Rocannon went to Fomalhaut II. The League (at least until its defeat) controlled the "technological enhancement" of newly discovered worlds to avoid further rebellions by newly armed aggressive peoples like the Faradayans. Hilfers like Rocannon were probably granted a more important role in inviting worlds into the League; the Law of Cultural Embargo, in fact, may have been drafted by an ethnologist, for it appears to be an extension of the practices an ethnologist would use during his fieldwork. (This all prefigures the methods of the Ekumen, which sends ethnologists to newly discovered worlds rather than exporting military hardware to them.)

This new emphasis on anthropology in the League's history is reflected in the whole structure of *Planet of Exile,* distancing it from space-opera conventions. Le Guin was beginning to free herself from the Asimov-Wollheim traditions by turning them inside out. If the Gaal hordes on Rolery's planet are named after Gaal Dornick, Hari Seldon's biographer, Le Guin may be suggesting that the real enemies of civilization are the techno-bureaucratic elites who run the Galactic Empire. It is in her handling of the narrative point of view, however, that Le Guin integrates anthropological values in the story (perhaps a case of "technique as discovery"). Rather than following the heroic adventures of a white male protagonist as she did in *Rocannon's World,* Le Guin begins *Planet of Exile* with Rolery's trip into Landin. Through an alien white woman's eyes, we first see the black Terrans as aliens, and we see their disintegrating science-fictional civilization as something strange and abnormal, something to be feared and distrusted. Not until chapter three of the novel are we introduced to the Terran point of view, and then we discover that ethnocentrism and fear of the alien other is reciprocal. "Man" (i.e., Occidental white males), Le Guin is telling us, is not the focal point of the universe; there are other, no more and no less valuable, points of view. The Terran adherence to the League's old Laws is as conservative as the Tevaran holding to the "Way of Man"(*PE,* p. 36). This relativistic, even egalitarian, view of cultural values, more catholic than the one implicit in the Asimov tradition, may be called a properly anthropological point of view.[19]

Yet for all its qualifications of the values and attitudes of conventional science fiction, *Planet of Exile* is still an Interregnum story. Like many others in that category, its plot turns on an evolutionary genetic change on an isolated world. The alliance between the Terrans and the Tevarans, as Jakob's analogies indicate, is a replication of the League's policy of banding together to meet an alien invader, and, to what extent, is again conventional. But as Le Guin worked out the plot of *Planet of Exile,* she discovered a theme, which grows inevitably from her handling of point of view, and which would influence the later history of the Hainish worlds: the problems of communication and love between aliens who happen to be distant kin. Moreover, teleological and etiological impulses begin to emerge. The Terrans, Jakob tells Rolery, want to "make a ship and go find out" what happened to Terra and the League. Their goal is to discover their origins, to connect beginning and end.

V

Six centuries later, a descendant of Rolery and Jakob does exactly that in *City of Illusions.* Le Guin's third novel, which advances the chronology of her future history forward in a customary manner, is one of her least successful works. She recognizes that "it has some good bits," but admits that it "is only half thought out. I was getting hasty," she says.[20] Twelve years after writing it, she put her finger on the major flaw: "villain trouble.... The Shing are the least convincing lot of people I ever wrote.[21] Her hero is not very convincing, either. Single-handedly, Falk-Ramarren outwits the Shing with his superior mindscience, escapes from Earth in a stolen Shing space ship, and sets in motion their ultimate defeat, bringing an end to the Age of the Enemy that followed upon the fall of the League. One senses that Le Guin was feeling cramped by the future history conventions she had been using, or perhaps had been used by, and was looking for a quick way to write herself out of a corner.

As she did so, she experimented with methods of integrating historical narrative into the plot of her novel, and tried out a technique that she would use in *The Left Hand of Darkness:* inserting and interpolating self-contained pieces of narrative that by themselves look back to origins but function to advance the plot into the future.[22] In *Planet of Exile,* Jakob's explanation of the League's history does no more to advance the plot than the extract from the League *Handbook* does to advance the plot of *Rocannon's World;* but Orry's "childish narrative" (*CI,* p. 100), the story of the Terran colony on Werel and its search for its roots on Earth, is an indispensible step in Falk's recovery of his identity as Ramarren, and thus necessary for his progress toward integrating his two selves and overpowering Ken Kenyek so that he and Orry can escape from the Shing.

Before Falk had left Zove's Clearing, he did learn what little history the Terrans had preserved during the 1,200 years since the fall of the League: "a few names of worlds and heroes, a ragtag of facts . . . patch[ed] into a history . . . but all that was vague and half-legendary, like all of man's history" (*CI,* pp. 18, 21).[23] Orry's history of Werel is likewise vague and half-legendary. He describes a world that "was rife with earthquakes, volcanoes, plants that walked, animals that sang, men who spoke and built cities: a catalogue of wonders" (*CI,* p. 98; note that Werelian geology, like the geology on Le Guin's other imaginary worlds, is "in the process of making itself"). Orry, who must enjoy spinning a yarn, tells Falk about the League's attempts to gain allies,

> ever since, generations before, warnings had come from beyond Hyades of a great wave of conquerers that moved from world to world, from century to century, closer toward the farflung cluster of eighty planets that so proudly called itself the League of All Worlds (*CI,* p. 98).

(Le Guin silently reduces the number of worlds in the League, and gently satirizes its pretensions to embrace the whole universe, as well as gently mocking her own use of the conventions of the Galactic Empire.) Orry goes on to explain how the Terran colony was stranded, cut off from Earth and "the Prime World Davenant" (*CI,* p. 98) (Le Guin's first explicit indication of the central place Hain-Davenant holds in the League), how it decayed for 600 years until the Terrans made an alliance with the Tevarans, discovered that they could reproduce, and founded a hybrid race:

> The new mixed stock and mixed culture of the Tevar-Alterran nation flourished in the years after the perilous Tenth Winter. The little cities grew; a mercantile culture was established on the single north-hemisphere continent. Within a few generations it was spreading to the primitive peoples of the southern continents, where the problem of keeping alive through the winter was more easily solved. Population went up; science and technology began their

exponential climb, guided and aided always by the Books of Alterra, the ship's library, the mysteries of which grew explicable as the colonists' remote descendants relearned lost knowledge. They had kept and copied those books, generation after generation, and learned the tongue they were written in—Galaktika, of course. Finally, the moon and sister-planets all explored, the sprawl of cities and the rivalries of nations controlled and balanced by the powerful Kelshak Empire in the old Northland, at the height of an age of peace and vigor the Empire had built and sent forth a light-speed ship (*CI*, p. 100).

It sounds as though Orry has been reading old Terran science fiction pulp magazines; that "history" is straight out of Wollheim's "Rise of the Galactic Empire" stage of the future—except for the "of course" that follows the word "Galaktika": with that ironic aside, and with the change from "Galactica" to "Galaktika," Le Guin mocks her own use of the hackneyed machinery of space opera.

Le Guin's attitude toward the Kelshak Empire, which is to say her attitude toward science fiction conventions, for that Empire is little more than a convention, is ambiguous. Ramarren, navigator of the Alterra, "the greatest prosteny, a mathematician-astronomer, in all Kelshy" (*CI*, p. 102), is the highest expression of that culture and, as the "good guy," has our sympathies throughout the story. The Kelshak art of mindguarding helps him foil the plans of the "bad guys," the Shing, so it must have our sympathy too. The conventions of the romance genre demand it. Thus, this description of the Kelshak code of secrecy must be sympathetic:

> The Kelshak code of secrecy concerning the Books of the Lost Colony had evolved along with a whole technique of mindguarding. The mystique of secrecy—or more precisely restraint—had grown over the long years from the rigorous control of scientific-technical knowledge exercised by the original Colonists, itself an outgrowth from the League's Law of Cultural Embargo, which forbade cultural importation to colonial planets. The whole concept of restraint was fundamental in Werelian culture by now, and the stratification of Werelian society was directed by the convention that knowledge and technique must remain under intelligent control. Such details as the True Name of the Sun were formal and symbolical, but the formalism was taken seriously—with ultimate seriousness, for in Kelshey knowledge was religion, religion knowledge. To guard the intangible holy places in the minds of men, intangible and invulnerable defenses had been devised. Unless he was in one of the Places of Silence, and addressed in a certain form by an associate of his own level, Ramarren was absolutely unable to communicate, in words or writing or mindspeech, the True Name of his world's sun (*CI*, pp. 142-43).

But stratification and Empires are not positive things elsewhere in Le Guin's work, even if restraint in some forms may be. Indeed, when she introduced a new edition of *City of Illusions* in 1978, she expressly rejects them: she says she is grateful to the book for the "chance to speak of civilization not as a negative force—restraint, constraint, repression, authority—but as an opportunity lost, an ideal of truth."[24] Is this a case where we must trust the tale, not the teller?

Was Le Guin cornered into inventing Kelshak culture in order to resolve her plot, to get rid of the Shing, who had got rid of the League, to move her future history out of the constraints of the conventions she had been using? I think so.

Although the content of the history in *City of Illusions* is a regression to pulp conventions, Le Guin's use of that content is an advance in the development of her narrative techniques. Just as the story that frames Orry's historical narrative tells of the return of the Werelians-Alterrans to their origins on Earth and of Falk's trek across North America, the story Orry tells Falk in Es Toch on Earth is also a return. A necessary moment in the process by which the Alterrans rediscover their origins on Earth is the rediscovery by an Alterran on Earth of his origins on Alterra (another instance of chiasmus in Le Guin's work). Orry's etiological tale augments the inherently teleological impulse of the narrative by contradicting it. Only by going back into the past can Falk move into the future. These paradoxes, which rise from the ways Le Guin mixes together the historical time of Hainish chronology with the narrative time in one episode in the Hainish cycle, blur the distinctions between "history" and "story."

The catalysts for this advance in Le Guin's storytelling technique might have been Dinesen and Taoism. Robert Langbaum identifies Dinesen's "most conspicuous narrative device" as a

> frequent use of tales within the tale as a kind of dialogue that advances the action. Inset tales are to be found within the stories of *The Arabian Nights;* they are to be found in Ovid, Cervantes, and the whole romance tradition—the tradition that presents the story as story rather than as an imitation of reality.[25]

In addition to writing in the romance tradition, in addition to modeling her own techniques of distancing after Dinesen's, Le Guin is a Taoist. Literary technique and philosophical orientation thus reinforce each other. Like the movement of the Tao that controls Falk's "way" when he loses it (the content of the story), the plot of *City of Illusions* is a reversion to roots and a search for origins (the technique of the story). Return is the movement of the Tao.

City of Illusions is also a springboard into the future, the last moment in the League's history before Le Guin jumped forward toward the Ekumen, a move she made when she wrote "Winter's King," the next Hainish story. From 1963 to 1965 she had written three novels, following rather conventionally the canons for inventing a science fiction future history, and had reached what was for her a dead end. She could no longer develop as an artist, could no longer develop her narrative techniques within the conventions established by Asimov in the early forties. "Winter's King" is not only a large step forward in the Hainish chronology; it is an even larger step backwards, back to the Fore-Eras of Hain.

VI

The story that generated Le Guin's League history in 1963, "The Dowry of Angyar," weaves together a Norse myth and time dilation, a science fiction convention borrowed from relativity physics. Three years later, when the forward movement of her history hit a snag, Le Guin backed off, returned to that earlier technique, and advanced her history past the snag: another circular journey in her artistic *Bildungsreise*. "Winter's King," the story that creates the Ekumen, is, like "The Dowry of Angyar," a weaving together of myth and time dilation, but this time the myth is mediated to Le Guin through a science, her father's anthropology. The dialectical interplay between literary convention and myth that generated her future history now reaches a higher, more complex level with the integration of anthropology's mythic substratum. Le Guin's stories shift from science *fiction* to *science* fiction, while her history simultaneously reaches back to its mythic beginning and forward to its mythic end: the *aitia* of Hain and the *telos* of the Ekumen.

Set six centuries after the Age of the Enemy ("WK," p. 77), "Winter's King" carries the Hainish chronology as far forward as Le Guin would take it; "the Ekumen of Known Worlds" ("WK," p. 74), mentioned now for the first time, is the utopian ideal at the end of her future history.[26] But Le Guin's Ekumen, a teleological myth, is a transformation of her father's etiological myth, her science fictional version of the *Oikoumenê* he proposed in 1945. Just as A.L. Kroeber hypothesized that Eurasian cultures are "an historic culture aggregate" with a single origin, Le Guin in "Winter's King" reveals for the first time in her future history that Hain is the single origin of the Ekumenical worlds, a fictional-historical culture aggregate. Interestingly enough, Kroeber's *idea* becomes the beginning of Le Guin's history, while the *name* of the idea becomes the end; in source and significance they are one. With "Winter's King" Le Guin joins beginning and end and mocks death. Alcmaeon would grasp her method instantly.

Le Guin makes her revelation in the form of a dialogue between King Argaven XVII of Karhide on the planet Winter, and Mr. Mobile Axt, Ambassador Plenipotentiary from the Ekumen to Winter:

> "Once you said something, Lord Axt, which seemed to imply that all men on all worlds are blood kin. Did I mistake your meaning?"
>
> "Well, as far as we know, which is a tiny bit of dusty space under the rafters of the Universe, all the men we've run into are in fact men. But the kinship goes back some five hundred and fifty thousand years, to the Fore-Eras of Hain. The ancient Hainish settled a hundred worlds."
>
> Argaven laughed, delighted. "My Harge dynasty has ruled Karhide for seven hundred years now. We call the times before that 'ancient.'"

"So we call the Age of the Enemy 'ancient,' and that was less than six hundred years ago. Time stretches and shrinks; changes with the eye, with the age, with the star; does all except reverse itself—or repeat."

"The Powers of the Ekumen dream, then, of restoring that truly ancient empire of Hain; of regathering all the worlds of men, the lost worlds?"

Axt nodded, chewing bread-apple. "Of weaving some harmony among them, at least. Life loves to know itself, out to its farthest limits. To embrace complexity is its delight. All these worlds and the various forms and ways of the minds and lives on them: together they would make a really splendid harmony."

"No harmony endures," said the young king.

"None has ever been achieved," said the Plenipotentiary. "The pleasure is in trying." He drained his tankard, wiped his fingers on the woven-grass napkin.

"That was my pleasure as king," said Argaven. "It is over" ("WK," p. 77).

Like the conversation between Jakob and Rolery in *Planet of Exile,* this dialogue demonstrates again the micro-macrocosm analogies between affairs of one part of the Ekumen and the affairs of the whole; it is another moment in the creative hermeneutic circle that is the process of Le Guin's invention-discovery of her future history. The Ekumen understands that "the equilibrium of the Whole rests in all its parts" ("WK," p. 76) and is therefore interested in Argaven because his way is its Way. Moreover, this scene, like the scene between Rolery and Jakob, is an instance of communication between aliens who are distant kin. Similarity and difference must both be present for human relations like love, and social relations like ethics, to be possible. Finally, Argaven and Axt are performing what may be the oldest social act: eating together. Their common meal of bread-apple and ale binds them into a unit.

Bread-apple in an arctic climate like Winter's seems an anomaly, because it calls to mind breadfruit. Breadfruit is a plant native to the tropics on Earth, where we might also find "woven-grass napkins." Breadfruit

> has been cultivated in the Malay Archipelago (where the species is held to be indigenous) since remote antiquity...[and] spread throughout the tropical South Pacific in prehistoric times.[27]

a dispersion in space and time not unlike the dispersion of the Hainish, who may be related (if not by name, then on a level before and beyond all naming) to Hainuwele, also indigenous to the Malay Archipelago:

> In a myth from Ceram (Molucca Islands), a beautiful girl, Hainuwele, has grown up out of a coconut plant. After providing the community with their necessities and luxuries, she is killed and her body cut into several pieces, which are thrown over the island. From each part of her body a coconut tree grows. It is only after the death of Hainuwele that mankind becomes sexual; that is, the murder of Hainuwele enables mankind to have some determination in the process of bringing new life into the world.[28]

The murder, dismemberment, and dispersion of Hainuwele's body is what Joseph Campbell calls a "mythological event...a single, unique, and critical moment of definitive precipitation at the close of the paradisal age and opening of the present."[29] In other words, a mythological event creates history, and not just any mythological event, but a murder. Death, usually in the form of murder, is the event that sets in motion historical time in Le Guin's fictional worlds; death is the ultimate beginning in her fiction.

Le Guin is not by any means elaborating a detailed account of the Hainish dispersion in "Winter's King"; she is only pointing to it, as it were, glancing back to the origins of the history she had been writing in her first three novels. She is announcing a discovery without publishing a full account of her exploration of that discovery. Such an exploration may not have been necessary, or may not have been possible as she was writing "Winter's King." The purpose of the myth of Hain is to show that all humans are related by virtue of their common origin, and that they have enough in common with each other to form an Ekumen. A.L. Kroeber's scientific hypothesis—that the ecumenical culture of the Eurasian landmass spread out from Mesopotamia, "that first hearth of all higher civilization"—had to include evidence so that his theory could be verified or refuted. But Le Guin's fictional hypothesis—that all known human cultures in our corner of the galaxy spread out from Hain, one of the "prime worlds of the Ekumen, the hearth-worlds of our race" (*LHD*, p. 280)—need not be verified or refuted. It is a contract myth that makes the Ekumen possible and accounts for the origin of her future history. Le Guin extracts the mythic core from her father's scientific theory and makes it the core of her science fiction, where it becomes a historical "fact," confirmed when Rolery gives birth to Jakob's child and when any other two aliens rediscover their kinship.

The relation between fact and myth and storytelling, or, more precisely, the relationship between linear historical time and circular mythic time and narrative time, is Le Guin's major concern in "Winter's King," which opens with these words:

> When whirlpools appear in the onward run of time and history seems to swirl around a snag, as in the curious matter of the Succession of Karhide, then pictures come in handy: snapshots, which may be taken up and matched to compare the young king to the old king, the father to the son, and which may also be rearranged and shuffled until the years run straight ("WK," p. 66).

The narrator is a historian, telling a familiar story, the succession of kings. But this is science-fictional history, and time-dilation makes it possible for King Argaven to succeed his son, who had succeeded him. When we first read the phrase "the young king to the old king, the father to the son," it appears as though Le Guin is using the familiar rhetorical device chiasmus; when we reread it after finishing the story, however, we realize that it is not chiasmus, but parallelism. Just as Le Guin's narrative techniques make it possible to synthesize crossed and parallel lines, bending them into a figure-eight, they also make possible her synthesis of linear and circular time, and thus foreshadow her synthesis of sequency and simultaneity in *The Dispossessed.*

"Winter's King" is a history in two senses. One is the familiar sense, and the other is history as *historia,* Medieval Latin for a row of windows with pictures on them that tell a story, pictures "which may be rearranged and shuffled till the years run straight." Each one of the nine "snapshots" that make up the narrative episodes in "Winter's King" (which, Le Guin told an interviewer, were taken by a photographer named "Lit'ry Device"),[30] each one of those nine putative historical documents that Le Guin arranges in chronological order, advances the narrative toward the end of the story. But from the point of view of those who welcome Argaven back to Winter at the end of the story, they carry them into the past. Argaven is caught in a whirlpool of time, as if Le Guin had poured history, myth, and narrative into a container and stirred them together. She has made "those events, which in real or imagined History move on in a *strait* Line, assume to our Understandings a *circular* motion—the snake with it's tail in it's Mouth," as Coleridge says.

To make that synthesis, Le Guin uses techniques she could have picked up from Dinesen. In Dineson's tales, says Robert Langbaum,

> the past appears not in sequence but through tales which advance the present situation, and we do not let go of one understood episode to move on to another but insert as it were the later episodes into the earlier in order to understand them . . . . [Dinesen's] method is a way of penetrating in depth. It is a way of penetrating, through a structure such as Kierkegaard often uses in his philosophical writing, a structure like that of Chinese boxes arranged one inside the other, to the heart of life.[31]

Chinese boxes are not unlike the whirlpool in the onward run of time in "Winter's King," nor are they unlike the sock turned inside out that Argaven experiences on Ollul:

> He learned a great deal. He had already learned in his first few days on Ollul that the Earth was, here, called Winter, and Ollul was the Earth: one of those facts which turn the universe inside out like a sock ("WK," p. 81).

Nor are Chinese boxes unlike the uroboros of time in "Winter's King," the unification of beginning and end, etiology and teleology, in the ecumenical contract-creation myth.

In "Winter's King" Le Guin binds together a device from popular fiction (science-fictional time-dilation) and a narrative technique from elite fiction (Dinesen's methods) to make it possible for King Argaven to "escape from [his] own time, in which [he has] become an instrument in evil" ("WK," p. 78): there is a moral purpose behind the manipulation of time in this story. Argaven leaves Winter, spends twelve years in the "Clearinghouse of the Ekumen for the West Worlds" on Ollul, twenty-four light years from Winter—where he knows himself "a barbarian" (i.e., a *barbaros* from outside the *oikoumenê*)—in order to learn "the nature and history of a kingdom that was a million years old," so that he can return to Winter to take command of a rebellion against his son King Emran, who is old enough to be his father ("WK," pp. 81ff.). His experience contradicts Axt's remark that "despite the tricks played by instantaneous inter-stellar communication and just-sub-lightspeed interstellar travel, time . . . does not reverse itself; nor is death mocked" ("WK," p. 66). Argaven does indeed mock death, and he does it by virtue of Le Guin's narrative techniques that connect beginning and end.

Interstellar travel and interstellar communication are not historical facts; they are literary conventions. The tricks played in this story (and there are a lot of them) are literary tricks with historical time, and they carry the historical time of Le Guin's League saga into the mythic time at the beginning and end of her Hainish cycle. She thus frees herself to speak in her own voice, unhampered by the tradition Asimov established in the early forties. She had returned to the forties, to her father's *Oikoumenê* and to creation myths like the myth of Hainuwele, to advance beyond the tired conventions of science fictional future histories that she could use rather than be used by.

Conversely, she moved beyond using myth as she had done in "The Dowry of Angyar," and allowed herself "to be used by myths," as she puts it, "to find the native symbology of [her] own creative unconscious."[32] When she recalled her father's *Oikoumenê* in 1966, as she was writing "Winter's King" and *A Wizard of Earthsea,* just before she began *The Left Hand of Darkness,* she found that native symbology, and she found it by telling a story: technique as discovery. When she used the storytelling techniques of Dinesen and science fiction, when she used the photographs taken by Lit'ry Device to penetrate to the heart of life, to the bottom of the whirlpool of time, she discovered death. The union of life and death, beyond all rational analysis and explanation, communicable only through myth, is the most potent symbol native to Le Guin's creative unconscious.

At the heart of "Winter's King" we find the shadow of a "mythological event," a creation myth similar to the creation myths that are at the center of *A Wizard of Earthsea* and *The Left Hand of Darkness.* The *Creation of Ea* in Earthsea is probably an allusion to Ea in the Mesopotamian creation myth, and "An Orgota Creation Myth" is clearly indebted to the Norse creation myth. Like Kroeber's *Oikoumenê,* like Le Guin's "Ekumen of the Known Worlds," the Ceram, Mesopotamian, and Norse creation myths have a common origin.

All three of them "embody the sacrificial motif as the basis of the cosmos"; in each of them, says Charles Long,

> the sacrificial victim is a residue of great power.... The killing or sacrifice of these powerful beings affects a redistribution of power. Instead of the power residing in one being, it now flows into every part of the universe. It is made accessible to all beings. The parts of the sacrificed beings become the stable and life-giving sources of the cosmos. But sacrifice is also the coming of death. *Life and death thus inhere in the same act.* Without the distribution of sacred power no cultural life is possible, but the generalizing of the power is accomplished in death.[33]

Whenever Le Guin makes a journey into her heart of darkness, whenever she lets her "imagination go groping around in...the dark"—her way of describing the prelude to writing a story—she discovers there life and death indistinguishably united into a whole that contains endless creative possibilities. She discovers the life-giving sources of her imaginary countries, worlds, even the whole cosmos of her art. "Winter's King" mocks death; on a much more profound level, though, every story Le Guin tells mocks death. By absorbing death into her fiction, by uniting death and creativity, Le Guin herself mocks death whenever she tells a story. The power to tell her stories comes from death.[34]

Rather like his creator who returns from encounters with death to weave a harmony by telling a story, King Argaven XVII comes back from the dead: he goes home again to try once more to gather into a harmony the factions in Karhide and to bind back together Winter and the Ekumen. Although he is greeted with a cliche turned inside out—"The King is dead, long live the King" ("WK," p. 87)—he does not begin his job as King. He leaves the symbol of Kingship on his dead son's finger and begins his reign as "Winter's king" ("WK," p. 87), the lower case "k" indicating that he has broken the endless cycle of madness and suicide, of Emran-Argaven-Emran-Argaven, and will bring Karhide out of the realm of eternal return into the realm of history. His trip to Ollul and his encounter with the Ekumen is thus a "mythological event" for Karhide. Before he could carry out his Ekumenical mission, he had to escape from his own time, enter the realm of myth, and return.

Before Le Guin could write *The Left Hand of Darkness* she likewise had to enter the realm of myth. The Fore-Eras of Hain and the Ekumen exist prior to "once upon a time" and after "they lived happily ever after"; as myths they are outside history and hence outside the narrative time of Le Guin's Hainish cycle. (This is not to say, however, that they do not exercise a profound influence on the shape of the narrative time and the history in the cycle.) Therefore, when Le Guin wrote the next piece of her future history, she did not extend the "strait Line" of time into the future, but reversed chronology. She tells us in "Winter's King" that "Horden Island, off the south coast of Karhide, was given as a freehold to the Ekumen by the Kingdom of Karhide during the reign of Argaven XV" ("WK," p. 83). *The Left Hand of Darkness,* which Le Guin says is set "several generations" before "Winter's King," tells the history behind the story of Argaven XV's gift. After that, every Hainish story Le Guin tells is set progressively farther in the past; each one explores a beginning that is older than the previous one.

VII

History usually entails chronological narration, so in one sense, when Le Guin reversed her straightforward exploration of Hainish history as she wrote *The Left Hand of Darkness,* she stopped writing history. She moved on from the kind of history embedded in the Asimov-Wollheim tradition, the ethnocentric kind that projects the arrow of time onward and upward to the stars. Having absorbed anthropology and anthropological myth into the internal dialectic impelling her future history forward, she turned her gaze around 180°, for anthropology is a science that attempts to understand our own culture by searching for its origins and its ecological relations with other cultures. Rather than projecting the male-dominated, techno-bureaucratic way of twentieth-century Western culture, as Asimov's science fiction does, the Hainish history Le Guin wrote after "Winter's King" tries to understand any present moment, and the future immanent in that moment—the immanent teleology of Romantic thought and imagination—in terms of its roots in the past. Like the Ekumen, Le Guin "considers beginnings to be extremely important" (*LHD,* p. 245); she therefore inserts a story about beginnings, "An Orgota Creation Myth," at the climax of the story that tells of the beginning of Gethen's relationship with the Ekumen.

That story, *The Left Hand of Darkness,* is, like "Winter's King," a set of documents, which comes to us as a historical document from the "Archives of Hain": the transcript of Genly Ai's "report" of his successful mission as the first Ekumenical Mobile on Gethen. Because Ai, a black Terran about thirty years old, was taught as a child that "Truth is a matter of the imagination" (*LHD,* p. 7), he makes his report in the form of a "story." Interpolated into the narrative he composes five years after Estraven's death are several documents: a "hearth-tale" from the "archives of the College of Historians in Erhenrang" (*LHD,* p. 26), a "story" and a "tale" he recorded in Gorinhering after his trek across the Ice (*LHD,* pp. 46, 120), four extracts from Estraven's journal, ethnological field notes made forty years earlier (*LHD,* p. 89), an extract from "the Yomesh Canon," 900 years old (*LHD,* p. 155), and a creation myth whose "origins....are prehistorical" (*LHD,* p. 224). Documentary headnotes and footnotes (*LHD,* pp. 15, 27, 121, 157, 212) and an appendix, "The Gethenian

Calendar and Clock" (*LHD,* pp. 284-86), give his report an aura of factual accuracy. None of these facts, he assures us, "are false, and it is all one story" (*LHD,* p. 7).

Since Ai has been trained by the Ekumen, it is only fitting that he should use the same methods to make a report (*rapport* in French) that the Ekumen uses to gather 83 worlds and 3,000 anthrotypic peoples into a harmony. The Ekumen knows that an individual's perception of reality is constituted and conditioned by the configurations and patterns of values in his native culture, and that truths are relative; similarly, Ai apparently knows (his creator surely does) that the truths yielded by any one of the narrative types he has collected will be partial and relative, because meaning is genre-bound: "at moments the facts seem to alter with an altered voice" (*LHD,* p. 7). To discover Truth, therefore, he must use his imagination to create a vision of the whole. So he weaves together into one story a broad range of narrative types: autobiography, documentary report, story, tale, field notes, journal entries, priestly sayings, and myth. Like the worlds that compose the Ekumen, the parts of Ai's story are interconnected by complex ecological relationships. In the same way that Le Guin's Ekumen (anarchism) replaces the Galactic Empire (imperialism) in her version of the cosmogony and cosmology of the future, her cooperative narrative types replace imperial authorial omniscience. Since "ecumenical" and "ecological" have a common root word (Greek *oikos,* house), we could call *The Left Hand of Darkness* a "house-tale," an ecological novel. Like the human cultures in the Ekumen which all come from a single hearth-world, the narrative types Ai assembles may all derive from a single "hearth-tale": "story" is an aphetic form of "history." "Story" means many different things, not the least important of which are "a report of facts" and "a lie.' When Ai says it is "all one story," he is being ecumenical; Truth comes out of the report *as* story, an imaginative rapport of complementary facts and lies, truths and illusions, reality and fantasy.

When we ask *why* Ai should make his report in the form of a story, we are on the way toward the heart of the novel. "The story," says a story-telling character in one of Dinesen's tales,

> the story only has authority to answer the cry of heart of each of its characters, that cry of heart of each of them: *"Who am I?"*[35]

And we can also recall Hannah Arendt:

> *who* somebody is or was we can only know by knowing the story of which he is himself the hero...everything else we know of him tells us only *what* he is or was.[36]

Thus, the only way Ai, whose name is "a cry of pain" (*LHD*, p. 218), can answer the "cry of heart . . . '*Who am I?*' " is by telling his own story. He creates himself, an "I," by telling the history of his rapport with Estraven, a "Thou." As Robert Langbaum says of Dinesen,

> you don't get at the truth about the world or yourself by going straight to it. You get at it by seeming to move away to an esthetic distance. You get at it through artifice and tradition— by assimilating your particular event to a recurring pattern, your particular self to an archetype. Readers of Yeats will be reminded of his evolution from the nineteenth-century doctrine of sincerity to the twentieth-century doctrine of the mask.[37]

Ai gets at the Truth about himself and his world by imagination, by making-a-report-telling-a-story that recounts his relationship with an archetype, Estraven the androgyne. He assimilates Estraven's story—the journal entries— into his own story, and assimilates the particular events of his mission to a recurring narrative pattern, the romance. The result of his rapport with Estraven is his report of who he is, his story, history.

Like her hero Ai, Le Guin also gets at the Truth about her world and her self by imagination and artifice, by moving away from herself to an aesthetic distance. Ai, a black Terran male, is a Yeatsian antithetical mask for the "I" of a white American female writing a novel in the late sixties. While Betty Friedan and Kate Millet were using nonfiction in those years to answer the question "Who am I?" Le Guin was answering the question by writing a science fiction novel addressed to a male audience. She defines herself as a woman, an "I," by communicating with a collective "Thou," the predominantly male readers of science fiction. Having learned on his quest with Estraven that an "I," Ai himself, can survive and exist *only* in a cooperative relationship with a "Thou," Ai assimilates Estraven's language, his journal entries, into his own when he makes his report; similarly, Le Guin assimilates her particular patterns, her particular self, to an archetype by telling a story with what Adrienne Rich calls "the oppressor's language."[38] Working in a tradition dominated by males, Le Guin creates a rapport between her own story and her readers by giving them "a man . . . to work with and sort of be changed with."[39] Like the relationship between Ai and Estraven, like the relationship between Ai's narrative and Estraven's journal entries, Le Guin's relationship with her readers is an eristic dialectic. Ai creates a synthesis, a whole self, only through the *aufheben* that reconciles the contradictions between himself with Estraven. Le Guin creates a novel and herself as a woman novelist by absorbing, negating, and transcending the contradictions between herself and the language available to her. The result is a synthesis, a new language, the whole novel itself, a "metaphor for what [her] language has no words for as yet, [an] experiment in imagination."[40] Like *A Wizard of Earthsea,* the novel that Le Guin wrote immediately before *The Left Hand of Darkness, The Left Hand of Darkness* is a story about death and coming of age. Just as Le Guin herself came of age when she was about thirty, her thirty year-old hero Ai comes of age after Estraven's death. By telling that story Le Guin herself came of age as a novelist. Before Friedan, Millet, and Le Guin wrote their books, they knew *what* they were; afterwards, they knew *who*. Instead of extrapolating past history into the future, instead of retelling Asimov's cosmogony of the future, Le Guin now creates her own story, her Hainish history, herstory.

That story is a quest for origins, an attempt to recover a creative potential long obscured by the sediment of custom and the historical accretions of convention—convention both in the sense of cultural patterns internalized in Ai and Estraven that keep them from understanding one another, and also in the sense of literary tradition, specifically the Galactic Empire and all it implies. *The Left Hand of Darkness* is a sophisticated elaboration of the quest in *Rocannon's World,* the search for integration and harmony in a mythic image; like *Planet of Exile* it is an interracial love story; and it is a complex development of the narrative techniques Le Guin had tried out in *City of Illusions* and "Winter's King," two stories which go forward by returning to and absorbing the past. What makes *The Left Hand of Darkness* a real advance is its synthesis of these strains: it presents Estraven's and Ai's adventure; it depicts the process by which they come to trust and love each other, and at the same time it is the process *and* result of Ai's quest to find a language that will enable him to comprehend his experiences on Gethen and thus make his report to the Stabile on Ollul. The diagram on the next page is designed to illustrate these quests.

The twenty chapters of the novel are separated into three groups, which may be understood as three "voices": ten chapters, seven in the left-hand column and three in the center column below the creation myth, are Ai's first-person narrative; the four chapters in the right-hand column are the extracts Ai took from Estraven's journals before he returned them to Estraven's parent; and the remaining six chapters in the middle column are (with the exception of Ong Tot Oppong's field notes) Gethenian texts Ai collected after Estraven's death. Ai's and Estraven's columns/voices/languages are separated at the top of the diagram to indicate the alienation and betrayal Ai feels when he completely misunderstands Estraven's motives and language (in the broadest sense of the word) at the beginning of the novel, and also to represent the geographical distance that separates them after Estraven goes into exile and Ai leaves Erhenrang for the Otherhord Fastness and Gorinhering. In Mishnory, notwithstanding their nearness in space, Ai and Estraven are as far apart as ever, but when Estraven rescues Ai from Pulefen Farm, Ai begins to comprehend Estraven, so their columns approach each other and then finally unite. The mindspeech they use on the Gobrin Ice is one metaphor for the common language they have found as they share the ordeal of a winter journey.

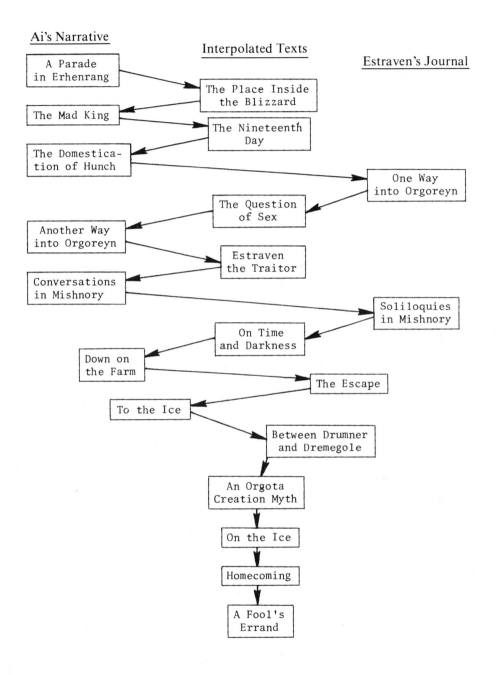

Ai's Narrative

Interpolated Texts

Estraven's Journal

A Parade
in Erhenrang

The Place Inside
the Blizzard

The Mad King

The Nineteenth
Day

The Domestica-
tion of Hunch

One Way
into Orgoreyn

The Question
of Sex

Another Way
into Orgoreyn

Estraven
the Traitor

Conversations
in Mishnory

Soliloquies
in Mishnory

On Time
and Darkness

Down on
the Farm

The Escape

To the Ice

Between Drumner
and Dremegole

An Orgota
Creation Myth

On the Ice

Homecoming

A Fool's
Errand

Another merging of their voices occurs when they arrive in Kurkurast Domain after coming off the Ice:

> Estraven spoke, a barely audible whisper. "We ask the hospitality of the Domain."
> Noise, buzz, confusion, alarm, welcome.
> "We came over the Gobrin Ice."
> More noise, more voices, questions; they crowded in on us.
> "Will you look to my friend?"
> I thought I had said it, but Estraven had (*LHD,* p. 257).

The mindspeech and confusion of voices are localized signs of the common language Ai shared with Estraven before he was killed. In the five years between Estraven's death and Ai's report to his superior, he searches for a language that will give him a deeper understanding of who Estraven was and why he acted as he did. He finds that language in the Gethenian myths and legends. Because Ai's Terran-Ekumenical language evolved on worlds alien to Gethenian realities, it is simply inadequate to comprehend the Gethenians, but Gethenian stories, like stories everywhere, are a metalanguage that can carry meaning across linguistic and cultural barriers, and presumably across biological and psychological ones as well. Consciously or unconsciously, Le Guin understands a principle enunciated by Lévi-Strauss:

> Whatever our ignorance of the language and the culture of the people where it originated, a myth is still felt as a myth by any reader in the world. Its substance does not lie in its style, its original music, or its syntax, but in the *story* which it tells. Myth is language, functioning on an especially high level where meaning succeeds practically at "taking off" from the linguistic ground on which it keeps on rolling.[41]

The middle column of the diagram, then, represents the mediation of the dialectical process by which Ai and Estraven come together. The stories are a language Ai has discovered that enables him at once to understand who Estraven was and to communicate that understanding to the Stabile on Ollul. The Gethenian tales Ai interpolates in his narrative become progressively older until they leave history altogether: the origins of the Orgota creation myth are prehistorical. This is the narrative pattern of *Rocannon's World* and *City of Illusions* writ large. Just as Rocannon returns to mythic sources before he can complete his mission, and just as Falk does not discover who he is until he returns to his origins via Orry's storytelling, Ai completes his mission and understands Estraven and himself only after he returns to the mythic and prehistorical origins of Gethenian storytelling. The goal of his quest is the recovery of a primal beginning; to go forward, he has to go backward. Le Guin seems to be proposing, implicitly, that this is the way to redeem history also: if, as Estraven says, the nations of Gethen have taken a dangerous historical direction, then the way to turn them away from their ultimately self-destructive course is to return to the beginning, tap the mythic sources of creativity, and inject into history a new purpose and goal.

This is in a sense what Le Guin herself was doing as she wrote *The Left Hand of Darkness*. By returning to mythic sources, she was able to direct her science fictional future history in a new direction. The two remaining major works in Le Guin's Hainish future history, *The Word for World is Forest* and *The Dispossessed,* are elaborations of the two basic myths in *The Left Hand of Darkness*. The creation myth that turns on a murder and the fall into mortality and history becomes the core of the clash between Athsheans and Terrans in *The Word for World is Forest,* and the teleological myth of the Ekumen is brought down to earth, as it were, and given historical form when Le Guin concretizes its anarchism and mystical politics, demystified, in the utopian society on Anarres in *The Dispossessed.*

VIII

The Word for World is Forest is set about twenty-five centuries before *The Left Hand of Darkness,* and about three centuries before the events in *Rocannon's World;* it deals with the impact of a Terran militaristic-colonialistic logging operation on the planet Athshe, 27 light years from Earth, and with the impact on that operation of the founding of the League of Worlds. Of all the novels in Le Guin's Hainish future history, it is the most engaged with contemporary history. References to the wars in Vietnam and Southeast Asia are far from subtle. Colonel Dongh remembers that series of wars and their lessons:

> There's three million of these aliens all scattered out all over every damned island, all covered with trees and undergrowth, no cities, no vital network, no centralised control. You can't disable a guerilla type structure with bombs, it's been proved, in fact my own part of the world where I was born proved it for almost thirty years fighting off major super-powers one after the other in the twentieth century (*WWF,* p. 91).

And in a passage written within a year after the Tet Offensive and the atrocity at My Lai 4, Le Guin enters Captain Davidson's consciousness to describe his retaliatory raid after Selver's attack on Smith Camp:

> Davidson had located the creechie town some weeks ago, and had saved up the treat for his men. He could have done it single-handed, but it was better this way. You got the sense of comradeship, of a real bond among men. They just walked into the place in broad open daylight, and coated all the creechies caught above-ground with firejelly and burned them, then poured kerosene over the warren-roofs and roasted the rest. Those that tried to get out got jellied; that was the artistic part, waiting at the rat-holes for the little rats to come out, letting them think they'd made it, and then just frying them from the feet up so they made torches. The green fur sizzled like crazy (*WWF,* p. 69).

Yet even as *The Word for World is Forest* is the Hainish novel most engaged with contemporary history, it is also in some ways the most mythical. Before the Terran soldiers and loggers arrive, the Athsheans live in "two realities, considered...as equal, the dream-time and the world-time" (*WWF*, p. 79). They "balance [their] sanity not on the razor's edge of reason but on the double support, the fine balance, of reason and dream" (*WWF*, p. 76). From the perspective of the Terrans, who have separated consciousness from the unconscious, reality from dream, inside from outside, who conceive history as linear progress, and who consider their environment as an object to be exploited, the Athsheans inhabit a timeless and mythic world, the *illud tempus* Eliade speaks of. Athshean dream-time, in fact, appears to be a science fictional version of the Australian Aboriginal Dreamtime,

> the days when creative acts were performed by the first ancestors of men, or by the spirits and heroes who established the pattern of Nature and Life and thereby created man's environment. "Dreaming" is a translation of the Aboriginal term commonly used, but a better term is Eternal Dreamtime. It had its beginning when the world was young and unformed, but it was a process as well as a period. It never ceased. Time entered into the concept...not as a period or even a succession of periods, but as an ever-present "now" that eternally perpetuated the Dreamtime....the Dreamtime was...the time of birth of the world, when man, animal, and spirit worked together and in harmony....[42]

Athsheans slip in and out of their dream-time several times a day, and this biological rhythm acts rather like a ritual that keeps them in a state of Eternal Dreamtime, in a time when the world is perpetually being born, a time of peace and harmony. Davidson knows that the Athsheans "didn't fight, didn't kill, didn't have wars" (*WWF*, p. 39), and Lyubov, who knows them better, realizes that "their unaggressiveness ran so deep in them, right through their culture and society and on down into their subconscious, their 'dream time,' and perhaps into their very physiology" (*WWF*, p. 72). When the Hainishman Lepennon hears of the Athshean way of life, he is excited:

> "Wonderful," Lepennon said, and his white skin paled further with pure excitement. "A human society with an effective war-barrier! What's the cost Dr. Lyubov?"
> "I'm not sure, Mr. Lepennon. Perhaps change. They're a static, stable, uniform society. They have no history. Perfectly integrated and wholly unprogressive. You might say that like the forest they live in, they've attained a climax state" (*WWF*, p. 58).

What the Terrans bring them is progress, change, and history, and they bring them in the form of defoliation and murder.

Just as murder is the "mythological event" that initiates history in the myth of Hainuwele, the Norse creation myth, and the Orgota creation myth, Davidson's rape and murder of Selver's wife brings murder into the world-time of the Athsheans, and thus into their dream-time. Talking with Selver after the raid on Smith Camp, Coro Mena recognizes that they live in "a new time for the world" (*WWF*, p. 52). Selver's act has made him a god, who, like the heroes of Aboriginal Dreamtime, establishes a new pattern of Nature and Life on Athshe. In one sense, then, *The Word for World is Forest* is a creation myth, a new beginning for the Athsheans. Lyubov, Davidson, and Selver will probably become, parallel to the ancestors of Australian Aboriginies, men who change into trees, totems of clans or tribes or individuals on Athshe, men who establish laws and patterns of behavior and who will continue to be as alive in the future as they were when they performed their original deeds. "Maybe after I die," says Selver at the end of the story, "people will be as they were before I was born, and before you [Lepennon and the other "yumens"] came. But I do not think they will" (*WWF*, p. 108). They have learned how to murder and have fallen from *illud tempus* into history.

Complementing this "mythological event" is another event in *The Word for World is Forest* that marks a turn and a new beginning in the history of the worlds seeded by the Hainish: the invention of the ansible and the consequent formation of the League of Worlds. If on the one hand there are Davidsons at large raping, killing, and burning, on the other hand the creation of the League at least makes them answerable for their actions. Thus the "Dreaming" that brings murder to Athshe is balanced with the creation of a society, which is to say the institution of a language-communication system that can connect humans in a network of ethical relationships, making them morally responsible. When the Terrans left Earth to establish the logging operation on Athshe, they could count on a time-gap between worlds that allowed anyone to commit any act and never answer for it in his lifetime. But ansible communication (answerable communication) changes all that. Commander Yung of the *Shackleton* explains to the Terrans as he leaves an ansible with them that "instantaneous transmission of a message over any distance ... is as important to us as an interstellar species as speech itself was to us earlier in our evolution. It'll have the same effect: to make society possible" (*WWF*, p. 60). Thus "there is no longer any excuse for acting on outdated orders; for ignorance; for irresponsible autonomy" (*WWF*, p. 61). Although this worries the military, it means hope to people like Lyubov:

> Reports back home meant something, now that this ansible, this *machina ex machina,* functioned to prevent all the comfortable old colonial autonomy, and make you answerable within your own lifetime for what you did. There was no more 54-year margin for error. Policy was no longer static. A decision by the League of Worlds might now lead overnight to the colony's being limited to one Land, or forbidden to cut trees, or encouraged to kill natives—no telling. How the League worked and what sort of policies it was developing could not yet be guessed from the flat directives of the Administration. Dongh was worried by these multiple-choice futures, but Lyubov enjoyed them. In diversity is life and where there's life there's hope (*WWF*, p. 80).

The ansible and the formation of the League are a contract myth that accounts for the society and government in the Asimovian future history Le Guin had written in the first three Hainish novels. Irresponsible autonomy and the anarchic exploitation of natural and human resources may make it necessary, but Le Guin does not give it her final assent. The true anarchy of the Athsheans before the coming of the Terrans is closer to her ideal, as is apparent in this exchange between Selver and Yung near the end of the story:

> "You decide matters all at once, your people," [Selver] said, [...] between statement and question.
> "How do you mean?" The Commander looked wary.
> "Well, you say that none of you shall cut the trees of Athshe: and all of you stop. And yet you live in many places. Now if a headwoman in Karach gave an order, it would not be obeyed by the people of the next village, and surely not by all the people in the world at once...."
> "No, you haven't one government over all. But we do—now—and I assure you its orders are obeyed. By all of us at once. But, as a matter of fact, it seems to me from the story we've been told by the colonists here, that when *you* gave an order, Selver, it was obeyed by everybody on every island here at once. How did you manage that?"
> "At that time I was a god," Selver said, expressionless (*WWF*, p. 106).

The Word for World is Forest thus contains two etiological contract myths, one centered on a god from the forest and the other on a god from the machine (even if Lyubov calls it a *machina ex machina,* the ansible still functions as a *deus ex machina,* albeit too late to produce a happy ending, and thus less blatantly than it does in *Rocannon's World*). The next major piece of Le Guin's future history goes yet further into the past to explore the beginnings behind these beginnings. The anarchist utopian society on Annarres has as its mythic core the conception of an ahistorical and homeostatic world that existed in *illud tempus,* but that society, unlike the fundamentally mythic society on prelapsarian Athshe, is elaborated and embodied more in political and economic terms than in biological, psychological, and anthropological terms, is more realistic in that it is peopled with humans like ourselves rather than "little green men" (Le Guin's original title for *The Word for World is Forest*), and is a goal or *telos* of history rather than a source or *aitia* in a prehistory as it is on Athshe. The other beginning in *The Dispossessed* is of course Shevek's General Temporal Theory. Just as Le Guin's utopian anarchism marries source and goal in history, Shevek's theory marries sequency and simultaneity—a scientific way of synthesizing what the Athsheans synthesize with their world-time and dream-time—and makes possible the invention of the ansible, the creation of the League of Worlds, and finally the creation of the Ekumen, the ultimate *telos* of Le Guin's whole future history and one mythic model for the anarchist society in which Shevek grows up, which itself is the *telos* of the history of the development of Le Guin's Hainish future history.[43]

IX

The Dispossessed is an anachronism. By the early 1970s a long series of "new maps of hell" had displaced the positive utopia in the system of literary genres; many people considered the utopian genre all but dead.[44] We could imagine a scene in a publisher's office between a reader of Le Guin's manuscript and Le Guin herself, and the reader might have said to her what the Terran Ambassador Keng says to Shevek in *The Dispossessed:*

> You are like somebody from our own past, the old idealists, the visionaries of freedom; and yet I don't understand you, as if you were trying to tell me of future things; and yet, as you say, you are here, now! (*TD,* p. 308).

Just so: the substance of Le Guin's "ambiguous utopia" is neither an outdated and naive vision of social perfection from a more innocent age, nor is it a blueprint for a society set in the never-never land of the far future. *The Dispossessed* is about the present, the "here, now," and it argues that the present is made real only when one has a full consciousness of the past (memory and history) and the future (intention, hope, and promise). Thus Le Guin could say to the publisher's reader what Shevek says to Keng:

> You don't understand what time is [...]. You say the past is gone, the future is not real, there is no change, no hope. You think Anarres is a future that cannot be reached, as your past cannot be changed. So there is nothing but the present, this Urras, the rich, real, stable present, the moment now. And you think that is something which can be possessed! You envy it a little. You think it's something you would like to have. But it is not real, you know. It is not stable, not solid—nothing is. Things change, change. You cannot have anything.... And least of all can you have the present, unless you accept with it the past and the future. Not only the past but also the future, not only the future but also the past! Because they are real: only their reality makes the present real (*TD,* pp. 307-8).

The Dispossessed is thus an anachronism about chronism. With a hero who studies "chronosophy"[45] and who conceives of the present as a chiasmus of the past and future—"not only the past but also the future, not only the future but also the past"—and with a chiasmatic narrative structure that connects beginning and end—the first chapter, "Anarres - Urras," the voyage out, and the last chapter, "Urras - Anarres," the return, complete a circle as Anarres-Urras, Urras-Anarres—*The Dispossessed* is a marriage of the etiological and teleological impulses present in the previous stories and novels in Le Guin's Hainish cycle, and a synthesis in the dialectic of beginnings and endings that began with "The Dowry of Angyar" and *Rocannon's World.* According to Northrop Frye, "the question 'Where is utopia?' is the same as the question 'Where is nowhere?' and the only answer to that question is 'here.' "[46] Le Guin's utopia argues implicitly that Frye's spatial concepts need a temporal dimension: the question "When is utopia" is the same as the question "When is never?" (or, perhaps, "When is 'once upon a time'?"), and the only answer to that question is "now." Shevek and *The Dispossessed* are "here, now."

The anarchist society on Anarres, fashioned out of the idea of the Taoists, William Godwin, Shelley, Kropotkin, Emma Goldman, Ghandi, and Paul Goodman, along with a fragment or two from Engels, is, if not a realistic elaboration of Ekumenical principles, then at least a concrete embodiment of the Ekumen *in* history (fictional history, to be sure, but history nevertheless).[47] In *The Left Hand of Darkness,* Genly Ai explains that

> the Ekumen doesn't rule, it coordinates. Its power is precisely the power if its member states (*LHD,* p. 22).
>
> The Ekumen is not a kingdom, but a coordinator, a clearinghouse for trade and knowledge (p. 38).
>
> ... the Ekumen is not essentially a government at all. It is an attempt to reunify the mystical with the political.... It is a form of education; in one respect it's a sort of very large school— very large indeed. The motives of communication and cooperation are of its essence.... The Ekumen as a political entity functions through coordination, not by rule. It does not enforce laws; decisions are reached by council and consent, not by consensus or command.... [It is] an experiment in the superorganic (pp. 132-33).[48]
>
> In a certain sense the Ekumen is not a body politic, but a body mystic. It considers beginnings to be extremely important. Beginnings, and means. Its doctrine is just the reverse of the doctrine that the end justifies the means. It proceeds, therefore... rather as evolution does, which is in certain senses our model.... (p. 245).[49]

The PDC (Production and Distribution Coordination) system on Anarres is the Ekumen brought down to earth; it is a "network of administration and management, ... a coordinating system for all syndicates, federatives, and individuals who do productive work" (*TD*, pp. 67-68). When Odo planned the society for Anarres,

> she had no intention of trying to deurbanize civilization.... She intended that all communities be connected by communication and transportation networks, so that goods and ideas could get where they were wanted, and the administration of things might work with speed and ease, and no community should be cut off from change and interchange. But the network was not to be run from the top down. There was to be no controlling center, no capital, no establishment for the self-perpetuating machinery of bureaucracy and the dominance drive of individuals seeking to become captains, bosses, chiefs of state.... However vast the distances separating settlements, they held to the ideal of complex organicism. They built the roads first, the houses second (*TD,* pp. 84-85).

Odo's plans and intentions, her promise, were for a utopia *in* history, a society that was to be alterable *in essence.* Unlike the mythic Ekumen, which does not change, the historicized utopia on Anarres does indeed evolve, but in its first two centuries it changes into a society that obstructs change and gives rein to the very impulses it was designed to rein in. Bedap, the novel's sharpest critic of counter-revolutionary trends on Anarres, sees bureaucratic machinery everywhere:

> Learning centers, mines, mills, fisheries, canneries, agricultural development and research stations, factories, one-product communities—anywhere that function demands expertise and a stable institution. But that stability gives scope to the authoritarian impulse. In the early years of the Settlement we were aware of that, on the lookout for it. People discriminated very carefully then between administering things and governing people. They did it so well that we forgot that the will to dominance is as central in human beings as the impulse to mutual aid is, and has to be trained in each individual, in each new generation. Nobody's born an Odonian any more than he's born civilized! But we've forgotten that. We don't educate for freedom. Education, the most important activity of the social organism, has become rigid, moralistic, authoritarian (*TD*, p. 149).

Shevek's goal—the purpose of the Syndicate of Initiative and his trip to Urras (and, not so incidentally, the purpose of Le Guin's science fiction as well)—is "to shake things up, to stir up, to break some habits, to make people ask questions. To behave like anarchists!" (*TD*, p. 339).

In a sense, Shevek's trip to Urras is King Argaven's trip to Ollul turned inside out. Instead of making a circular journey from the realm of history to the realm of myth and back again in order to learn "the nature and history of a kingdom that was a million years old," Shevek makes a circular journey from the realm of myth (historicized) back into history to learn something about the eight millennia of Urrasti history that preceded the Settlement and the century and a half that followed it—to return to roots and thus regenerate the social organism on Anarres. The Ekumen, a teleological myth that marks the *terminus ad quem* of Hainish history, may therefore be understood as the "cause" of the utopia on Anarres, which is itself the goal, or, in retrospect perhaps the final cause, of the history of the evolution of Le Guin's future history. Yet one product of the utopia, Shevek's General Temporal Theory, makes possible the invention of the ansible, without which there would be no Ekumen; and Shevek's dialectics of simultaneity and sequency, a microcosmic analogy for the dialectics of history (sequency, linear time) and myth (simultaneity, circular time) that informs the whole macrocosm of the Hainish saga, is inconceivable apart from Anarresti social conditions and Odonian modes of cognition, themselves anticipated by, and even a product of, the Ekumen. Since Shevek's theory makes ansible communication possible, and since ansible communication makes society possible (as Commander Yung argues in *The Word for World is Forest* and as Ambassador Keng hopes in *The Dispossessed*), it is part of what Frye would call "an account of the origins of society," a social contract myth which projects an analysis of the present into the past and "passes off a fiction as a fact." But *The Dispossessed* is also a utopia, in Frye's words, "a *speculative* myth" which projects an analysis of the present "into the future or some distant place," and "presents an imaginative vision of the *telos* or end at which social life aims." Within the horizons of Le Guin's future history, *The Dispossessed* is *both* social contract *and* utopia; not only does it present "a theory connecting social facts together," but it also "contain[s] or provide[s] a vision of [Le Guin's] social ideas."

By marrying these two mythically conditioned social conceptions, which, says Frye, "begin in an analysis of the present," Le Guin turns them around so that they *end* in an analysis of the present, in the "here, now." Le Guin's purpose in *The Dispossessed* is to constitute and explore "the landscape of time, in which the spirit may, with luck and courage, construct the fragile, makeshift, improbable roads and cities of fidelity: a landscape inhabitable by human beings" (*TD*, p. 295). In order for a landscape to be inhabitable by human beings, it not only must permit, but also should encourage *human* acts, that is to say ethical acts, and those occur only in the present, "within the landscape of the past and the future" (*TD*, p. 295): not on Urras, where the future is denied, nor on Anarres, where the past is denied, but in the process of a journey from one to the other and back again. Shevek does not go back home again; his going creates the home he returns to. As Ai says in *The Left Hand of Darkness,* "it is good to have an end to journey towards, but it is the journey that matters, in the end" (p. 209).

Rather than going to Urras to report that he has been into the future and that it works, Shevek wants to reconnect the future to its roots in the past so that the administrative machinery in the future will not work as well as it did in the past and the revolution that began in the past will continue in the future. He wants to make of the present not a wall separating the past and the future but an open door allowing free interplay between them. He hopes that by recovering the Urrasti history his world has denied, he will end ignorance, prevent the wrong that comes from ignorance, and return Anarres from its exile from history. One of his first requests on Urras is for books:

> pictures, stories, anything. Maybe they should be books for children. You see, I know very little.... We ignore you; you ignore us. You are our history. We are perhaps your future. I want to learn, not to ignore. It is the reason I came.... Such ignorance is wrong, from which wrong will arise (*TD*, pp. 66-67).

After he becomes acclimated to the home of his ancestors, his hosts take him to see the people (but not to talk to them), to see the country, the cities, Odo's grave, and Fort Drio, where Odo was imprisoned. Little of the fort is left, Shevek discovers, because the Urrasti considered Drio "a moribund sort of town, and the Foundation just wiped out and started fresh" (*TD*, p. 77). The Urrasti are as accomplished as the Anarresti are in closing themselves off from history, particularly threatening history, and thus insure its return. If the authoritarian impulse stays alive on Anarres, the revolution reemerges on Urras.

Shevek's hosts' carefully planned tours let him see "all the grace and beauty" of Urras, isolate him from the ugly underside, and weigh him down not with the burden of history, but with the costs of denying it:

> He was a frontiersman, one of a breed who had denied their past, their history. The Settlers of Anarres had turned their backs on the Old World and its past, opted for the future only. But as surely as the future becomes the past, the past becomes the future. To deny is not to achieve. The Odonians who left Urras had been wrong, wrong in their desperate courage, to deny their history, to forgo the possibility of return. The explorer who will not come back or send back his ships to tell his tale is not an explorer, only an adventurer; and his sons are born in exile (*TD*, p. 79).

True to the chiasmatic structure of the novel and the dialectic of the romance, Shevek's quest to return from exile, to go home again, carries him into the very heart of Urras: it is an exile-turned-inside-out: jail and cellar and death and a box without freedom. Finally realizing, after Vea's party, that by coming to Urras he had "locked himself in jail," Shevek tries to "act as a free man" by locking himself in his room and formulating the General Temporal Theory (*TD*, pp. 241ff.). Efor's gentle and healing touch during his illness breaks through the wall that had separated them, opens up to Shevek the other side of Urrasti history, and finally permits him to experience the real historical roots of Odonianism—violent repression of revolutionary hopes by the military arm of the authoritarian State. He discovers that the essence of Urrasti history is a room below ground and death, and he discovers it by *participating* in history, by acting, not by reading children's books and taking guided tours. Thus he can explain to Ambassador Keng:

> There is no way to act rightly, with a clear heart, on Urras. There is nothing you can do that profit does not enter into, and fear of loss, and the wish for power. You cannot say good morning without knowing which of you is "superior" to the other, or trying to prove it. You cannot act like a brother to other people, you must manipulate them, or command them, or obey them, or trick them. You cannot touch another person, yet they will not leave you alone. There is no freedom. It is a box—Urras is a box, a package, with all the beautiful wrapping of blue sky and meadows and forests and great cities. And you open the box, and what is inside it? A black cellar full of dust, and a dead man. A man whose hand was shot off because he held it out to others. I have been in Hell at last . . . . it is Urras; Hell is Urras (*TD*, pp. 305-6).

But without Urras, there would be no Anarres, and the only way Shevek discovers the real Anarres (and at the same time the unity of Sequency and Simultaneity) is by going to Urras, "the world that had formed Odo's mind and had jailed her eight times for speaking it , . . . the human suffering in which the ideals of his society were rooted, the ground from which they sprang" (*TD*, 251).

"The ground from which they sprang" is the goal of all of Le Guin's questers—Semley, Rocannon, Ramarren-Falk, Ged, Genly Ai, Estraven, and Shevek—as it is the goal of Le Guin's Hainish history. Only by returning to roots, by connecting beginning and end, by "binding time into a whole" (*TD*, p. 295) is it possible to create the "Circle of Life," a nearly closed circle that symbolizes "a landscape inhabitable by human beings" who are free because they are bound together by promises, fidelity, and loyalty—responsibilities and commitments that assert "the continuity of the past and future" (*TD*, p. 295) and so create a real present.[50] The significance of Le Guin's narrative forms, and the real, human significance of Shevek's chronosophy, whatever its relevance to physics, is *ethical,* and is clustered about the idea of the promise. The shy man at Vea's party is quite right when he remarks, "It seems to me the application of temporal physics is in ethics." After a feeble attempt to evade that issue—Shevek says, "Well I don't know. I do mostly mathematics, you know. You cannot make equations of ethical behavior"—Shevek makes the connection:

> it's true, chronosophy does involve ethics. Because our sense of time involves our ability to separate cause and effect, means and end. The baby, again, the animal, they don't see the difference between what they do now and what will happen because of it. They can't make a pulley, or a promise. We can. Seeing the difference between *now* and *not now,* we can make the connection. And there morality enters in. Responsibility. To say that a good end will follow from a bad means is like saying that if I pull a rope on this pulley it will lift the weight on that one. To break a promise is to deny the reality of the past; therefore it is to deny the hope of a real future. If time and reason are functions of each other, if we are creations of time, then we had better know it, and try to make the best of it. To act responsibly (*TD*, p. 199).

Using an analogy between a promise and a pulley may be a contrived way to marry temporal physics and ethics; more enlightening is the dialectic of freedom and the promise *in* marriage, Le Guin's "central, consistent theme":

> The validity of the promise, even promise of indefinite term, was deep in the grain of Odo's thinking; though it might seem that her insistence on freedom to change would invalidate the idea of promise or vow, in fact the freedom made the promise meaningful. A promise is a direction taken, a self-limitation of choice. As Odo pointed out, if no direction is taken, if one goes nowhere, no change will occur. One's freedom to choose and to change will be unused, exactly as if one were in jail, a jail of one's own building, a maze in which no one way is better than any other. So Odo came to see the promise, the pledge, the idea of fidelity, as essential in the complexity of freedom (*TD*, p. 216).

and

> There was process: process was all. You could go in a promising direction or you could go wrong, but you did not set out with the expectation of stopping anywhere. All responsibilities, all commitments thus understood took on substance and duration....

Fulfillment . . . is a function of time. The search for pleasure is circular, repetitive, atemporal. The variety seeking of the spectator, the thrill hunter, the sexually promiscuous, always ends in the same place. It has an end. It comes to the end and has to start over. It is not a journey and return, but a closed cycle, a locked room, a cell.

Outside the locked room is the landscape of time. . . .

It is not until an act occurs within the landscape of the past and the future that it is a human act. Loyalty . . . is the root of human strength; there is no good to be done without it (*TD*, pp. 294-95).

The Circle of Life is not closed; closed, it would be a jail or a locked room or a cellar full of death. Rather, it is a unity of sequency and simultaneity, of the arrow of time "without which there is no change, no progress, no direction, or creation" and the circle of time, "without which there is chaos, meaningless succession of instants, a world without clocks or seasons or promises" (*TD*, p. 198). It is journey and return, a process of renewal, a recreation of the present.

The Dispossessed ends with Shevek still in space, orbiting Anarres in the Hainish starship *Davenant* and making plans to land with Ketho, the Hainish first mate. In one sense, Shevek has not completed the journey he began on Anarres in the first chapter, but in another sense he has. One of the reasons he went to Urras was to "help keep the Revolution alive" (*TD*, p. 332), and he learns, just prior to landing, that "things are . . . a little broken loose, on Anarres" (*TD*, p. 339; ellipses in original). The future is open, as the Circle of Life is open, because it is grounded in history, as life is grounded in death, as Anarres is rooted on Urras, as Odo's ideals begin in a dusty cellar and a dead man.

X

One last beginning concludes Le Guin's Hainish saga. Set several generations before *The Dispossessed*, "The Day Before the Revolution" is a portrait of the aged revolutionary Odo as she goes through what appears to be her last day. Like *The Dispossessed*, it is a journey and a return: for the first time since a crippling stroke, Odo leaves the communal House in which she has been confined, and walks toward a park "to sit there and be old" ("DBR," p. 29). She is not strong enough to get that far, however, so she turns back toward the House, finds a doorstep and sits down to rest. "Who am I?" she mutters to an invisible audience. Only a story can answer that question; she remembers her life, returning to the beginning:

She was the little girl with scabby knees, sitting on the doorstep staring down through the dirty golden haze of River Street in the heat of late summer, the six-year-old, the sixteen-year-old, the fierce, cross, dream-ridden girl, untouched, untouchable. She was herself. Indeed she had been the tireless worker and thinker, but a bloodclot in a vein had taken that from her. Indeed she had been the lover, the swimmer in the midst of life, but Taviri, dying,

> had taken that woman away with him. There was nothing left, really, but the foundations. She had come home; she had never left home . . . . Dust and mud and a doorstep in the slums. And beyond, at the far end of the street, the field full of tall dry weeds blowing in the wind as night came ("DBR," pp. 29-30).

Odo never arrives at that field where the wind (freedom) blows, nor does she live to see the Revolution the next day. "I won't be here tomorrow," she says when someone asks her to speak at a meeting to plan a demonstration, a march, a general strike. Her story finished, she bequeaths to a younger generation of revolutionaries the task of making history not in a promised land flowing with milk and honey, but on an arid planet where the wind blows and where it is possible "to act rightly, with a clear heart."

No mythical law-giving patriarch, but a girl with scabby knees who grows up into a revolutionary anarchist with corns, discolored and shapeless nails, and knotted veins on her feet—*this* is the *telos* of the future history that germinated from Le Guin's combining the Norse myth of Freya and the Brisingamen Necklace with the conventions of pulp science fiction. Le Guin's Hainish future history thus ends as it began, with a story about a woman, but instead of portraying a member of a feudal aristocracy, a mythic figure who rides windsteeds and quests for a jewel to salve her ego, Le Guin presents a tough revolutionary from the working class who had

> mined the shipyards of Seissero, and had cursed Premier Inoilte to his face in front of a crowd of seven thousand, telling him he would have cut off his own balls and had them bronzed and sold as souvenirs, if he thought there was any profit in it—she who had screeched, and sworn, and kicked policemen, and spat at priests, and pissed in public on the big brass plaque in Capitol Square that said HERE WAS FOUNDED THE SOVERIGN NATION STATE OF A-IO ETC ETC, pssssssss to all that! ("DBR," p. 26).

That can stand as the epitaph of the Asimovian Galactic Empire and the beginning of a new and open history for science fiction.

Notes

Notes to the Preface

1. "A Citizen of Mondath," *Foundation* 4 (July 1973), 24.

2. "Dreams Must Explain Themselves," *Algol* 21 (November 1973), 12.

3. "Introduction to the 1978 Edition," *Planet of Exile* (New York: Harper & Row, 1978), pp. xii-xiii.

4. *Encyclopedia Britannica*, 15th ed. (1974), s.v., "yin-yang."

5. "A Response to the Le Guin Issue," *Science-Fiction Studies*, 3 (March 1976), 45.

6. *Science and the Common Understanding* (New York: Simon and Schuster, 1954), p. 76.

7. See Gerald Holton, "The Roots of Complementarity," *Daedalus*, 99 (Fall 1970), 1015-55.

8. See Jung's "On the Nature of the Psyche," *The Structure and Dynamics of the Psyche* (vol. 8 of the *Collected Works*) (New York: Pantheon, 1960), pp. 226-34; and "Synchronicity: An Acausal Connecting Principle," *The Structure and Dynamics of the Psyche*, pp. 477, 489.

9. *The Psychology of Consciousness* (1972; rpt., New York: Penguin, 1975).

10. *Science and Humanism* (Cambridge: At the University Press, 1951), p. 51.

11. "The Cardinal's First Tale," *Last Tales* (New York: Random House, 1957), p. 19.

12. *Science and Humanism*, p. 5. Great twentieth-century scientists like Einstein, Bohr, Heisenberg, and Schrödinger all tried to relate their specialized knowledge with the rest of knowledge.

Notes to Chapter 1

1. *City of Illusions*, in *Three Hainish Novels* (Garden City, N.Y.: Doubleday, 1978), p. 350. This edition of Le Guin's first three novels contains the best texts; subseqeunt references to *City of Illusions*, indicated parenthetically, are to this edition, which was issued by the Science Fiction Book Club.

2. *The Secular Scripture* (Cambridge: Harvard University Press, 1976), p. 186.

3. "Prophets and Mirrors: Science Fiction as a Way of Seeing," *The Living Light: A Christian Education Review*, 7 (Fall, 1970), 111-12. Compare Sir Karl Popper's thesis: "what is most characteristic of the human language is the possibility of story telling," quoted by George Steiner, *After Babel* (London: Oxford University Press, 1975), p. 224n.

4.   "The Cardinal's First Tale," *Last Tales* (New York: Random House, 1957), p. 23.

5.   "In Defense of Fantasy," *Horn Book*, 49 (1973), 239.

6.   *Rocannon's World* in *Three Hainish Novels*, p. [3].

7.   *The Left Hand of Darkness* (New York: Ace Books, 1976), p. 1.

8.   Erwin H. Hiebert, "Mach's Use of the History of Science," *Minnesota Studies in the Philosophy of Science*, vol. 5, *Historical and Philosophical Perspectives of Science*, ed. Roger H. Stuewer (Minneapolis: University of Minnesota Press, 1970), p. 200.

9.   See Thomas Scortia, "Science Fiction as the Imaginary Experiment," *Science Fiction: Today and Tomorrow*, ed. Reginald Bretnor (Baltimore: Penguin, 1975), pp. 135-47. For Le Guin's remarks on the thought experiment, see her "Is Gender Necessary?" *Aurora: Beyond Equality*, ed. Vonda McIntyre and Susan Anderson (Greenwich, Conn.: Fawcett, 1976), pp. 130-39; and her "Introduction," *The Left Hand of Darkness*, pp. [xii]-[xvi].

10. Tzvetan Todorov, "Literary Genres," in his *The Fantastic: A Structural Approach to a Literary Genre*, trans. Richard Howard (Ithaca, N.Y.: Cornell University Press, 1975), pp. [3]-23.

11. "The Significant Context of SF," *Science-Fiction Studies*, 1 (Spring 1973), 47.

12. *Validity in Interpretation* (New Haven: Yale University Press, 1967), pp. 100-101.

13. *Ibid.*, p. 82.

14. "On the Uses of Literary Genres," *Literature as System: Essays Toward the Theory of Literary History* (Princeton: Princeton University Press, 1971), p. 121. "The crucial point," says Guillén earlier in this essay, "is this: *form is the presence in a created, man-made object of a 'cause'*" (p. 111, emphasis in original).

15. "Spenser: From Magic to Miracle," *Four Essays on Romance*, ed. Herschel Baker (Cambridge: Harvard University Press, 1971), p. 18.

16. *Ibid.* This applies to Le Guin's romances only in the most general way: the reconciliation of opposites in her fiction does not come with an image of permanence and perfection, but rather signals a momentary balance which is of course subject immediately to change.

17. *The Secular Scripture*, p. 4.

18. "Magical Narratives: Romance as Genre," *New Literary History*, 7 (Autumn 1975), 153.

19. "Romance: A Perdurable Pattern," *College English*, 36 (October 1974), 143. Subsequent quotations from Hume's essay are indicated parenthetically.

20. "The Quest Hero," *Texas Quarterly*, 4 (Winter 1961), 85, my emphasis.

21. *The Secular Scripture*, pp. 57, 58.

22. *Ibid.*, p. 4.

23. Fromm, *The Forgotten Language* (New York: Holt, Rinehart and Winston, 1951); and Le Guin, "Fantasy, Like Poetry, Speaks The Language of the Night," *World* (Sunday Supplement to the San Francisco *Examiner & Chronicle*), November 21, 1976, p. 41.

24. "The Quest Hero," p. 84.

25. *Anatomy of Criticism*, (Princeton: Princeton University Press, 1957), p. 187.

26. *The Secular Scripture,* pp. 15, 60. The following paragraphs contain several references to Frye's book; they are indicated parenthetically. It will be obvious that Frye's account of the structure of the romance contains a marked orientation around a vertical axis, while Hume's account seems oriented more to journeys on a horizontal plane. Hume's orientation is probably more compatible with Le Guin's fiction, but again, Frye's ideas are helpful apart from his ulterior motives.

27. See Le Guin's "The Child and the Shadow," *Quarterly Journal of the Library of Congress,* 32 (April 1975), esp. 147-48, where Le Guin argues that a writer should offer self-knowledge to readers, which includes their accepting their personal capacity for evil.

28. "Magical Narratives," p. 141.

29. *Ibid.*

30. Ibid., p. 142.

31. *The Left Hand of Darkness,* pp. 260, 261.

32. Two good discussions of the difficult term *aufheben* are Walter Kaufmann, *Hegel: A Reinterpretation* (Garden City: Doubleday Anchor, 1966), pp. 144 and 181; and M.H. Abrams, *Natural Supernaturalism,* (New York: W.W. Norton, 1971), pp. 177, 182, 212-13, 219-20, and 230.

33. *The Secular Scripture,* p. 58.

34. *A Wizard of Earthsea* (Berkeley: Parnassus Press, 1968), pp. 202, 203.

35. "The Child and the Shadow," p. 141.

36. *Ibid.,* p. 144.

37. *Ibid.,* p. 141.

38. "American SF and the Other," *Science-Fiction Studies,* 2 (November, 1975), 209-10.

39. "The Child and the Shadow," p. 144.

40. *Ibid.,* p. 145.

41. *Ibid.,* p. 147.

42. *The Farthest Shore* (New York: Atheneum, 1972), pp. 104-5.

43. "The Child and the Shadow," p. 147.

44. *Ibid.*

45. For Le Guin's own perceptive comments on her own fiction vis-à-vis the fantasy-science fiction split, see her "A Citizen of Mondath," *Foundation* 4 (July 1973), 23; and "Ursula K. Le Guin: An Interview," *Luna Monthly,* No. 63 (March, 1976), 1-2.

46. "On the Poetics of the Science Fiction Genre," *College English,* 34 (December 1972), 375.

47. "Magical Narratives," p. 142.

48. This is the central thesis of Max Horkheimer and Theodor Adorno, *Dialectic of Enlightenment* (New York: Herder and Herder, 1972). See also Samuel R. Delany, "About Five Thousand One Hundred and Seventy Five Words," *SF: The Other Side of Realism* (see note 14, above), pp. 130-45. Delany notes that "virtually all the classics of speculative fiction [his term for science fiction] are mystical" (p. 144).

49. "On the Poetics of the Science Fiction Genre," p. 377.

50. "*Entfremdung, Verfremdung:* Alienation, Estrangement," trans. Darko Suvin, *The Drama Review,* 15 (Fall 1970), 124-25.

51. "Is Gender Necessary?" pp. 138-39.

52. "A Response to the Le Guin Issue," *Science-Fiction Studies,* 3 (March 1976), 45.

53. "Magical Narratives," p. 153.

54. "Varieties of Literary Utopias," *Utopias and Utopian Thought,* ed. Frank Manuel (Boston: Beacon Press, 1967), p. 49.

55. "Defining the Literary Genre of Utopia: Some Historical Semantics, Some Genology, a Proposal, and a Plea," *Studies in the Literary Imagination,* 6 (Fall 1973), 123.

56. "Introduction," *The Left Hand of Darkness,* p. [xv].

57. "Is Gender Necessary?" p. 132. I return to this whole idea at the end of chapter 3 when I discuss Le Guin's story "Schrödinger's Cat."

58. "Introduction," *The Left Hand of Darkness,* p. [xiii].

59. *The Secular Scripture,* p. 179.

60. This is, of course, a very old and quite common idea, stemming at least from Socrates who thought of learning as a reawakening of what was once known but has been forgotten. That Le Guin has first-hand knowledge of it is apparent in *The Farthest Shore:* Ged tells Arren "we find ourselves facing what is yet to be in what was long forgotten" (p. 86).

61. "The Crab Nebula, the Paramecium, and Tolstoy," *Riverside Quarterly,* 5 (February 1972), 90, 91.

62. "Vaster then Empires and More Slow," *The Wind's Twelve Quarters* (New York: Harper & Row, 1975), p. 208.

63. There is a good deal of word-play in Le Guin's fiction, and Genli Ai's play on the words "alien" and "other" is one of the most significant. Recalling one of their nights on the Ice, Ai reports this exchange: "'Good night, Ai,' said the alien, and the other alien said, 'Good night, Harth'" (p. 213). Both Ai and Estraven are exiles, both are aliens, and both are the Other to each other. These relationships suggest the hypothesis that the rhetorical device of chiasmus may be the root of nearly everything in Le Guin's fiction. The way she shifts points of view, the way she engineers complementary estrangements, the way she structures *The Dispossessed,* alternating the Urras and Anarres chapters, the way hunter and hunted switch roles in *A Wizard of Earthsea*—all of this is chiasmus on one level or another, a rhetorical manifestation of the dialectical poetics of the romance genre.

64. Two sources, both recommended by Le Guin, for an understanding of Taoist *wu wei* are Holmes Welch, *Taoism: The Parting of the Way* (Boston: Beacon Press, 1957), pp. 18-35; and Joseph Needham, *Science and Civilisation in China,* vol. 2, *History of Scientific Thought* (Cambridge: Cambridge University Press, 1965), pp. 68-70, 562-63, and 576-77.

65. *The Left Hand of Darkness,* p. 287, my emphasis.

66. Quoted by Paula Brookmire, "She Writes about Aliens—Men Included," *Milwaukee Journal,* July 21, 1974; rpt., *Biography News* (Detroit: Gale, 174), p. 1155.

67. *The Left Hand of Darkness,* p. 12.

68.   *Ibid.,* p. 248.

69.   *Ibid.,* p. 95.

70.   "In Defense of Fantasy," p. 239.

Notes to Chapter 2

1.   Le Guin, personal correspondence, March 7, 1977. The name *Orsinia* and the adjective *Orsinian* appear nowhere in the text of *Orsinian Tales.* Le Guin's imaginary country is neither realistic nor fantastic; to have named it would have been defining it too clearly, and she does not want the boundaries of Orsinia to be well defined.

2.   "A Citizen of Mondath," *Foundation* 4 (July 1973), 22.

3.   *Ibid.,* pp. 22-23.

4.   "Folksong from the Montayna Province," *Prairie Poet* (Charleston, Ill.), Fall 1959, p. 75; and *"An die Musik," Western Humanities Review,* 15 (Summer 1961), 247-58, are Le Guin's first published poem and first published story.

5.   Darrell Schweitzer, "The Vivisector," *Science Fiction Review* (Portland), 6 (February 1977), 36-38.

6.   "Foreword," *The Wind's Twelve Quarters* (New York: Harper & Row, 1975), p. vii.

7.   Le Guin, personal correspondence, March 7, 1977.

8.   Eleanor Cameron, apparently on the basis of information supplied by Le Guin, writes that "almost all of what [Le Guin] wrote before publication was fantasy in the style of Isak Dinesen's tales or Austen Tappan Wright's *Islandia*" ("High Fantasy: *A Wizard of Earthsea,*" *Horn Book,* 47 [1917], 131). Le Guin herself says "I read Islandia first at 13 [Le Guin was 13 when *Islandia* first appeared in 1942] and so of course its influnce is generic in all my work" (personal correspondence, September 15, 1976). Even a cursory glance at both *Islandia* and *The Left Hand of Darkness* would reveal the extent of the influence.

9.   See Hugh Seton-Watson, *The "Sick Heart" of Modern Europe: The Problem of the Danubian Lands* (Seattle: University of Washington Press, 1975), and Mircea Eliade, *The Myth of the Eternal Return,* trans. Willard Trask (Princeton: Princeton University Press, 1954), pp. 139-62.

10. *Orsinian Tales* (New York: Harper & Row, 1976), p. 157. Subsequent references are to this edition and are indicated parenthetically.

11. That presumably objective historical narratives are also profoundly poetic is the thesis of Hayden White's *Metahistory: The Historical Imagination in Nineteenth-Century Europe* (Baltimore: Johns Hopkins University Press, 1973). Conversely, profoundly poetic works may aim at historical "objectivity": *War and Peace* is one of Le Guin's favorite novels.

12. On the Romantic "circuitous journey," see M.H. Abrams, *Natural Supernaturalism* (New York: W.W. Norton, 1971), pp. 141-324.

13. *Moulds of Understanding: A Pattern of Natural Philosophy,* ed. Gary Werskey (London: Allen & Unwin, 1976), pp. 221ff. Le Guin knows and admires Needham's work.

14. *Les Systèmes socialistes,* 2 vols. (Paris: Giard & Brière, 1902-03), II, 332. My translation. For this ancedote I am indebted to Bertell Ollmann, *Alienation: Marx's Conception of Man in Capitalist Society,* 2nd ed. (Cambridge: Cambridge University Press, 1976), p. 3.

15. "The Magic Art and the Evolution of Words: Ursula Le Guin's Earthsea Trilogy," *Mosaic,* 10 (Winter 1977), pp. 148f.

16. *The Farthest Shore* (New York: Atheneum, 1972), p. 133.

17. "The Vivisector," p. 37.

18. "Sisters and Science Fiction," *The Little Magazine,* 10 (Spring-Summer 1976), 89.

19. I refer here to the philosophy of internal relations, discussed by Ollmann, *Alienation,* passim. Pareto's bird and mouse are internally related parts of a whole, as are the complementary Chinese concepts Yin and Yang. These are concepts, not independent entities: one cannot exist without the other any more than reality can exist without fantasy and vice versa. The epigraph to chapter one above, from Horkheimer and Adorno, is most apposite for an understanding of the relationships between reality and fantasy.

20. "A Citizen of Mondath," p. 22.

21. Two essays on landscape and setting in Le Guin's science fiction are Ian Watson, "The Forest as Metaphor for Mind," *Science-Fiction Studies,* 2 (1975), 231-37, and Elizabeth Cummins Cogell, "Setting as Analogue to Characterization in Ursula K. Le Guin," *Extrapolation,* 18 (1977), 131-41. Neither Watson nor Cogell refers to landscape painting. Le Guin says that J.M.W. Turner has probably helped her "make a world out of chaos" more than her literary influences have ("A Response to the Le Guin Issue," *Science-Fiction Studies,* 3 [1976], 46). Turner was influenced by seventeenth- and eighteenth-century French painters of the *paysage moralisé* like Claude, Poussin, and Watteau. See Le Guin's story about a landscape painter, "The Eye Altering," *The Altered* I, ed. Lee Harding (Melbourne: Norstrilia Press, 1976), pp. 108-17.

22. "Is Gender Necessary?" p. 131. Le Guin's full statement merits quotation: "The fact is that the real subject of the book is not feminism or sex or gender or anything of the sort; as far as I can see, it is a book about betrayal and fidelity."

23. *The Dispossessed,* p. 227.

24. *Collected Shorter Poems 1927-1957* (New York: Random House, 1966), pp. 238-41.

25. Le Guin refers to Auden as perhaps the only twentieth-century poet with enough science to bridge the gap between Lord Snow's Two Cultures from the side of the humanists ("The Crab Nebula," p. 96). "In Praise of Limestone" appeared first in *Horizon,* July 1948, p. 1-3, and then in Auden's *Nones* (New York: Random House, 1951). Le Guin wrote the first Orsinian tale in 1951.

26. Le Guin lists "Rilke's one novel" *(Die Aufzeichnungen Malte Laurids Brigge)* as part of the "tradition into which [she] fit[s] by disposition and choice" ("The View In," *A Multitude of Visions,* ed. Cy Chauvin [Baltimore: T-K Graphics, 1975], p. 6). In her "Response to the Le Guin Issue," she lists Rilke as one of the poets who have influenced her (p. 46). According to Le Guin's mother, Theodora Kroeber, she introduced Rilke to her father in the late fifties *(Alfred Kroeber* [Berkeley: University of California Press, 1970], p. 261). Le Guin has published translations of six of Rilke's French poems in *Mr. Cognito* (Forest Grove, Ore.), 1 (Winter 1975), 8-13. There are some astonishingly clear echoes of Rilke's Tenth Duino Elegy in *The Farthest Shore,* and Rilke may have helped Le Guin invent the Orsinian Karst. *Schloss Duino,* near Trieste, where Rilke conceived the *Duino Elegies,* is on the edge of the Adriatic Karst. Sonnet xi in Part 2 of *Sonnets of Orpheus* is about the Karst. For Rilke's influence on Auden, see Monroe K. Spears, *The Poetry of W.H. Auden* (New York: Oxford University Press, 1968), pp. 141-42.

27.   "Rilke in English," *The New Republic,* September 6, 1939, pp. 135-36.

28.   "A Response to the Le Guin Issue," p. 45.

29.   *The Poetry of W.H. Auden,* p. 142.

30.   "Dreams Must Explain Themselves," *Algol* 21 (November 1973), p. 12.

31.   For the biographical facts, see Theodora Kroeber, *Alfred Kroeber,* pp. 139-42.
      I am not suggesting that the Egideskar family is an exact photographic reproduction of the Kroeber family, any more than I would argue that Shevek in *The Dispossessed* is a realistic portrait of J. Robert Oppenheimer. Le Guin has used the same distancing techniques in "Imaginary Countries" that she uses throughout *Orsinian Tales.* Besides shifting her parents from California to Orsinia and transforming them into a baron and a baroness, she reduces the number of children from four to three, and adds Josef Brone so that the tale has a character who can contribute an outside perspective on the family (most of the tale is told through his point of view). Kishamish, Theodora Kroeber explains, got its name when "Karl, the youngest of the boys, was in his myth-making period in imitation of Greek and Norse myths. [He] saw the two nearer knolls as being Thor and Kishamish (the latter an invented giant), the two recumbent after a fight to the finish: hence the name Kishamish's Place" (p. 140). Le Guin is still in her myth-making period.
      Nor am I suggesting that any of this biographical information accounts for the aesthetic qualities that make "Imaginary Countries" and *Orsinian Tales* worthwhile reading experiences. I am sympathetic with the position on biographical approaches taken by Karl Kroeber (a professor of English at Columbia), but I certainly do not accept his extreme statement of that position: "to know these [biographical] sources is to know nothing of significance about the stories as stories. Bad stories often are raw biography. Literary art consists in transforming one kind of reality, that of physical experience, into another kind of reality, that of literary experience" ("Sisters and Science Fiction," p. 87). It does not necessarily follow from this that raw biography is bad art; in any case, "Imaginary Countries" is not raw biography. Take, for example, these two descriptions:

> The Kishamish guestbook kept during those years [the thirties] can be read as a roster of graduate students in anthropology stopping by, to and from the field; of California Indians and other Indians; of visiting writers and scholars; of the children's friends; of family. Among the names are those who stayed for days or weeks and whose repeated names tell the story of the circle of intimacy which completed itself there—very California Indian, very Kishamishian (*Alfred Kroeber,* p. 142).

> All summer in tides and cycles the house had been full or half full of visitors, friends of the children, friends of the baroness, friends, colleagues and neighbors of the baron, duck-hunters who slept in the disused stable since the spare bedrooms were full of Polish historians, ladies with broods of children the smallest of whom fell inevitably into the pond about this time of the afternoon. No wonder it was so still, so autumnal now: the rooms vacant, the pond smooth, the hills empty of dispersing laughter (*Orsinian Tales,* pp. 174-75).

Having placed these two passages together, we can see more clearly the way Le Guin uses Rilkean *Dinge* and landscape to create atmosphere and meaning. The shift in her passage from fullness and activity to emptiness and stillness, and from the house to the hills beyond, is similar to the landscape painting we find not only in *Orsinian Tales,* but also in the Earthsea trilogy, where Le Guin often pauses in her narration to direct our gaze toward distant hills and the horizon.

Although both Le Guin and her mother are writing in the elegiac mode, neither passage can be reduced to the other, nor can either be reduced to the raw experience that stands behind each of them. Both are works of art, but they are in different genres: biography and fiction. One is written by a woman who was an adult when she lived the experiences she describes; the other is written by a woman who was a child when she experienced what she describes. Like Wordsworth's "Lines Composed a Few Miles Above Tintern Abbey," "Imaginary Countries" is "emotion recollected in tranquillity." Where Le Guin's mother emphasizes the circle of intimacy at Kishamish, Le Guin evokes the mood and atmosphere of endings as moments in "tides and cycles" at Asgard. The imminent change from summer to autumn and winter is analogous to other changes in the tale, personal and public. Zida is on the verge of passing from childhood into an awareness of time and season, and *Mitteleuropa* in 1935 is on the verge of total war between totalitarian superpowers. Ragnarok is a game played both in the Egideskar family and by the nations of Europe. Much of the aesthetic effect of the tale, in fact, comes from the contrasts between the masterfully delicate and sensitive portrayal of Zida's world and the ominous and brooding shadows of a war more destructive and barbaric than anything history had ever witnessed.

32. *Collected Letters of Samuel Taylor Coleridge,* 6 vols., ed. Earl Leslie Griggs (Oxford: At the Clarendon Press, 1956-71), IV, 545.

33. Without disparaging the imagination, the baron can distinguish between fantasy and reality, and respect the value each has for the other. Note that the pig, though "real," is imaginary:

> "What is that?" [the baron asks Zida].
> "A trap for catching a unicorn." She brushed hair and leafmold off her face and arranged herself more comfortably on him.
> "Caught any?"
> "No."
> "Seen any?"
> "Paul and I found some tracks."
> "Split-hoofed ones, eh?"
> She nodded. Delicately through twilight in the baron's imagination walked their neighbor's white pig, silver between birch trunks.

34. "The View In" is an essay in which Le Guin explains why she writes science fiction (see note 26, above), and *A Very Long Way from Anywhere Else* (London: Gollancz, 1976) is the British edition of Le Guin's juvenile novella published in the USA as *Very Far Away From Anywhere Else* (New York: Atheneum, 1976). Owen Griffiths, the narrator and principal character, has invented an imaginary country named "Thorn": "a very small country, on an island in the South Atlantic, only about sixty miles across, and a very long way from anywhere else. The wind blew all the time in Thorn" (Atheneum ed., p. 51). When Owen's friend Natalie Field helps him to take imaginary countries seriously (she introduces him to Angria and Gondal, the Brontës' imaginary countries), he begins to escape the ideology of consumerism and mediocrity that smothers his parents in a fog. The wind on Thorn, which would of course keep the island free of fog, means the same thing to Owen that the breeze in Book I of *The Prelude* means to Wordsworth: freedom.

Just as Owen discovers an Archimedes point in his imaginary country, Le Guin and the baron discover Archimedes points in their imaginary countries. The baron uses myth and history to discover his, while his creator uses myth and history along with the estrangement techniques of science fiction to discover hers.

35. "I grew up," said Le Guin in an interview, "reading the Norse myths and they have always

meant incomparably more to me than the Greek or any other. They are in fact of my 'childhood lore,' *they shaped my imagination;* to me the reality of Ragnarok lies on the same profound, subrational level as the Crucifixion or the Resurrection lies for one brought up as a Christian. One may no longer 'believe in' it, but it remains a basic symbol, a mode of one's imagination—both a limiting, and an enabling mode" ("Ursula K. Le Guin: An Interview," *Luna Monthly* no. 63 [March 1976], p. 3, my emphasis).

36.   *Planet of Exile,* in *Three Hainish Novels,* p. 166.

37.   *Letters to Friends, Family, and Editors,* trans. Richard and Clara Winston (New York: Schocken, 1978), quoted by V.S. Pritchett, "The Incurable," *New York Review of Books,* February 25, 1978, p. 4.

38.   In the discussion of *"An die Musik"* that follows, I cite the text as first published in 1961. When Le Guin revised it for publication in *Orsinian Tales,* she removed most of the allusions to Romantic poets and musicians.

39.   See John Huntington, "Public and Private Imperatives in Le Guin's Fiction," *Science-Fiction Studies,* 2 (November 1975), 237-42.

40.   "The Crab Nebula," p. 96.

41.   Eichendorff, *Neue Gesamtausgabe der Werke und Schriften,* 4 vols. (Stuttgart: J.G. Cotta'sche Buchhandlung, 1957), I, 294. My translation. *"Es wandelt, was wir shcauen"* is one of five lyrics grouped under the title *"Der Umkehrende,"* "Turning Back" or "Return."

42.   This image is recycled in "Schrödinger's Cat," a science fiction story written more than a decade after *"An die Musik."* See the last section of chapter 3 for a discussion of the later story.

43.   That Le Guin should have chosen Lotte Lehmann to be the vehicle for Gaye's epiphany is but one instance among many in this remarkable tale of the way each element resonates in all the others. Lotte Lehmann, born in Prussia in 1888, became "one of the most eminent lyric-dramatic sopranos of her time" (Richard Capell, "Lotte Lehmann," *Grove's Dictionary of Music and Musicians,* 5th ed., V, 116). Lehmann was a product of the culture of *Mitteleuropa,* a culture Le Guin eulogizes in *Orsinian Tales,* a culture Lehmann gave voice to: "the lyric stage of the time knew no performance more admirably accomplished: it seemed to embody a civilization, the pride and elegance of old Vienna, its voluptuousness, chastened by good manners, its doomed beauty" (Capell, p. 116). Lehmann was barred by the Nazis from singing in Germany, and when Hitler took Austria, she emigrated to the USA.

   Lehmann's attitude toward the relationship between music and politics is consonant with Le Guin's in *"An die Musik"* (though not in her later fiction). In her autobiography, Lehmann writes,

   I cannot serve politics. I can only serve that which always has been and still is the mission in my life. I cannot paint political boundaries on the measureless ways of the art-world. I will not, and cannot probe whether the people to whom I give my art are good or bad, believers or unbelievers; nor does it interest me to know what race they belong [to], or to what politics they subscribe.... God put music into my heart and a voice in my throat. I serve Him when I serve music ("Postscript, May 1938," *Midway in My Song* [Indianapolis: Bobbs-Merrill, 1938], p. vii).

Le Guin says that Lehmann "has been my favorite woman singer for many years.... She ended many concerts—and the last of her whole career—by singing *"An die Musik"* (personal correspondence, September 9, 1977). Lehmann's performance of *"An die Musik"* may be heard on Camden 1015 (S.S. Prawer, "Discography," *The Penguin Book of Lieder* [Harmondsworth: Penguin, 1964], p. 195). This recording is out of print and difficult to find, but one ought really to hear the song performed to appreciate fully Le Guin's tale.

Lehmann died in Santa Barbara, California, one month before Harper & Row published *Orsinian Tales.*

44. *The Fischer—Dieskau Book of Lieder,* trans. George Bird and Richard Stokes (New York: Knopf, 1977), p. 53, slightly altered to conform to the way Schubert wrote the song to be performed. See Franz Schubert, *Complete Works,* 19 vols. (New York: Dover, 1965), XV, 86-87.

45. Auden, "In Memory of W.B. Yeats (d. Jan. 1939)," *Collected Shorter Poems,* pp. 142, 143. (Note that Auden's poem, like Le Guin's Orsinian tales, includes a date: it is a meditation on history as well as an elegy).

46. See Walter A. Strauss, *Descent and Return: The Orphic Theme in Modern Literature* (Cambridge: Harvard University Press, 1971).

47. Quoted by J.B. Leishman, "Introduction," *Duino Elegies,* trans. J.B. Leishman and Stephen Spender (New York: W.W. Norton, 1939), p. 15. Auden quotes this passage in his review of *Duino Elegies,* and adds these comments:

> This ... is not to be dismissed with the cheery cry "defeatism." It implies not a denial of political action, but rather the realization that if the writer is not to harm both others and himself, he must consider, and very much more humbly and patiently then he has been doing, what kind of person he is, and what may be his real function. When the ship catches fire, it seems only natural to rush importantly to the pumps, but perhaps one is only adding to the general confusion and panic: to sit still and pray seems selfish and unheroic, but it may be the wisest and most helpful course ("Rilke in English," p. 135).

Le Guin has had to make these choices. With *The Word for World is Forest,* she rushed to the pumps, and has said since that she regrets it and hopes never to do it again. She would not, like Auden, pray, but she might meditate: that would be in keeping with the quietist ethic of Taoism, *wu wei,* which Le Guin translates as "action through stillness" ("Introduction to the 1978 Edition," *Planet of Exile* [New York: Harper & Row, 1978], p. ix).

48. Quoted by J.B. Leishman, "Introduction," *Sonnets to Orpheus,* trans. J.B. Leishman (London: Hogarth Press, 1936), p. 23.

49. Hynes, *The Auden Generation: Literature and Politics in England in the 1930s* (New York: Viking Press, 1977), p. 353. Hynes's account of "Auden Country" bears at a number of points on Le Guin's fiction of the late sixties and early seventies. The historical pressures on artists in the thirties were not unlike those on artists in the sixties, and may have made it necessary for writers like Auden and Le Guin to invent imaginary countries, to use Kafka's "strategic considerations" to make possible the exchange of truthful words.

Notes to Chapter 3

1. "The Science Fiction of Ursula K. Le Guin," *Science-Fiction Studies,* 2 (November 1975), 204.

2. *The Farthest Shores of Ursula K. Le Guin* (San Bernardino, Calif.: Borgo Press, 1976), p. 32.

3.   *City of Illusions* in *Three Hainish Novels* (Garden City, N.Y.: Nelson Doubleday, 1978), p. 350.

4.   Coleridge, paraphrased by M.H. Abrams, *Natural Supernaturalism* (New York: W.W. Norton, 1971), p. 185.

5.   Le Guin, "Dreams Must Explain Themselves," *Algol* 21 (November 1973), 8.

6.   See Scribner's advertisement on p. 13 of the *L.A. Con Program Book,* distributed at the 30th World Science Fiction Convention, September 1-4, 1972.

7.   *Natural Supernaturalism,* pp. 172-95.

8.   This account of the process of artistic creation is, as Susan Wood has pointed out, distinctively Romantic ("Discovering Worlds: The Fiction of Ursula K. LeGuin"). *Voices for the Future,* vol. 2, ed. Thomas D. Clareson [Bowling Green, Ohio: Bowling Green University Popular Press, 1979].

9.   "The Word of Unbinding," *The Wind's Twelve Quarters* (New York: Harper & Row, 1975), p. 72. Subsequent quotations from this story, from "The Rule of Names," and from "Semley's Necklace" are from this edition, and are indicated parenthetically.

10.   *The Left Hand of Darkness* (New York: Ace Books, 1976), p. 73.

11.   Le Guin mentions her "obsession" in the headnote to "The Word of Unbinding" in *The Wind's Twelve Quarters* (p. 71). See also Ian Watson, "The Forest as Metaphor for Mind: 'The Word for World is Forest' and 'Vaster than Empires and More Slow,'" *Science-Fiction Studies,* 2 (November 1975), 231-37, for a treatment of the obsession in two of Le Guin's science fiction stories.

12.   *The Phenomenology of Mind,* trans. J.B. Baillie (1910; rpt., New York: Harper & Row, 1967), p. 790, slightly altered.

13.   Le Guin, statement made while sitting on a panel at Aussiecon, the 33rd World Science Fiction Convention, Melbourne, August 14-17, 1975.

14.   For discussions of this aspect of Le Guin's style, see Eleanor Cameron, "High Fantasy: *A Wizard of Earthsea,*" *Horn Book,* 47 (April 1971), 129-38, and T.A. Shippey, "The Magic Art and the Evolution of Words: Ursula Le Guin's Earthsea Trilogy," *Mosaic,* 10 (Winter 1977), 147-63.

15.   Quoted by Jay Williams, "Very Iffy Books," *Signal: Approaches to Children's Books,* no. 13 (January 1974), 26.

16.   "Dreams Must Explain Themselves," p. 10.

17.   *Natural Supernaturalism,* pp. 184, 191.

18.   "A Citizen of Mondath," *Foundation* no. 4 (July 1973), 24.

19.   The parallelisms are obvious:

     a.   Rocannon on Fomalhaut II for 400 days when he is stranded, eight light years from home.

     a.   Genly Ai on Gethen for two years when his mission is "betrayed," five years from rescue.

     b.   Faradayan attack cuts off Rocannon's Ethnological Survey.

     b.   Tibe's rise ends Ai's mission in Erhenrang.

     c.   Mogien offers help.

     c.   Estraven helps (but Ai doesn't realize it).

d.	Rocannon captured at Oafs-castle after crossing the sea to Southern Continent.		d.	Ai captured after crossing the Ey River into Orgoreyn.
e.	Rocannon and Mogien separated.		e.	Ai and Estraven separated.
f.	Rocannon fascinated at first by the precision and order of the hive city.		f.	Ai hopeful that his mission will succeed in the orderly politics of Orgoreyn.
g.	Rocannon realizes he's imprisoned.		g.	Ai in Pulefen Farm.
h.	Amid snow and ice at high altitude, Rocannon enters cave and receives mindspeech.		h.	On Gobrin Ice, in the "Place Inside the Blizzard," Ai "sees" Estraven, and they try mind speech.
i.	Mogien dies flying into helicopter.		i.	Estraven dies skiing into Karhide border guards' foray guns.
j.	Lady Ganye's son asks Rocannon for stories about other lands.		j.	Estraven's child asks Ai for story of crossing the Ice and stories of other lands.

20. "A Citizen of Mondath," p. 23. For a more detailed discussion of genre-mixing in *Rocannon's World,* see Le Guin's "Introduction," *Rocannon's World* (New York: Harper & Row, 1977).

21. This account is from Jeff Levin, Le Guin's bibliographer, and from Terry Carr, who was a junior editor at Ace at the time (conversation at MidAmeriCon, 34th World Science Fiction Convention, Kansas City, September 1-4, 1976).

22. *The Human Condition* (Chicago: University of Chicago Press, 1958), p. 186.

23. "Myth and Archetype in Science Fiction," *Parabola,* 1 (Fall 1976), 45.

24. *The Best from Amazing* (New York: Manor Books, 1973), p. 83.

25. Le Guin discusses myth and science fiction in "Ursula K. Le Guin: An Interview," *Luna Monthly,* no. 63 (March 1976), 1-4, in "Myth and Archetype in Science Fiction," and in her "Introduction" to *Rocannon's World.*
    Her primary source for Freya's story is Padraic Colum, *The Children of Odin* (New York: Macmillan, 1920), which she read as a child so thoroughly that she "practically knew it by heart" (personal correspondence, March 14, 1977). Part II of Colum's book, "Odin the Wanderer," is the source for a few episodes of *Rocannon's World.* As "Olhor the Wanderer," Rocannon is a reincarnation of Odin.

26. "Ursula K. Le Guin: An Interview," p. 3.

27. "European SF: Rottensteiner's Anthology, the Strugatskys, and Lem," *Science-Fiction Studies,* 1 (Spring 1974), 182.

28. R.R. Marett, "Magic," *Encyclopaedia of Religion and Ethics,* ed. James Hastings (New York: Scribner's 1928), VIII, 245.

29. *A Wizard of Earthsea* (Berkeley: Parnassus Press, 1968), p. 185. The following paragraphs contain several references to *A Wizard of Earthsea* and *The Farthest Shore,* and are indicated with the abbreviations *WE* and *FS.*

30.   *Structural Fabulation: An Essay on Fiction of the Future* (Notre Dame: University of Notre Dame Press, 1975), pp. 82, 86-87.

31.   My discussion of druidism is drawn mainly from *Encyclopaedia Britannica,* 11th ed., s.v. "druidism," and J.A. MacCulloch, "Magic (Celtic)," *Encyclopaedia of Religion and Ethics,* VIII, 257-59.

32.   Barry Barth, "Ursula Le Guin interview: Tricks, anthropology create new worlds," *Portland Scribe,* May 17-May 23, 1975, p. 8.

33.   "Preface," *Aftermath* (New York: Macmillan, 1936), p. vi.

34.   *Argonauts of the Western Pacific* (1922; rept., New York: E.P. Dutton, 1961), p. xiii.

35.   "Dreams Must Explain Themselves," p. 10.

36.   *Argonauts of the Western Pacific,* pp. 83, 92.

37.   *Magic, Science, and Religion and Other Essays* (Garden City, N.Y.: Doubleday Anchor, 1954), pp. 86-87.

38.   *Argonauts of the Western Pacific,* pp. 427, 451. Belief in the magical power of words is, of course, nearly universal in human cultures. See Malinowski, "The Power of Words in Magic—Some Linguistic Data," *Argonauts of the Western Pacific,* pp. 428-63, and also his "An Ethnographic Theory of the Magical Word," *Coral Gardens and Their Magic,* 2 vols. (Bloomington: Indiana University Press, 1965), II, 213-50.

39.   "Dreams Must Explain Themselves," p. 10.

40.   *Argonauts of the Western Pacific,* p. 401.

41.   *Magic, Science and Religion,* p. 75, my emphasis.

42.   *Argonauts of the Western Pacific,* p. 409.

43.   "Schrödinger's Cat," *Universe 5,* ed. Terry Carr (New York: Random House, 1974), pp. 32-40. Because the story is so short, I have omitted page numbers when I quote the text.

44.   "After the Book?" *On Difficulty and Other Essays* (New York: Oxford University Press, 1978), p. 187.

45.   The fascinating and often dramatic controversies over the correct interpretation of the quantum theory and its philosophical implications have already produced volumes, and cannot be neatly summarized here. For the nonspecialist, chapter 44, "More Theory and Experiment: Physics Today," in Eric M. Rogers, *Physics for the Inquiring Mind* (Princeton: Princeton University Press, 1960), pp. 714-59, provides a superb introduction, beautifully illustrated, to the twentieth-century revolutions in physics. Norwood Hanson's "Quantum Mechanics, Philosophical Implications of," *Encyclopedia of Philosophy,* ed. Paul Edwards (New York: Macmillan, 1967), VII, 41-49, offers an orientation to the philosophical issues.

     For the Copenhagen interpretation, see the essays of Bohr, and Heisenberg's *Physics and Philosophy: The Revolution in Modern Science* (1958; rept., New York: Harper & Row, 1962).

     Schrödinger and Einstein, old fashioned rationalists who believed in the existence of an objective, comprehensibly ordered reality independent of a perceiving subject, never accepted the Copenhagen interpretation. Schrödinger, in fact, invented his *Gedankenexperiment* with the "smeared-out cat" to burlesque the "mixed-up model" *(verwaschenes Modell)* that came out of Bohr's institute in Copenhagen. We don't know, says Schrödinger, whether we're looking at "a blurred or unfocussed photograph" or a photograph of "clouds and foggy vapors" *(einer verwackelten oder unscharf eingestellen Photographie... Wolken und Nebelschwaden)* ("Die gegenwärtige Situation in der Quantenmechanik," *Die Naturwissenschaften,* 23 [1934], 812).

Einstein's crack "God does not play dice with the world" was made, though not in those exact words, during his debate with Born and Bohr in the twenties and thirties. See Ronald W. Clark, *Einstein: The Life and Times* (New York: World Publishing Co., 1970), p. 340. "Einstein believed," writes Clark, "that the universe had been designed so that its workings could be comprehensible, therefore these workings must conform to discoverable laws; thus there was no room for chance and indeterminancy—God, after all, did not play the game that way" (p. 346). During the forties, Einstein wrote to Born, "The great initial success of quantum theory cannot convert me to believe in that fundamental game of dice.... However, I cannot provide logical arguments for my conviction, but can only call on my little finger as a witness, which cannot claim any authority to be respected outside my own skin" (Max Born, *Natural Philosophy of Cause and Chance* [1949; rpt. New York: Dover, 1964], pp. 122, 123).

46. Wigner, 1963 Nobel Laureate in Physics, argued that the paradox of the half-live and half-dead cat must be resolved by including the observer in the experiment. See his "Remarks on the Mind-Body Question," *The Scientist Speculates: Anthology of Partly-Baked Ideas,* ed. Irving J. Good (New York: Basic Books, 1962), pp. 284-302. See also Bryce S. De Witt, "Quantum Mechanics and Reality," *Physics Today,* September 1970, pp. 30-33.

47. De Witt, pp. 31, 33-35.

48. Le Guin's narrator is not the first to have recalled the myth of Pandora's Box and to have forgotten Hope. In *Pandora's Box: The Changing Aspects of a Mythical Symbol,* 2nd ed., rev. (1962; rpt., New York: Harper & Row, 1965), Dora and Erwin Panofsky report that Marc-Antoine de Murret commented (in 1578) on an allusion to Pandora in Ronsard's *Les Amours* XXXII (1552) by relating "after Hesiod, the story of Pandora at great length... but omitting the motif of Hope" (p. 58n6). Le Guin, who wrote her MA thesis on Ronsard, may have encountered this.

49. *Shelley's Poetry and Prose,* ed. Donald H. Reiman and Sharon B. Powers (New York: W.W. Norton, 1977), p. 210.

50. *Physics and Philosophy,* p. 58.

Notes to Chapter 4

1. "Foreword," *The Wind's Twelve Quarters* (New York: Harper & Row, 1975), p. viii.

2. *The Journal of the Royal Anthropological Institute of Great Britain and Ireland,* 75 (1945), 9. The lecture is reprinted in Kroeber, *The Nature of Culture* (Chicago: University of Chicago Press, 1952), pp. 379-95.

3. On Asimov's debt to Gibbon, see Donald A. Wollheim, "The Decline and Fall of the Galactic Empire," *The Universe Makers* (New York: Harper & Row, 1971), pp. 37-41; on the Spenglerian element in Asimov see Robert Scholes and Eric S. Rabkin, *Science Fiction: History - Science - Vision* (New York: Oxford University Press, 1977), pp. 59-60; and on Asimov's use of history in general and Toynbee and Marx in particular, see Charles Elkins, "Issac Asimov's 'Foundation' Novels: Historical Materialism Distorted into Cyclic Psycho-History," *Science-Fiction Studies,* 3 (March 1976), 26-36.

4. "Preface," *Caesar and Christ* (New York: Simon and Schuster, 1944), p. viii.

5. "Varieties of Literary Utopias," *Utopias and Utopian Thought,* ed. Frank E. Manuel (Boston: Beacon Press, 1967), p. 25.

6. *The Foundation Trilogy* (New York: Avon, 1974). The three volumes in this edition are not paged consecutively. The quotation is from p. 101 of *Second Foundation.* Elkins' characterization is in his "Issac Asimov's 'Foundation Novels,'" p. 35.

7. "The Ancient *Oikoumenê,*" p. 10.

8. For an alternate reading of Le Guin's development, see Ian Watson, "Le Guin's *Lathe of Heaven* and the Role of Dick: The False Reality as Mediator," *Science-Fiction Studies, 2* (March 1975), 67-75.

9. "Technique as Discovery," *The World We Imagine: Selected Essays* (New York: Farrar, Straus and Giroux, 1968), p. 10.

10. References in what follows to Wollheim's *The Universe Makers* are indicated in parenthesis. Asimov's future history was not the only one—only the one that found "general acceptance in the main current of science fiction and produce[d] a framework and inspiration for a thousand later stories [by other writers], which would fill in that framework with details" (James Gunn, *Alternate Worlds: The Illustrated History of Science Fiction* [Englewood Cliffs, N.J.: Prentice-Hall, 1975], p. 169).

11. Gunn, p. 169.

12. "A Citizen of Mondath," p. 22.

13. Quoted by Vonda McIntyre, "Ursula K. Le Guin: 'Using the Language with Delight,'" *Encore* (Portland), 1 (April/May 1977), 7.

14. Sources for these dates are as follows: for "The Dowry of Angyar": headnote to "Semley's Necklace," *The Wind's Twelve Quarters,* p. 1; for *Rocannon's World:* inferred from other dates; for *Planet of Exile:* "Introduction to the 1978 Edition," *Planet of Exile* (New York: Harper & Row, 1978), p. viii; for *City of Illusions:* "Introduction," *City of Illusions* (New York: Harper & Row, 1978), p. vi; for "Winter's King": headnote in *The Wind's Twelve Quarters,* p. 93; for *The Left Hand of Darkness:* letter from Le Guin cited by Elizabeth Cogell, "Taoist Configurations: *The Dispossessed,*" *Ursula K. Le Guin: Voyager to Inner Lands and to Outer Space,* ed. Joe De Bolt (Port Washington, N.Y.: Kennikat, 1979), p. 154; for *The Word for World is Forest:* "Author's Introduction," *The Word for World is Forest* (London, Gollancz, 1977), p. 7; for "Vaster than Empires and More Slow": letter from Le Guin, cited by Cogell; for *The Dispossessed:* letter from Le Guin, cited by Cogell; and for "The Day Before the Revolution": inferred from Le Guin's "Foreword," *The Wind's Twelve Quarters,* p. viii. In the discussion of these stories and novels that follows, I cite the *first* publication of each text, and use these abbreviations in my parenthetical references:

"DA"	"The Dowry of Angyar"
RW	*Rocannon's World*
PE	*Planet of Exile*
CI	*City of Illusions*
"WK"	"Winter's King"
LHD	*The Left Hand of Darkness*
WWF	*The Word for World is Forest*
"VTE"	"Vaster than Empires and More Slow"
TD	*The Dispossessed*
"DBR"	"The Day Before the Revolution"

15. J.J. Pierce, "Cordwainer Smith: The Shaper of Myths," *The Best of Cordwainer Smith*, ed. J.J. Pierce (Garden City, N.Y.: Nelson Doubleday [for the Science Fiction Book Club], 1975), p. 4.

16. Pierce, "Cordwainer Smith," pp. 1-8.

17. This dialectical interplay between part and whole in the development of Le Guin's Hainish future history would almost inevitably lead to microcosm-macrocosm analogies, and is probably the explanation for the "iconicity" that Rafail Nudelman identifies as the "essential structural principle" of Le Guin's science fiction ("An Approach to the Structure of Le Guin's SF," *Science-Fiction Studies*, 2 [November 1975], 213).

18. Le Guin confirmed these speculations in a letter dated April 21, 1978: she says Davenant comes from "avenant (plus) avenir (=future) You know this is the name the Terrans called Hain?"

19. See A.L. Kroeber and Clyde Kluckhohn, *Culture: A Critical Review of Concepts and Definitions* (New York: Vintage, [1963]), esp. p. 61.

20. "A Citizen of Mondath," p. 23.

21. "Introduction," *City of Illusions* (1978), p. vi.

22. Whether Le Guin started doing this in the Orsinian tales she had been writing for fifteen years is something we cannot know. It is clear, however, that she uses the technique whether she writes science fiction, fantasy, or "mundane" fiction, as science fiction fans call it.

23. That "all men's history" is "vague and half-legendary" is an observation Le Guin could have derived from her study of Jean Lemaire's *Illustrations de Gaule et singularitez de Troie* (1511-13), a universal history (if we can call it that) tracing a line beginning with Noah, running through Priam, and culminating in Charlemagne. It concludes with an appeal, based on their common ancestry, to unite *Gaule orientale* (Germany; the Teutons) and *Gaule occidentale* (France; the Franks). Like Lemaire's history, which begins with the dispersion of a primal family (Noah's), then describes the dispersion of a later primal family (Priam's), in order to lead up to an "ecumenical" civilization in Western Europe, Le Guin's Hainish history begins with the dispersion of a primal family (the Hainish), goes on to recount a regathering of that family's members and descendants (the League of All Worlds), which is followed by another dispersion (the Age of the Enemy), only to culminate in the civilization of the Ekumen.

24. "Introduction," *City of Illusions*, p. vii.

25. *The Gayety of Vision: A Study of Isak Dinesen's Art* (New York: Random House, 1965), p. 24.

26. The text of "Winter's King" I am citing was published in *Oribt 5*, ed. Damon Knight (New York: G.P. Putnam's Son's [for the Science Fiction Book Club], 1969). The pagination may differ slightly from the regular trade edition.
     When Le Guin revised this story for *The Wind's Twelve Quarters*, she changed not only all masculine pronouns for Gethenians to the feminine (see her headnote in *WTQ*, pp. 93-94, for her reasons), but also made other changes (mark the house metaphor for the universe; it signals an ecumenical [from Gk. *oikos*, house] consciousness):

"Winter's King" (1969)	"Winter's King" (1975)

"Once you said something, Lord Axt, which seemed to imply that all men on all worlds are blood kin. Did I mistake your meaning?"

"Well, so far as we know, which is a tiny bit of dusty space under the rafters of the universe, all the men we've run into are in fact men. But the kinship goes back some five hundred and fifty thousand years, to the Fore-Eras of Hain. The ancient Hainish settled a hundred worlds."...

"The Powers of the Ekumen dream, then, of restoring that truly ancient empire of Hain; of regathering all the worlds of men, the lost worlds?"

"Of weaving some harmony among them, at least. Life loves to know itself, out of its farthest limits. To embrace complexity is its delight. All these worlds and the various forms and ways of the minds and lives on them: together they would make a splendid harmony" (p. 77).

"Once you said, Lord Axt, that different as I am from you, and different as my people are from yours, yet we are blood kin. Was that a moral fact, or a material one?"

Axt smiled at the very Karhidish distinction. "Both, my lord. As far as we know, which is a tiny corner of dusty space under the rafters of the Universe, all the people we've run into are in fact human. But the kinship goes back a million years and more, to the Fore-Eras of Hain. The ancient Hainish settled a hundred worlds."...

"The dream of the Ekumen, then, is to restore that truly ancient commonality; to regather all the peoples of all the worlds at one hearth?"

"To weave some harmony among them, at least. Life loves to know itself, out to its farthest limits; to embrace complexity is its delight. Our difference is our beauty. All these worlds and the various forms and ways of the minds and bodies on them—together they would make a splendid harmony" (pp. 105-6).

Here is evidence (if any is needed) to corroborate Le Guin's saying that she is a discoverer, not a planner. Between the 1969 and the 1975 texts stand *The Left Hand of Darkness* and *The Dispossessed*. Between 1969 and 1975, she discovered that her writing, like much of science fiction, was sexist (though not as much as most science fiction), and that the source of her future history, the Fore-Eras of Hain, was, again like much of science fiction, imperialist. So "men" become "people" and an "empire" becomes a "commonality," which turns out to be twice as old as the empire. "Difference," after an "ambiguous utopia" becomes an important complement to harmony.

27. *Encyclopaedia Britannica*, 15th ed. (1974), s.v. "bread-fruit."

28. C[harles] H. L[ong], "Creation, Myths and Doctrines of," *Encyclopaedia Britannica*, 15th ed. (1974), vol. 5, p. 242. For the full text of the myth, see Long's *Alpha: The Myths of Creation* (New York: Braziller, 1963) or Joseph Campbell, *The Masks of God: Primitive Mythology* (1959; rpt., New York: Penguin, 1976), pp. 173-76, where it is presented in a section entitled "The Descent and Return of the Maiden," words directly applicable to Le Guin and her fiction (cf. my reference to Orpheus at the end of chapter 2). Le Guin pleads "ignorance" of this myth (personal communication, April 21, 1978).

29. Campbell, *The Masks of God: Primitive Mythology*, p. 182.

30. *Entropy Negative* #3 (1971), p. 4 of "Le Guin (II)."

31. *The Gayety of Vision,* p. 25.

32. "Ursula K. Le Guin: An Inteview," *Luna Monthly,* No. 63 (March 1976), 3.

33. Long, *Alpha,* p. 223, 224; my emphasis.

34. In order to understand (but not necessarily explain) how life and death and murder and creation are complementary and internally related parts of an organic whole in Le Guin's fiction, we might review some of the story of which she herself is the heroine. Biographical criticism of a living author sometimes carries the distasteful flavor of premature forensic surgery; I hope to avoid that here.

    Noting that the French *haine* means "hate," Gerard Klein has already made a foray into the subject by speculating about Le Guin's "guilt and hate sustained by the contemplation or the fantasy of the 'original scene,'" suggesting that she has "incorporated the 'original scene,' has taken it up as a woman, has installed herself as mother." Klein hypothesizes that this may be one source specifically of the Hainish worlds and generally of the fecundity of Le Guin's writing ("Le Guin's 'Aberrant' Opus," pp. 293-94). Klein's Freudian analysis is far from simplistic, nor is it vulgar. He understands that psychological factors cooperate with the social determinants of artistic creativity. I will assemble some of Le Guin's statements, add some material from her mother's biography of her father, and will try to see how the circumstances of her life may have put her in situations that could have called up powerful archetypal images. Further, I will note some of the similarities between those situations and their apparent reflection in Le Guin's fiction with what Joseph Campbell calls "the mythological event," the model of which is the Hainuwele myth from the Molucca Islands. Finally, I believe that all this will help us recognize the common sources of Le Guin's fantasy and science fiction. I will try to understand how the fantasy and science fiction that Le Guin wrote after 1966—regarded by many of her readers as her best work—is "all one story."

    In 1965, Le Guin was asked to write a book for young people by Herman Schein, who with his wife Ruth Robbins (an illustrator), is Parnassus Press, just as Leonard and Virginia Woolf were Hogarth Press. Parnassus had published in 1964 Theodora Kroeber's *Ishi, Last of His Tribe,* a fictionalized children's version of her *Ishi In Two Worlds* (Berkeley: University of California Press, 1961). It was probably not long after that that Schein asked Theodora Kroeber's daughter for a juvenile. "He wanted something for older kids," explains Le Guin:

    > till then Parnassus had been mainly a young-juvenile publisher, putting out the handsomest and best-made picture books in America [for a sample of their work, see Theodora Kroeber's *A Green Christmas,* published a year before *A Wizard of Earthsea*]. He gave me complete freedom as to subject and approach. Nobody until then had ever asked me to write anything; I had just done so, relentlessly. To be asked to do it was a great boon. The exhilaration carried me over my apprehensions about writing "for young people," something I had never seriously tried. For some weeks or months I let my imagination go groping around in search of what they wanted, in the dark. It stumbled over the Islands, and the magic employed there [the Islands and magic that she had discovered in "The Rule of Names" and "The World of Unbinding" two or three years earlier]. Serious consideration of magic, and of writing for kids, combined to make me wonder about wizards. Wizards are usually elderly or ageless Gandalfs, quite rightly and archetypically. But what were they before they had white beards? How did they learn what is obviously an erudite and dangerous art? Are there colleges for young wizards?... And so on.
    >
    > The story of the book is essentially a voyage, a pattern in the form of a long spiral. I began to see the places where the young wizard would go. Eventually I drew a map. Now that I knew where everything was, now was the time for cartography. Of course a great deal of it only appeared above water, as it were, in drawing on the map ("Dreams Must Explain Themselves," *Algol* 21 [November 1973], p. 10).

This account of the genesis of *A Wizard of Earthsea,* like the map of the archipelago, leaves a lot below the surface. "Serious consideration of magic," as I argue in chapter 3, may have included looking into Celtic lore about druids for models of "colleges for young wizards," and may have included reading or rereading (besides Sir James's and Lady Frazer's books) Bronislaw Malinowski, and that means looking at the Malay Archipelago: islands and magic. "Serious consideration of writing for kids" included serious consideration of death, "the ultimate Ultimate" (Ibid.). She had written a story about a prince from Havnor a couple of years earlier, a story that "never worked itself out at all well," perhaps because all the elements, personal and aesthetic, needed to come to terms with death were not yet within her grasp.

The subject of *A Wizard of Earthsea,* she says, is "the most childish thing about" it: "coming of age." She continues:

> Coming of age is a process that took me thirty years; I finished it, so far as I ever will, at about age 31; and so *I feel rather deeply about it.* So do most adolescents. It's their main occupation, in fact (*Ibid.,* pp. 12-14, my emphasis).

Le Guin was seventeen days short of her thirty-first birthday when her father died. By the time she was thirty-two, she had written "Coming of Age" (the longest poem in *Wild Angels* [Santa Barbara, Calif.: Capra Press, 1975], pp. 8-16), and "Imaginary Countries," which became the central tale in *Orsinian Tales* (see chapter 2, pp. 41-45). The subject of the second book of the Earthsea trilogy is, "in one word, sex . . . . "More exactly, you could call it a feminine coming of age. Birth, rebirth, destruction, freedom are the themes" ("Dreams," p. 14). *The Farthest Shore,* the third book, "is about death." Death, writes Le Guin,

> seemed an absolutely suitable subject to me for young readers, since in a way one can say that the hour when a child realizes, not that death exists—children are intensely aware of death—but that he/she, personally, is mortal, will die, is the hour when childhood ends, and the new life begins. Coming of age again, but in a larger context *(Ibid.).*

Just before *The Farthest Shore* was published, Le Guin told a newspaper reporter that adolescents

> want to face the issues . . . . You raise a problem and they really live through it. It fills a need. They are so intense about life. *You never take it quite that hard again after the teens . . . .* But when you're older you have to respect them. Some people lose touch with their adolescence, those passionate hates and loves. If you remember them you won't be so difficult (Helen L. Mershon, "'Teen Passions' Motivate Author Here," [Portland] *Oregon Journal,* September 8, 1972, sec. 2, p. 1, my emphasis).

When Le Guin was thirteen, her father nearly died. At the beginning of the summer of 1943, Kroeber was in a "state of near exhaustion" from working in the Army Specialized Training Program in Berkeley (Theodora Kroeber, *Alfred Kroeber* [Berkeley: University of California Press, 1970], p. 186). He was persuaded to take two weeks off, and along with Theodora, Karl and Ursula (the two eldest sons were in the Navy and Air Corps), went to Lake Tahoe. Kroeber did not feel well, wanted to "get to a lower altitude," so Karl and a local doctor arranged for an ambulance to take the family (Theodora herself was quite ill) back to Berkeley. In Berkeley, Kroeber suffered a "severe thrombosis." He "did not expect to survive . . . nor did Dr. Donald pretend to any confidence that he would" (p. 187). He did, though and the next summer,

> Kroeber, Urusla, and I decided to try Kishamish, the three of us alone . . . . Ursula and Kroeber wrote prodigiously—poetry and science, respectively (p. 190).

Having returned to life from the edge of death, Kroeber soon formulated his theory of the *Oikoumenê;* Ursula, in the shadow of death and at the beginning of adolescence, "wrote prodigiously" (cf. Alcmaeon and Kermode's *The Sense of an Ending:* fictions "make tolerable one's moment between beginning and end") A year and a half later, Kroeber sailed on the *Queen Mary* to England to address the Royal Anthropological Society.

Twenty years later, Le Guin transformed her father's *Oikoumenê* into her science fictional Ekumen—"an in-memoriam in-joke," she calls it (personal correspondence, March 21, 1977)—and wrote "Winter's King," a time-loop story that mocks death by connecting beginning and end, the story of a king who returns from the dead to weave his country into a harmony and to reunite it to the Ekumen. At about the same time, she was beginning *A Wizard of Earthsea,* a story "in the form of a long spiral" about death and coming of age. Several things seem to have coalesced in Le Guin's creative unconscious as her imagination was groping in the dark in 1966 or threabouts, after Schein asked her for a book. She was giving serious consideration to magic (a metaphor for her art, and therefore for creation), reading or thinking about creation myths, thinking about death, thinking about coming of age, thinking about adolescents, probably remembering on some level her father's near-death when she was an adolescent, remembering her father's 1945 Huxley Memorial Lecture, perhaps looking at the Malay Archipelago and the breadfruit indigenous to those islands, thinking about Antarctica, finding in Scott's journals "a landscape of the mind" (personal correspondence, September 15, 1976) which congealed into the frozen landscape of the planet Winter, whose staple food is the bread-apple. All of this was something like a primal egg, a swarm of potentiality, undifferentiated and single in her creative unconscious, all clustered around the idea of death, waiting for and at the same time motivating its own expression in aesthetic form. At a time of life the Jungians are extremely interested in, middle age, Le Guin at thirty-six or thirty-seven again "wrote prodigiously"—seven novels and several short stories between 1966 and 1972—wrote the works that established her reputation as "probably the best writer of speculative fabulation working in this country today, [who] deserves a place among our major contemporary writers of fiction" (Robert Scholes, *Speculative Fabulation* [Notre Dame: University of Notre Dame Press, 1975], p. 80).

I believe that Le Guin experienced what Joseph Campbell calls "the mythological event" in the summer of 1943 and then lived with it in her creative unconscious until 1966, when it rose into consciousness as she wrote "Winter's King," *A Wizard of Earthsea,* and *The Left Hand of Darkness;* it found expression in aesthetic form in the circular journeys her heroes and heroines make through Earthsea Archipelago and the Hainish future history, journeys which connect beginning and end. It may have been a crucial and determining factor in her decision to reverse the Hainish chronology after she wrote "Winter's King." She had let herself be used by myths and had found her own voice.

When asked if the name "Hain" was connected in any way with the murder and dismemberment of Hainuwele, Le Guin answered, "No—I plead ignorance" (personal correspondence, April 21, 1978). She need not have knowledge of this particular myth, however, to have experienced the power of the archetype. The Norse and the Mesopotamian creation myths are images of the same archetype. (I refer to the Jungian distinction between an archetype and an archetypal image. The archetype would overwhelm and obliterate consciousness while the image allows consciousness to assimilate the power of the archetype and use it creatively. Commenting on the Hainuwele myth, Campbell writes,

> The leading theme of the primitive-village mythology of the Dema is the coming of death into the world, and the particular point is that death comes by way of murder.... Moreover, as we learn from other myths and mythological fragments in this culture sphere, the sexual organs are supposed to have appeared at the time of this coming of death. Reproduction without death would be a calamity, as would death without reproduction.

We may say, then, that the interdependence of death and sex, their import as complementary aspects of a single state of being, and the necessity of killing . . . this deeply moving, emotionally disturbing glimpse of death as the life of the living is the fundamental motivation supporting the rites around which the social structure of the early planting villages was composed (pp. 176-77).

Death came into Le Guin's world when she was in early adolescence. "This deeply moving, emotionally disturbing" combination of events ("You never take it quite that hard again after the teens") may be the fundamental motivation supporting the fictions around which her life as a writer is composed. In the culture sphere of the Moluccas, "the mythological image, the mythological formula is rendered present, here and now, in the rite"; in the modern West, it is actualized in Le Guin's life and in her fiction. If, as Campbell says,

the festival is an extension into the present of the world-creating mythological event through which the force of the ancestors (the eternal ones of the dream) became discharged into the rolling run of time and where what then was ever present in the form of a holy being without change now dies and reappears, dies and reappears—like the moon, like the yam, like our animal food, or like the race (pp. 179-80),

then Le Guin's creation of imaginary worlds is likewise an extension into the present of the same world-creating mythological event. The whole Hainish cycle, from the Fore-Eras of Hain to the League, the Age of the Enemy, and the Ekumen, shows a race dying and reappearing like the moon, one of those heavenly bodies that Alcmaeon and Heraclitus knew to be ever present because in their circular motions they connect beginning and end: they provide a model of and justification for Plato's doctrine of the immortality of the soul.

Like her father's *Oikoumenê,* itself a fundamentally mythic, as well as a scientific construct, Le Guin's best fantasy and science fiction, themselves as mythic as they are scientific, seem to grow from a single source, some moment when her imagination went groping in the dark, allowing itself to be used by myth, so that it could discover its native symbology. Her fantasy and science fiction, as different as the two halves of the brain, as separate as adjacent colors on the spectrum, as distinguishable as two veins in marble (all metaphors she has used), seem to flow from some moment in 1966. When she concluded her autobiographical "A Citizen of Mondath" with the statement that "Outer Space, and the Inner Lands are still, and always will be my country" (p. 24), she located those two realms in *one* country, going against many critics who try to draw sharp boundaries around them (Le Guin recognizes distinctions; see her "Do-It-Yourself Cosmology," *Parabola,* 2, iii [1977], 14-17). Le Guin takes that position as a result, I believe, of her creative experiences in or around 1966, when she invented-discovered Earthsea and Gethen and the Ekumen at the same time and structured both *A Wizard of Earthsea* and *The Left Hand of Darkness* as circular journeys around the image of the Shadow: death.

35. "The Cardinal's First Tale," *Last Tales* (New York: Random House, 1957), p. 26.

36. *The Human Condition,* p. 186.

37. *The Gayety of Vision,* p. 20.

38. "The Burning of Paper Instead of Children," quoted by Donna Gerstenberger, "Conceptions Literary and Otherwise: Women Writers and the Modern Imagination," *Novel,* 9 (Winter 1976), 141.

39. Quoted by Paula Brookmire, "She Writes about Aliens—Men Included," *Milwaukee Journal,* July 21, 1974; rpt., *Biography News* (Detroit: Gale, 1974), p. 1155.

40. "Is Gender Necessary?" p. 132.

41. *Structural Anthropology,* trans. Claire Jacobson and Brooke Schoepf (New York: Basic Books, 1963), p. 310.

42. A.W. Reed, *An Illustrated Encyclopedia of Aboriginal Life* (Sydney: A.H. & A.W. Reed, 1969), pp. 56-57. See also W.E.H. Stanner, "Religion, Totemism and Symbolism," in *Aboriginal Man in Australia,* ed. Ronald M. and Catherine H. Berndt (Sydney: Angus and Robertson, 1965), pp. 207-37.

43. I am passing over "Vaster than Empires and More Slow," a story written between *The Word for World is Forest* and *The Dispossessed.* It is only tangentially related to the internal dynamic of Le Guin's Hainish history that I am tracing. Unlike the other stories—"The Dowry of Angyar," "Winter's King," and "The Day Before the Revolution"—it does not occupy an inaugural, transitional, or terminal position in the development of the whole saga, but instead is another development of the themes and metaphors in Le Guin's other works.

44. See Kingsley Amis, *New Maps of Hell* (New York: Harcourt, 1960). Robert C. Elliott, author of *The Shape of Utopia: Studies in a Literary Genre* (Chicago: University of Chicago Press, 1970), announced in 1975 that "although the search for utopia, for the good life, continues, literary utopia is all but dead" ("Literature and the Good Life: A Dilemma," *Yale Review,* 65 [October 1975], 37). Not long after making that pronouncement, however, he discovered *The Dispossessed,* whose theme, he says, is "anachronistically positive," and went on to review it enthusiastically in the issue of the *Yale Review* that followed the one continuing his premature obituary of the genre ("A New Utopian Novel," *Yale Review,* 65 [Winter 1976], 256-61).

45. *Chronosophy* is a neologism coined by J.T. Fraser, whose collection *The Voices of Time* (New York: Braziller, 1966) may be the single most important source, after the writings of several anarchists, of Le Guin's ideas in *The Dispossessed.* An interviewer once asked Le Guin how she "came up with" the theory of Simultaneity. She answered:

    My physics is even shakier than my social science. I have a physicist friend who says it's all right. I was so relieved. What's really wierd—there are shelves of books about space and space-time, but there's *one* main reference for thinking about time, either from a physics point of view or from philosophy. It's called *The Voices of Time,* an anthology. He's collected all the main articles from all the way back, from China and India and everywhere else. Sequency and Simultaneity seem to be the basic question. As well as I understood it I tried to work it into the book. It got absolutely fascinating. (Barry Barth, "Ursula Le Guin interview: Tricks, anthropology create new worlds," *Portland Scribe,* May 17-May 25, 1975, p. 8).

46. Frye, "Varities of Literary Utopias," p. 49.

47. Le Guin's anarchism is ably treated by Philip E. Smith II, "Unbuilding Walls: Human Nature and the Nature of Evolutionary and Political Theory in *The Dispossessed,*" in *Ursula K. Le Guin,* ed. Joseph D. Olander and Martin H. Greenberg (New York: Taplinger, 1979), pp. 77-96, and Victor Urbanowicz, "Personal and Political in Le Guin's *The Dispossessed,*" *Science-Fiction Studies,,* 5 (1978), 110-17.

48. See A.L. Kroeber, "The Superorganic," *The Nature of Culture* (Chicago: University of Chicago Press, 1952), pp. 22-51.

49. The evolutionary theory on which the Ekumen is modeled is probably closer to Pierre Teilhard de Chardin's than Darwin's (see *The Phenomenon of Man,* trans. Bernard Wall [New York: Harper & Row, 1965]). Anarresti society is also modeled on evolution, but evolutionary law in *The Dispossessed,* unlike the mystical and metaphysically oriented evolution in *The Left Hand of Darkness,* has ethical significance. Vea and Shevek rehearse the debate between Thomas Huxley and Kropotkin:

> "Life is a fight, and the strongest wins. All civilization does is hide the blood and cover up the hate with pretty words!"
>
> "Your civilization, perhaps. Ours hides nothing. It is all plain. Queen Teaea wears her own skin, there. We follow one law, only one, the law of human evolution."
>
> "The law of evolution is that the strongest survives!"
>
> "Yes, and the strongest, in the existence of any social species, are those who are the most social. In human terms, most ethical" (*TD,* pp. 194-95).

50. Le Guin says that the Circle of Life is not the *t'ai chi,* the yin-yang circle; "it's just a *circle*—not quite closed." (personal correspondence, September 9, 1977).

Bibliography

Listed below are only those works cited in this book. For a complete listing of Le Guin's works, see Elizabeth Cummins Cogell, *Ursula K. Le Guin: A Primary and Secondary Bibliography* (Boston: G. K. Hall, 1983).

I. Works by Le Guin

A. Books

Rocannon's World (New York: Ace, 1966; New York: Harper & Row, 1977).
Planet of Exile (New York: Ace, 1966; New York: Harper & Row, 1978).
City of Illusions (New York: Ace, 1967; New York: Harper & Row, 1978).
Three Hainish Novels (Garden City: Doubleday, 1978).
A Wizard of Earthsea (Berkeley: Parnassus Press, 1968).
The Left Hand of Darkness (New York: Ace, 1969, 1976).
The Farthest Shore (New York: Atheneum, 1972).
The Dispossessed: An Ambiguous Utopia (New York: Harper & Row, 1974).
The Wind's Twelve Quarters (New York: Harper & Row, 1975).
Orsinian Tales (New York: Harper & Row, 1976).

B. Stories

"An die Musik," Western Humanities Review, 14 (1961).
"The Dowry of Angyar," *Amazing Stories,* September, 1964.
"Winter's King," *Orbit 5,* ed. Damon Knight (New York: Putnam, 1969).
"The Word for World is Forest," *Again, Dangerous Visions,* ed. Harlan Ellison (Garden City: Doubleday, 1972).
"The Day Before the Revolution," *Galaxy,* August 1974.
"Shrödinger's Cat," *Universe 5,* ed. Terry Carr (New York: Random, 1974).

C. Essays and Interviews

"Prophets and Mirrors: Science Fiction as a Way of Seeing." *The Living Light,* 7 (Fall 1970), 111-21
"The View In," *A Miltitude of Visions,* ed. Cy Chauvin (Baltimore: T-K Graphics, 1975)
"The Crab Nebula, the Paramecium, and Tolstoy," *Riverside Quarterly,* 5 (1972), 89-96.
"In Defense of Fantasy," *Horn Book,* 49 (1973), 239
"A Citizen of Mondath," *Foundation,* no. 4 (1975), 20-24

"Dreams Must Explain Themselves," *Algol* 21 (November 1973), 7ff.

"The Child and the Shadow," *Quarterly Journal of the Library of Congress,* 32 (April 1975), 139-48

"American SF and the Other," *Science-Fiction Studies,* 2 (1975), 208-10.

"A Response to the Le Guin Issue," *Science-Fiction Studies,* 3 (1976), 43-46

"Is Gender Necessary?" *Aurora: Beyond Equality,* ed. McIntyre and Anderson (Greenwich: Fawcett, 1976)

"Myth and Archetype in Science Fiction," *Parabola* 1 (Fall 1976), 9-12

"Le Guin (II)," *Entropy Negative,* no. 3 (1971) A science fiction fanzine published in Vancouver, B.C.

"She Writes About Aliens—Men Included," *Biography News* (Detroit: Gale, 1974), 1155

"Ursula Le Guin Interview," *Portland Scribe,* May 14-May 25, 1975, pp. 8-9

"Ursula K. Le Guin: An Interview," *Luna Monthly,* no. 63 (March 1976), 1-7

II. Works about Le Guin

Cameron, Eleanor. "High Fantasy: *A Wizard of Earthsea.*" *Horn Book,* 47 (1971), 129-38.

Cogell, Elizabeth. "Setting as Analogue to Characterization in Ursula Le Guin." *Extrapolation,* 18 (1977), 131-41.

Delany, Samuel, "To Read *The Dispossessed.*" In his *The Jewel-Hinged Jaw: Notes on the Language of Science Fiction.* Elizabethtown, N.Y.: Dragon Press, 1977, pp. 239-308.

Elliott, Robert C. "A New Utopian Novel." *Yale Review,* 65 (1976), 256-61.

Gerstenberger, Donna. "Conceptions Literary and Otherwise: Women Writers and the Modern Imagination." *Novel,* 9 (1976), 141-50.

Huntington, John. "Public and Private Imperatives in Le Guin's Novels." *Science-Fiction Studies,* 2 (1975), 237-43.

Klein, Gérard. "Ursula Le Guin, ou la sortie du piège." In his *Malaise dans la science-fiction.* Metz: L'Aube Enclavée, 1977, pp. 48-78; trans. and abridged by Richard Astle as "Le Guin's 'Aberrant' Opus: Escaping the Trap of Discontent." *Science-Fiction Studies,* 4 (1977), 287-95.

Kroeber, Karl. "Sisters and Science Fiction." *The Little Magazine,* 10, No. 1 & 2 (Spring-Summer 1976), 87-90.

Nudelman, Rafail. "An Approach to the Structure of Le Guin's SF." Trans. Alan G. Myers. *Science-Fiction Studies,* 2 (1975), 210-20.

Remington, Thomas J. "A Touch of Difference, a Touch of Love: Theme in Three Stories by Ursula K. Le Guin." *Extrapolation,* 18 (1976), 28-41.

Scholes, Robert. "The Good Witch of the West." *The Hollins Critic,* 11 (April 1974), 2-12. Rpt. in his *Structural Fabulation: An Essay on Fiction of the Future.* Notre Dame, Ind.: University of Notre Dame Press, 1975, pp. 77-99.

Shippey, T.A. "The Magic Art and the Evolution of Words: Ursula Le Guin's Earthsea Trilogy." *Mosaic,* 10 (Winter 1977), 147-63.

Slusser, George E. *The Farthest Shores of Ursula K. Le Guin.* San Bernadino, Calif.: The Borgo Press, 1976.

Smith, Philip E., II. "Unbuilding Walls: Human Nature and the Nature of Evolutionary Political Theory in *The Dispossessed.*" In *Ursula K. Le Guin.* Ed. Olander and Greenberg. New York: Taplinger, 1979, pp. 77-96.

Urbanowicz, Victor. "Personal and Political in Le Guin's *The Dispossessed.*" *Science-Fiction Studies,* 5 (1978), 110-17.

Watson, Ian. "The Forest as Metaphor for Mind: 'The Word for World is Forest' and 'Vaster than Empires and More Slow.'" *Science-Fiction Studies,* 2 (1975), 231-37.

———. "Le Guin's *Lathe of Heaven* and the Role of Dick: The False Reality as Mediator." *Science-Fiction Studies,* 2 (1975), 67-75.

Williams, Raymond. "Utopia and Science Fiction." *Science-Fiction Studies,* 5 (1978), 203-14.

Wood, Susan. "Discovering Worlds: The Fiction of Ursula K. Le Guin." In *Voices for the Future.* Vol. 2. Ed. Thomas D. Clareson. Bowling Green, Ohio: Bowling Green University Popular Press, 1979.

III. General Works

Abrams, M.H. *The Mirror and the Lamp: Romantic Theory and the Critical Tradition.* New York: Oxford University Press, 1953.

———. *Natural Supernaturalism: Tradition and Revolution in Romantic Literature.* New York: W.W. Norton, 1971.

Amis, Kingsley. *New Maps of Hell: A Survey of Science Fiction.* New York: Harcourt, Brace, 1960.

Arendt, Hannah. *The Human Condition.* Chicago: University of Chicago Press, 1958.

Asimov, Isaac. *The Foundation Trilogy.* New York: Avon, 1974.

Auden, W.H. *Collected Shorter Poems 1927-1957.* New York: Random House, 1966.

———. "The Public v. the Late Mr. William Butler Yeats." *Partisan Review,* 6 (Spring 1939), 46-51.

Auden, W.H. "The Quest Hero." *Texas Quarterly,* 4 (Winter 1961), 81-93.

———. "Rilke in English." *New Republic,* September 6, 1939, pp. 135-36.

Bloch, Ernst. "*Entfremdung, Verfremdung:* Alienation, Estrangement." Trans. Darko Suvin. *The Drama Review,* 15 (Fall 1970), 120-25.

Bohr, Niels. *Atomic Physics and Human Knowledge.* New York: John Wiley, 1958.

Born, Max. *Natural Philosophy of Cause and Chance.* New York: Dover, 1964.

Campbell, Joseph. *The Masks of God: Primitive Mythology.* New York: Penguin, 1976.

Capell, Richard. "Lotte Lehmann." *Grove's Dictionary of Music and Musicians.* Ed. Eric Blom. 10 vols. London: Macmillan, 1954-61, V. 116.

Clark, Ronald W. *Einstein: The Life and Times.* New York: World Publishing Col., 1970.

Coleridge, Samuel Taylor. *Collected Letters.* Ed. Earl Leslie Griggs. 6 vols. Oxford: At the Clarendon Press, 1956-71.

Colum, Padraic. *The Children of Odin.* New York: Macmillan, 1920.

Delany, Samuel R. "About Five Thousand One Hundred and Seventy Five Words." In *SF: The Other Side of Realism.* Ed. Thoams D. Clareson. Bowling Green: Bowling Green University Popular Press, 1971.

De Witt, Bryce S. "Quantum Mechanics and Reality." *Physics Today,* September 1970, pp. 30-35.

Dinesen, Isak. *Last Tales.* New York: Random House, 1957.

"Druidism." *Encyclopaedia Britannica.* 1910 ed.

Durant, Will. *Caesar and Christ.* New York: Simon and Schuster, 1944.

Eichendorff, Joseph. *Neue Gesamtausgabe der Werke and Schriften.* 4 vols. Stuttgart: J.G. Cotta'sche Buchhandlung, 1957.

Eliade, Mircea. *Australian Religions: An Introduction.* Ithaca: Cornell University Press, 1973.

———. *The Myth of the Eternal Return.* Trans. Willard R. Trask. Princeton: Princeton University Press, 1954.

Elkins, Charles. "Issac Asimov's 'Foundation' Novels: Historical Materialism Distorted into Cyclic Psycho-History." *Science-Fiction Studies,* 3 (1976), 26-36.

Elliott, Robert C. "Literature and the Good Life: A Dilemma." *Yale Review,* 65 (Autumn 1975), 24-37.

———. *The Shape of Utopia: Studies in a Literary Genre.* Chicago: University of Chicago Press, 1970.

Fischer-Dieskau, Dietrich. *The Fischer-Dieskau Book of Lieder.* Trans. George Bird and Richard Stokes. New York: Knopf, 1977.

Fraser, J.T., ed. *The Voices of Time: A Cooperative Survey of Man's Views of Time as Expressed by the Sciences and by the Humanities.* New York: George Braziller, 1966.

Frazer, Sir James G. *The Golden Bough: A Study in Magic and Religion.* New York: Macmillan, 1922.

Frazer, Lady [Lilly]. *Leaves from the Golden Bough,* culled by Lady Frazer. New York: Macmillan, 1924.

Frye, Northrup. *Anatomy of Criticism: Four Essays.* Princeton: Princeton University Press, 1957.

————. *The Secular Scripture: A Study of the Structure of Romance.* Cambridge: Harvard University Press, 1976.

————. "Varieties of Literary Utopias." In *Utopias and Utopian Thought.* Ed. Frank E. Manuel. Boston: Beacon Press, 1967.

Giamatti, A. Bartlett. "Spenser: From Magic to Miracle." In *Four Essays on Romance.* Ed. Herschel Baker. Cambridge: Harvard University Press, 1971.

Guillén, Claudio. *Literature as System: Essays Toward the Theory of Literary History.* Princeton: Princeton University Press, 1971.

Gunn, James. *Alternate Worlds: The Illustrated History of Science Fiction.* Englewood Cliffs, N.J.: Prentice-Hall, 1975.

Hanson, Norwood. "Quantum Mechanics, Philosophical Implications of." *Encyclopedia of Philosophy.* Ed. Paul Edwards. New York: Macmillan, 1967.

Hegel, G.W.F. *The Phenomenology of Mind.* Trans. J.B. Baillie. New York: Harper & Row, 1967.

Heisenberg, Werner. *Physics and Philosophy: The Revolution in Modern Science.* New York: Harper & Row, 1962.

Hirsch, E.D., Jr. *Validity in Interpretation.* New Haven: Yale University Press, 1967.

Horkheimer, Max, and Theodor W. Adorno. *Dialectic of Enlightenment.* Trans. John Cumming. New York: Herder and Herder, 1972.

Hume, Kathryn. "Romance: A Perdurable Pattern." *College English,* 36 (October 1974), 129-46.

Hynes, Samuel. *The Auden Generation: Literature and Politics in England in the 1930s.* New York: Viking Press, 1977.

Jameson, Frederic. "Magical Narratives: Romance as Genre." *New Literary History,* 7 (Autumn 1975), 136-63.

Kaufmann, Walter. *Hegel: A Reinterpretation.* Garden City, N.Y.: Doubleday Anchor, 1966.

Kroeber, A.L. *The Nature of Culture.* Chicago: University of Chicago Press, 1952.

————, and Clyde Kluckhohn. *Culture: A Critical Review of Concepts and Definitions.* New York: Vintage, 1963.

Kroeber, Theodora. *Alfred Kroeber: A Personal Configuration.* Berkeley: University of California Press, 1970.

Langbaum, Robert. *The Gayety of Vision: A Study of Isak Dinesen's Art.* New York: Random House, 1965.

Lehmann, Lotte. *Midway in My Song.* Indianapolis: Bobbs-Merrill, 1938.

Lévi-Strauss, Claude. *Structural Anthropology.* Trans. Claire Jacobson and Brooke Schoepf. New York: Basic Books, 1963.

Long, Charles H. "Creation, Myths and Doctrines of." *Encyclopaedia Britannica: Macropaedia.* 1974 ed.

Malinowski, Bronislaw. *Argonauts of the Western Pacific.* New York: E.P. Dutton, 1961.

————. *Magic, Science, and Religion and Other Essays.* Garden City, N.Y.: Doubleday Anchor, 1954.

Marett, R.R. "Magic." *Encyclopaedia of Religion and Ethics.* Ed. James Hastings. New York: Scribner's, 1928.

Needham, Joseph. *Moulds of Understanding: A Pattern of Natural Philosophy.* Ed. Gary Werskey. London: Allen & Unwin, 1976.

Ollmann, Bertell. *Alienation: Marx's Conception of Man in Capitalist Society.* 2nd ed. Cambridge: Cambridge University Press, 1976.

Oppenheimer, J. Robert. *Science and the Common Understanding.* New York: Simon and Schuster, 1954.

Ornstein, Robert. *The Psychology of Consciousness.* New York: Penguin, 1975.

Panofsky, Dora and Edwin. *Pandora's Box: The Changing Aspects of a Mythical Symbol.* 2nd ed., rev. New York: Harper & Row, 1965.

Pareto, Vilfredo. *Les Système socialistes.* 2 vols. Paris: Giard & Brière, 1902-3.

Pritchett, V.S. "The Incurable." Rev. of Franz Kafka, *Letters to Friends, Family, and Editors,* trans. Richard and Clara Winston. *New York Review of Books,* February 25, 1978, pp. 3-4.

Reed, A.W. *An Illustrated Encyclopedia of Aborginal Life.* Sydney: A.W. Reed, 1969.

Rilke, Rainer Maria. *Duino Elegies.* Trans. J.B. Leishman and Stephen Spender. New York: W.W. Norton, 1939.

———. *Sonnets to Orpheus.* Trans. J.B. Leishman. London: Hogarth Press, 1936.

Rogers, Eric M. *Physics for the Inquiring Mind: The Methods, Nature, and Philosophy of Physical Science.* Princeton: Princeton University Press, 1960.

Rose, Mark, ed. *Science Fiction: A Collection of Critical Essays.* Englewood Cliffs, N.J.: Prentice-Hall, 1976.

Scholes, Robert. *Structural Fabulation: An Essay on Fiction of the Future.* Notre Dame: University of Notre Dame Press, 1976.

Schorer, Mark. "Technique as Discovery." In his *The World We Imagine: Selected Essays.* New York: Farrar, Straus and Giroux, 1968.

Schrödinger, Erwin. "Die gegenwärtige Situation in der Quantenmechanik." *Naturwissenschaften,* 23 (1935), 807-12, 323-28, 844-49.

———. *Science and Humanism: Physics in Our Time.* Cambridge: At the University Press, 1951.

Schubert, Franz. "An die Musik." In his *Complete Works.* 19 vols. New York: Dover, 1965, XV, 86-87.

Scortia, Thomas. "Science Fiction as the Imaginary Experiment." In *Science Fiction: Today and Tomorrow.* Ed. Reginald Bretnor. Baltimore: Penguin, 1975.

Seton-Watson, Hugh. *The "Sick Heart" of Modern Europe: The Problem of the Danubian Lands.* Seattle: University of Washington Press, 1975.

Shelley, Percy Bysshe. *Shelley's Poetry and Prose.* Ed. Donald H. Reiman and Sharon B. Powers. New York: W.W. Norton, 1977.

Spears, Monroe K. *The Poetry of W.H. Auden.* New York: Oxford University Press, 1968.

Steiner, George. *On Difficulty and Other Essays.* New York: Oxford University Press, 1978.

Stevenson, Lionel. "The Artistic Problem: Science Fiction as Romance." In *SF: The Other Side of Realism.* Ed. Thomas D. Clareson. Bowling Green: Bowling Green University Popular Press, 1971.

Strauss, Walter A. *Descent and Return: The Orphic Theme in Modern Literature.* Cambridge: Harvard University Press, 1971.

Suvin, Darko. "Defining the Literary Genre of Utopia: Some Historical Semantics, Some Geology, a Proposal, and a Plea." *Studies in the Literary Imagination,* 6 (Fall 1973), 121-45.

———. "On the Poetics of the Science Fiction Genre." *College English,* 34 (December 1972), 372-83.

———. "The Significant Context of SF." *Science-Fiction Studies,* 1 (1973), 44-50.

Todorov, Tzvetan. *The Fantastic: A Structural Approach to a Literary Genre.* Trans. Richard Howard. Ithaca: Cornell University Press, 1975.

White, Hayden V. *Metahistory: The Historical Imagination in Nineteenth-Century Europe.* Baltimore: Johns Hopkins University Press, 1975.

Wigner, Eugen. "Remarks on the Mind-Body Question." In *The Scientist Speculates: An Anthology of Partly-Baked Ideas.* Ed. Irving J. Good. New York: Basic Books, 1962.

Williams, Jay. "Very Iffy Books." *Signal: Approaches to Children's Books,* No. 13 (January 1974), 26.

Wollheim, Donald A. *The Universe Makers.* New York: Harper & Row, 1971.

Wright, Austin Tappan. *Islandia.* New York: New American Library, 1975.

Index

17 3/09